PRAISE FOR

The Transcended Christian

"A work of encouragement and hope. If one cares for the church as it ought to be, rather than as it has been or is now, this book will be essential and constructive reading. It is a brave book by a brave man, and I am happy to commend it to all, especially to those for whom the future is more important than the past."

—Rev. Prof. Peter Gomes, Chaplain of Harvard's
Memorial Church

"Daniel Helminiak relates to his readers as teacher, priest, spiritual director, and guide. He challenges us to expand our understanding; he sinks roots deeply in scripture; he affirms our personal journeys; he points us in new directions. *The Transcended Christian* is a spiritual guidebook in a world where division and fear threaten our call to community and peacemaking."

—Rev. Dr. Jean Richardson, Director Kirkridge Retreat
and Study Center, Bangor, PA

"In *The Transcended Christian*, Daniel Helminiak reaches out to all those on the spiritual path seeking to grow into a new and deeper relationship with God. The richness and clarity he brings to this topic is both stimulating to the mind and stirring to the soul.

—Oreon Masters, Ph.D., President,
Universal University

"This is a wonderful book, so simply and powerfully written, and much needed in a time of change and struggle for many Christians. Anyone questioning her or his faith MUST read this book. It challenges, but offers the hope of discovering a new stance as a Transcended Christian."

—Richard P. Hardy, Adjunct Professor, Pacific School
of Religion at Berkeley

THE
TRANSCENDED
CHRISTIAN

SPIRITUAL LESSONS

FOR THE

TWENTY-FIRST
CENTURY

DANIEL A. HELMINIAK

alyson books
NEW YORK

To Bruce Jarstfer
surgeon
musician
political activist
father
dear friend

© 2007 BY DANIEL A. HELMINIAK.
FOREWORD © 2007 BY PETER J. GOMES.
ALL RIGHTS RESERVED.

MANUFACTURED IN THE UNITED STATES OF AMERICA.

THIS TRADE PAPERBACK ORIGINAL IS PUBLISHED BY ALYSON BOOKS,
245 WEST 17TH STREET, NEW YORK, NEW YORK 10011.
DISTRIBUTION IN THE UNITED KINGDOM BY TURNAROUND PUBLISHER
SERVICES LTD., UNIT 3, OLYMPIA TRADING ESTATE, COBURG ROAD,
WOOD GREEN, LONDON N22 6TZ ENGLAND.

FIRST EDITION: APRIL 2007

07 08 09 10 11 **a** 10 9 8 7 6 5 4 3 2 1

ISBN 1-55583-860-X
ISBN-13 978-1-55583-860-7

LIBRARY OF CONGRESS CATALOGING-IN-PUBLICATION DATA
IS ON FILE.

CONTENTS

FOREWORD

MOST OF WHAT people hear in church these days doesn't make any sense, which perhaps explains the glazed look on the faces of the people in the pews when the scripture lessons appointed by ecclesiastical authorities are read. It also explains the looks of boredom, bewilderment, and utter incredulity that abound during most sermons. Listening to ancient texts and the sermons based on them takes work, and while many people are prepared to pay deference to scripture and limited attention to preaching, more than most simply endure until they can do more interesting things. All of the Bible classes and all of the sermons cannot transform the fact that we are trying to manipulate our understanding to comprehend the incomprehensible, and to watch preachers and listeners try to do so is both painful and unedifying.

Now comes Daniel A. Helminiak with a heroic and challenging effort to seek and speak the truth that transcends these texts and allows both preachers and listeners to hear about a God and a Jesus who are too important to be locked up in a theological worldview centuries removed from our own. Based on a series of sermons preached over the course of a thoughtful and active ministry to those for whom the Bible often consists of texts of terror rather than of freedom and joy, and for whom the good news is not always good, *The Transcended Christian: Spiritual Lessons for the*

Twenty-first Century delivers on its promise to offer spiritual wisdom for the twenty-first century. The title alone tells us that it is no good to offer something in the twenty-first century that, while it may have made sense a hundred or a thousand years ago, strains the mental processes of honest twenty-first-century listeners, and makes it necessary for such listeners to leave both their heads and their hearts outside the door of the church.

This book addresses those who have outgrown their religion. They are not people who have repudiated their faith and embraced a mindless secular hedonism or have chosen to become wanton libertines. This is not about people who have chosen to follow other gods or who have embraced a form of contemporary idolatry. The people to whom this book is directed are those who, while trying to take their Christian faith and its biblical theology seriously, find that in good conscience they can no longer do so, not because science or secularism has made a better offer but because the religion as communicated uncritically in text and theology does not speak to the present realities of the human condition. This is not a triumph of the secular but rather a failure of faith—not the faith of the would-be believer but the faith in which the would-be believer is required to believe.

Most thoughtful twenty-first-century Christians have forged a religion of personal conviction and faith that exists within, and at times even contradicts, the religious tradition they have inherited. Most do not stand up in church and protest the reading of scriptures that no longer make sense or contest the theological presuppositions and conclusions of the sermons they are obliged to hear, and most do not leave the church or create a new religion for themselves. Most stay put, but they exist as resisters, quiet but consistent, within the prevailing polity: Most are too polite, too well socialized to offer resistance or public rebuke. They simply pick and choose among that which is offered, rejecting that which gives offense and makes no sense and holding fast to that which continues to work and appeal. Theology is not a lay person's forte, and most people are not trained to do the critical exegetical work, thus, within the prevailing traditions, most people have constructed their own system of faith and belief, and those systems often have very little to do with what is routinely read and preached in church.

It is to those persons that Helminiak hopes to speak. He is a trained theologian and an experienced preacher, and he understands that the purposes of theology are to make things clear rather than to maintain an orthodoxy based on obscurantist conformity. This makes both him and his work dangerous to those for whom inquiry is dangerous, and appealing to those who have been waiting for an honest clarity that will allow them to own their faith. In a world where, as the author writes, "Spiritual crisis is the symptom of our age," the "old-time religion" simply will not do; it is a part of the problem, not of the solution.

Daniel Helminiak writes as a theologian and biblical scholar, a Catholic priest, and a gay man. The Vatican has never accepted his resignation from the priesthood and he writes within a church that considers his sexual orientation "intrinsically disordered." This must be a painful situation, one in which what one says, however true and useful, can be condemned or ignored because it comes from someone whose very existence is contrary to the moral position of his own church. This, however, is the position in which millions find themselves, millions to whom no one but the most partisan of extremists speak, who are thus left to either conform or to deny their faith.

While this is not just another book on homosexuality and the Christian tradition, it is a book in which the Christian tradition in all of its forms is forced to confront a set of social and existential realities that can neither be denied nor made to conform. In order to do the work of faith in the twenty-first century, Helminiak argues that one must move beyond the church. As the author puts it, "I had to leave the priesthood to be able to genuinely do the work of Jesus as I understood it." In this conviction he is not alone; hundreds of clergy and believers are where he is, and this book speaks both out of that condition and to it. The book represents a struggle "to hold on to my valid religious past and to update it for living in the present." There is a paradox here that provides the creative tension of the book and will speak to the many who share it:

IN MANY WAYS, I have found my religion narrow, restrictive, and even downright mistaken, and I have grown beyond it. At the same time, much of the wisdom that let me grow came from my religious upbringing. This book is about this combination of staying rooted in one's Christianity and also growing beyond it.

Like most authentic writing, this book is autobiographical, drawing upon the deep experiences, wide learning, and often painful sensibilities of the author. Yet, as he professes, it is not his story alone, and therefore it will surely resonate with those millions who are "in" the church but no longer "of" it.

The Transcended Christian, while appealing, will be a difficult read for many who seek simple answers to complex questions. The mutual curse of fundamentalism and orthodoxy is that they offer simplicities in the form of incredulities in the face of complexities that compel credibility. Helminiak acknowledges that there are inevitable misunderstandings of certain Bible texts that are routinely read out in church. For example, he tells us that those passages about Jesus' supposed self-sacrifice in supposed obedience to God, the substitutionary blood atonement, make God a jealous perversity. The sacrifice of Isaac, which provokes murder in response to God's command, paints an unsatisfactory image of God: "Heard in contemporary English and without detailed exegesis, these scriptural passages present perversity."

Perversity should not be proclaimed as the "word of God," and to persist in doing so simply "perpetuates neurotic guilt in simple believers," working against "honest and sane responsibility among Christians." These texts, Helminiak argues, should be stricken from public lectionaries and replaced by texts that emphasize compassion, forgiveness, and thanksgiving. "The criterion should be to convey God's message to a contemporary congregation, not to hold fast to ancient texts and subtle theologies."

These are strong strategies and tough words, and while many will not hear them gladly, many more will, for honesty, clarity, and charity are the only assurances that will help the church transcend its own limited self-interest and be fit to take its place in the world of the twenty-first century. "Change in the outlook and practice of Christianity is inevitable," he writes. "The writing is already on the wall."

Appeals to the Bible, tradition, and God's eternal decrees cannot forever resist the tides of history, so, despite a lot of pessimism and some very heavy-hitting criticism, this is a work of encouragement and hope. If one cares for the church as it ought to be rather than as it has been or is now, this book will be essential and constructive reading. It is a brave book by a brave man, and I am happy to commend it to all, especially to those for whom the future is more important than the past.

—*Rev. Prof. Peter J. Gomes*
Cambridge, Massachusetts
September 25, 2006

ONE

THE TRANSCENDED CHRISTIAN

WHAT DO YOU DO when you've outgrown your religion? When your life experience exceeds that of your clergy? When the learning that life forced on you challenges your religious beliefs? When you can no longer deny that something new is afoot and your church is out of touch?

THE CURRENT SPIRITUAL CHALLENGE

Many people today are in this exact situation and for many different reasons. I know a wonderful woman who stands for the best of what Christianity means, who no longer goes to church and who now has grave doubts about all religion. Her father was a minister. She grew up in a devout and genuinely good home. Her dear, aged mother, loving but confused, continued to the end to pray for her, anxious and fearful of her daughter's eternal damnation. This woman herself is the finest of people: concerned, helpful, honest. She is a highly successful professional, and the whole of her work at nonprofit organizations is dedicated to helping other people. Who could be more Jesus-like?

But her marriage became unworkable. All efforts to salvage it failed. Even her deep concern for her son could not justify staying in that relationship. So she divorced and was summarily ostracized from the church that had professed for years to be her "Christian family."

She was no longer welcome. She had suddenly become a "wayward daughter" and a "lost sister." Now she found neither understanding nor support in her church. Already deeply hurt by the divorce and agonizing in conscience over the religious implications of her decision, she was left without the encouragement and spiritual counsel that now, of all times, she really needed and that the church always claimed to provide.

Her experience forced her to look at things differently. She believes in God and loves Jesus and respects all the positive values for which religion stands, but the course of her life made her unable to deny that religion is simplistic. Oftentimes life just does not follow the rules that religion lays down. Unexpected twists of fate bring on complications that religion is not willing to address. So anybody living a real life is liable not to fit into the standard religious picture.

Being an intelligent woman, she read, talked with people, attended conferences, and joined a spiritually based, nondenominational support group. Gradually, she put together a new outlook on life and a new understanding of spirituality. She salvaged the goodness of her upbringing and whatever wisdom she gained through religion. She combined these with her new learning and forged her own spiritual position.

THE TRANSCENDED CHRISTIAN

That is what my friend did when she outgrew her religion. Through her actual living and continued seeking, she took her religion to the next level. She went beyond the Christianity of her upbringing and morphed it into something new. She became a transcended Christian. She remained a genuine believer—she grew up a Christian and remains a Christian. But her life experience forced her to sift through her Christianity. She retains the valid spiritual core of her religious upbringing, but she has moved beyond the limits of institutional religion. She transcended her Christianity: She expanded it to include the complexities of life in the twenty-first century and to be open to truth and goodness in any of its guises.

I believe that she represents the new wave of religious believers. She is part of the next generation of Christians. She is the kind of Christian who can live comfortably and contribute generously to a pluralistic and even secular global society of the twenty-first century. But, of course, most churches today will have none of it.

No doubt, it was her religious upbringing itself that allowed her to take this step forward. Her religion instilled in her the moral commitment and supplied the spiritual insight that carried her through the crisis of her divorce. Indeed, I would say that in her case religion did exactly what it is supposed to do: It pointed out the stepping stones that lead to spiritual maturity.

Religion is not made to serve itself. Its goal is not to gather a larger congregation and rake in a higher collection each week. Like families, religion is supposed to help us grow up and move on. Religion is supposed to foster spiritual adulthood and free us from the necessary but limiting confines of spiritual childhood. In fact, then my friend is a stunning religious success. The tools she got from her religion allowed her to honestly and lovingly deal with her life. Now she is a blessing to all she meets. Broken out of a religious cocoon, she is a butterfly of spiritual beauty.

But, of course, she is no longer at home with the church, nor can she be comfortable with her family when questions of religion come up. She cannot discuss her spiritual life with any of them. Daughter of a respected minister's family, she lives on the fringes of organized religion. In general, churchgoers in the Bible Belt put her down. Naïvely they invite her to church, offering their sugar-coated-candy religion as an enticement. Sincerely, presumptuously, and blindly, not recognizing Jesus when they see him, they tell her that her life would be so much better if she'd only come to church with them and turn to Jesus. She tells them, "God makes house calls," and they are baffled. She and they are living in different worlds.

My friend grew beyond her religion because of a personal crisis. The religious rules she was taught did not square with the real life she had to live. Many people begin to question their religion because of personal crises. But today, spiritual questions and religious doubts affect all of us, personal crisis or not.

We live in difficult times. I doubt that any period in human history has known as much turmoil as our own. Because of TV, movies, the Internet, and easy travel, our world is becoming one global village. We know about different countries, different cultures, different religions. We cannot avoid them. It would be rare today to find someone who does not know well at least one person of a different religion. And when we get to know those others, we are challenged. Not only do they believe differently from us; they also often turn out to be good people. Sometimes they downright inspire us—like the remarkable Japanese woman I met in Mexico who reverently gave a coin to every beggar who asked. We can't just write those others off as "heathens" the way cocky preachers might. If we have any decency in us at all, we recognize their goodness and take them seriously. But taking them seriously, we cannot help but begin to wonder about our own religious beliefs.

Religions differ. We know that. We know it all too well. But the religions also all claim to be true, especially the Western religions: Judaism, Christianity, and Islam. Still, they cannot all be true when their teachings differ. Even the many Christian churches have different beliefs. So we are left wondering whether any of them is true. Is there even such a thing as truth? How does one know what to believe? Unless we are sure that our beliefs are true, they don't serve us very well. What good is a belief if you really can't rely on it? Nonetheless, heartlessly, our pluralistic world is forcing us to question our beliefs. Like it or not, if we are at all in tune with our world, we are thrust into a crisis of faith. Spiritual crisis is symptomatic of our age.

Some people resolve their crisis by going fundamentalist. They shut their eyes to other religions, stop questioning and thinking, hold to their own religion unbendingly, and walk lock-step in the security of the company of their fellow believers. One Bible-believing woman I knew dealt with her divorce in just this way. For the well-being of her children, she had to get away from her husband. Bravely she did, but thinking that God operates on unbending rules, she lives with constant guilt, prays that God will forgive her, and, compelled by her religion to also point out other people's "sins," she consoles herself and softens her rebukes with "We are all sinners."

More thoughtful, more insightful people cannot go that route. Religion itself has taught them to be honest about the facts. Even in the name of God, they cannot just shut down their minds and package up their lives. They want to continue living, exploring, growing. They learned that God is good. Precisely because they are religious, they want a life about which they can rejoice, be thankful, give praise. So they suffer a spiritual crisis because most churches have not yet stepped into the twenty-first century.

This book is written for that dear divorced friend and for so many other good-willed people who have outgrown their religion. In these chapters I have applied my own experience and my broad education to the meaning of Christian belief in the contemporary world. This book addresses the questions that arise in the minds of deeply spiritual people who can no longer find nourishment in that "old-time religion."

MY OWN EXPERIENCE

My friend is not the only one whose life led her beyond the church. There is the African-American college co-ed who came to my office in tears after a class on abortion: She had had one, and she had no one to whom she could turn. There is the intelligent college junior, raised Baptist in a small southern town, who came to me with questions about Jesus: His high-school–educated minister knew nothing of the early church councils, which debated the very questions that were troubling that boy's faith. There are the women, bright, gifted, generous women, who aced my theology courses: They wanted to be priests but, as Catholics, hadn't a prayer. And, of course, my own life has taken a similar trajectory through and beyond organized religion.

Born and raised in South Side, Pittsburgh, in a small Polish community whose center was the local Catholic church, I grew up intensely pious and considerably naïve. No one in that community, including my parents and relatives, had ever finished high school, let alone gone to college. Only the parish priests and the sisters who taught in the schools were well educated. Still, the people there were honest, hard working, deeply religious, and, as I later realized, shrewd and intelligent. I could not have had a better childhood home and neighborhood.

My all-consuming interest was science, but for a number of reasons—community expectations, ignorance of other options, my religious sensitivity, and personal factors of which I was not aware (I was running away from something)—after graduating from high school, I entered the seminary. Through college in the States and four years of graduate studies in Rome, I soared right along to ordination. Through all those years and for a good number afterward, I lived a supremely sheltered life. In fact, I believe, I was more open to other religions and to secular pursuits than my seminary classmates and fellow priests were. Nonetheless, my environment, my associations, and my thinking were Catholic through and through.

I spent my first four ordained years as an associate pastor in a suburban parish in Pittsburgh. Within two years, I was uncomfortable there. My mind wanted depth, but ministry pulled me in a hundred different directions. I was intensely lonely in the parish. I had always been. I missed the camaraderie and intellectual community that made seminary so appealing.

What's more, away from the protective routines of the seminary, my supposed virtue quickly proved shallow. No wonder celibacy was an easy commitment to make: I had no attraction to women and no desire to be married. After I had my first guilt-ridden sexual relationship, however, it finally dawned on me: I was using the hallowed requirement of priestly celibacy to avoid having to deal with sex. Of course I was the perfect seminarian and young priest! I was using celibacy exactly as the Catholic Church had designed it.

At that same time, I also suffered my first major disillusionment with the institutional Catholic Church. I had a close friend who was involved in the "birth-control controversy" in the Archdiocese of Washington, D.C., and over some months I watched the Church methodically crush a large group of priests, including my friend, for their public opposition to Pope Paul VI's condemnation of "the pill." I was dumbfounded. I was dismayed to realize that the official Catholic Church had so little concern for people that it would ruthlessly destroy anyone who publicly opposed its corporate policy. I was later to relearn that lesson in my own case. And the Church's evasive response to the recent sex-abuse cases was to drive that lesson home ruthlessly. Amazingly, the Catholic Church preserves a façade of holiness and, Teflon-clean, manages to slip away from even the most outrageous of scandals. Yes, indeed, my first years as a priest were a real eye-opener.

Trying to find a more congenial ministry, I left the Diocese of Pittsburgh and joined an association of priests in Baltimore, the Society of Saint Sulpice, the "Sulpicians," who specialize in seminary education. The idea was that this new work would serve my need for community, my intellectual bent, and my interest in psychology and spirituality all at once.

Within a year on the fast track, I was pursuing a doctorate in systematic theology in Boston. There, I had the extreme good fortune to study with Professor Bernard Lonergan, S.J., one of the geniuses of the twentieth century. I learned to think critically about religion, and I acquired the intellectual tools to apply my scientist's mind to it. Finally I began to construct my own understanding of Christianity.

I also began to deal with my sexuality. I realized and admitted that I was gay, and I began to explore intimate relationships. I also began serving as chaplain to Dignity/Boston, one of a national chain of support groups for gay, lesbian, bisexual, and transgender Catholics, their families, and friends.

By that time, at least in my own mind, I was already living on the fringes of the Catholic Church, almost standing on the outside looking in. Nonetheless, for years I attempted to reconcile my gay life, my reservations about the institutional Church, and my status as a Catholic priest. I taught graduate theology and spirituality at Oblate School of Theology in San Antonio. In those days, when there was still hope that Catholicism would respond positively to the reality of lesbian and gay people, I even served as the official chaplain of the Archdiocese of San Antonio to the gay community. But more and more I realized that there would eventually be no way I could be true to myself and remain a Catholic priest in good standing. So, with the intention of eventually resigning from the priesthood, I moved to Austin and earned a second PhD in psychology.

Through all those years from Boston to Austin, I continued to do priestly ministry: teaching and lecturing, weekend assistance in local parishes, and, of course, chaplaincy to Dignity/Boston, Dignity/San Antonio, and Dignity/Austin. I decided that, as long as I was able, I would use my priestly office to do what good I could.

Then, with the completion of that psychology degree and with my hiring by the Department of Psychology at the University of West Georgia in 1995, I submitted to my bishop and the Vatican a formal resignation from active priestly ministry. Part of my thinking was that, as an official priest, I was restricted from doing the honest and compassionate ministry that I thought I was ordained to do. I could not publicly say what needed to be said nor freely do what needed to be done. I had to leave the priesthood to be able to genuinely do the work of Jesus as I understood it. I have heard other ex-priests phrase the matter in exactly the same way.

The Vatican never accepted my resignation. I take this response to mean that the Vatican is giving me permission to continue to officially represent the Catholic Church. Hence, I write as a priest, and I do so in good conscience. Besides, according to Catholic teaching, once a priest, always a priest. One may be dispensed from priestly duties, but one can never undo ordination. So "in my soul" I remain a priest. That is to say, my priestly training, experience, and education make me in part what I am. This part of me cannot be lost or taken away. My history has formed and shaped my very being. My "priesthood" remains with me forever. In these pages I exercise a ministry of spiritual leadership.

THE SHAPE OF MY SPIRITUAL LIFE

My education, ordination, and priestly experience—not only these, but also my personal life inform this ministry and color my writing here. Through the years of seminary and priesthood and beyond until today, I continue to dedicate myself to the spiritual life. This dedication flows into this book. Indeed, in some ways I am not only spiritual, as they say these days, but also still religious. I still consider myself a Roman Catholic.

I attend Sunday Mass regularly—but always at a church where the service nourishes me spiritually. I find it useful to worship with others, to be encouraged and challenged by good preaching, to be inspired by beautiful music, to be moved to tears by soul searching, and to hold hands with fellow believers and pray aloud the Lord's Prayer. I sift through what comes down from the Catholic Church, and, as they say in twelve-step programs, I take what is useful and leave the rest. I use my church attendance to support my spiritual quest. I also often attend non-Catholic churches and even non-Christian religious ceremonies. Wherever I find spiritual nourishment, I am at home. Wherever I meet people who are committed to peace and justice, I feel connected.

Nonetheless, despite my fierce opposition to some Catholic teaching and my periodic outrage at some proclamations from the Vatican and the Catholic bishops, I cannot imagine giving up my Catholic identity. I know enough about religion to realize that I would find reason for similar opposition in any other church or religion, and I am encouraged by the infallibly defined Catholic teaching that there can be no true conflict between religion and science, faith and reason, because God's truth is one. Catholicism has always insisted on the goodness of creation in addition to the promise of eternal life—the natural and the supernatural—and insists that these two hang together. As an ancient Christian adage has it, "Grace builds on nature." So I stick with my own tradition, the one that I know best, the one with which I am most comfortable, and the one that makes most sense to me. I use religion to nurture my spirituality. In my understanding, to nurture spirituality is the purpose of organized religion.

Besides church attendance, I also have other spiritual practices. I meditate regularly. Usually I use a technique called "Centering Prayer," something similar to Transcendental Meditation. So my "prayer" is most often done without words. My goal in meditation is to open myself to my own depths and to whatever is beyond. Having learned about meditation during retreats at a Tibetan Buddhist monastery in Vermont, I have been practicing for decades. My *Meditation Without Myth* details my understanding of meditative practice.

I also sometimes pray in more standard ways—not really expecting God to step in and rescue me, to be sure, but using words and traditional "prayers," nonetheless. Oftentimes I fall asleep reciting by memory one of my favorite psalms. The Prayer of Saint Francis and the Buddhist Wish of Noble Sympathy are favorites of mine. I also sometimes use religious texts for inspiration and learning, such as passages from the Bible or from other spiritual writings, Christian and otherwise.

From time to time, often after my meditation, I will sing a Gregorian chant. The beauty of the Latin verses and the calm of the melodies soothe my soul. Besides, the chants call up memories of my seminary days, and in my gut I remember the religious community that I loved and, often sadly, the shining hope for religion that I used to have. The Latin takes me right back to the medieval world from which those chants emerged, and in my own soul I work to harmonize a long-standing and beautiful religious tradition with my current spiritual awareness.

Much of my spiritual practice involves an effort to hold on to my valid religious past and to update it for living in the present. This book is one fruit of this effort.

This work of updating also fills much of my professional life. Because I am now a professor of psychology whose specialization is spirituality, my study and research focus on spiritual growth. Thus, my work itself is an important part of my personal spiritual quest. Like many people who view their work—whether menial or lofty—as a sacred task, I see my research, teaching, lecturing, and writing as a ministry. I am performing a service. No longer functioning officially as a priest, I serve God's people as a professor, lecturer, and author. The discipline that my profession requires is central to my spiritual life. So I view the whole of my day as a spiritual exercise.

I find it hard to think of my spirituality as separate from my everyday living. All my encounters with others are aspects of my spiritual life. The Christian ideal of love or the Buddhist ideal of universal compassion—these I try to live. Whether teaching my students, advising them one-on-one, writing e-mail to a friend, attending to business with colleagues, greeting staff and fellow residents at my condo building, meeting a stranger at the mall, participating in political campaigns, or contributing to worthy causes, I strive to be patient, understanding, forthright, and compassionate. Overall, I try to be a person who is contributing to the common good, not part of the problems of our times but part of the solution.

For me, spirituality has less to do with church or prayer and more to do with daily living. In many ways I have found my Catholic religion narrow, restrictive, and even downright mistaken, and I have grown beyond it. At the same time, much of the wisdom that let me grow came from my religious upbringing. This book is about this combination of staying rooted in one's Christianity while also growing beyond it. In these pages I am actually sharing my spiritual journey and the spiritual quest of many other people in our age.

THE TITLE OF THIS BOOK

Ironically, one important credential of my spiritual leadership is my resignation from priestly ministry. A dear friend, Toby Johnson, made this very point. Toby, who also spent time in the seminary of a Catholic religious order, is a prolific author: He has edited *White Crane Journal*, a quarterly on gay spirituality, and for a wide range of people, he functions as a spiritual guru. His comment: "These days, being a saint requires leaving the church!"

I do not quite fit Toby's model. I did resign from the priesthood, but I do not intend to leave the Church. I grew up with earthly things interwoven within my soul—water, oil, real wine, candles, incense, statues, holy pictures, organ music, stained-glass windows, fellow-human saints, and flawed human priests, bishops, and popes. As I got older, I learned a theology that held earth and heaven together. So it was relatively easy for me to open my spirituality to secular and even non-Christian angles. Catholicism has served me well. I do not want to cut my Catholic roots.

Brilliantly creative and still committed to his initial insight, Toby referred to me as "a transcended Catholic." That comment gave me the idea for the title of this book. It is about me, a transcended Christian, and about so many others on this same pilgrimage.

THE ORIGINS OF THESE ESSAYS

During the years between my coming out and my resignation from the priesthood, I regularly preached to gay Catholic groups. Each time, I had to find in the scripture readings or in the feast of the day some spiritual lesson that would speak to people who are on the fringes of the church. What message can one preach to people who, according to official Catholicism and the Biblical Literalists, are sinners and destined for hell? Being one of those people myself, I had better have some idea.

For the sake of my own integrity, I had to work through difficult questions of conscience and to rethink traditional practices
and doctrines. So that I myself could continue believing and remain on a pilgrim's path, I had to reintegrate my upbringing, my
seminary training, and my spiritual commitments.

Week after week, I shared my rethinking as I preached to an
outcast church. In the depths of my anguished probing, I believe
that I more and more truly touched the core of Christianity. After
all, Jesus himself was taunted as being "a friend of tax collectors
and sinners" (Matthew 11:19), and he pointed to them as his examples of godly living: "Truly I tell you, the tax collectors and the
prostitutes are going into the kingdom of God ahead of you [chief
priests and elders]" (Matthew 21:31). Religion's true meaning
only comes out when it faces the burning issues of the day head-
on. Only in the cauldron of spiritual crisis does insight bubble to
the surface. I have been living in such a crisis for decades.

These essays are the fruit of my own spiritual quest. These
spiritual lessons summarize my up-to-date understanding of
Christianity. I write as a Roman Catholic, but I am certain that my
message is relevant to Christians of all denominations in these
turbulent times. I write as a Christian, but I reach out also to non-
Christians and to totally nonreligious people. I want to emphasize
the spiritual wisdom that bonds us all. Of this I have no doubt:
Any genuinely spiritual person in the third millennium identifies
with spiritual seekers of every stripe.

THE SPIRITUAL HERITAGE
OF CHRISTIANITY

My intent is to show that Christianity does bear a profound spiritual heritage. But of late, Western religion has been pushing a
cold and shallow agenda: a literal Bible, rote doctrinal formulas,
opposition to science, relentless moralizing, and unbending institutional allegiance. Christianity seems simpleminded. Therefore,
many people have looked to spiritual movements from the East
for guidance. People tend to forget that what we read of Eastern

philosophy and religion is the very best of what the East has to offer; only the best gets translated. In contrast, we are familiar with every dirty detail of our own religion. Besides, few of us actually know of the great classics of Christianity: Irenaeus, Athanasius, Augustine, Dionysius the pseudo-Areopagite, Benedict of Nursia, Bernard of Clairvaux, Thomas Aquinas, Francis of Assisi, Catherine of Sienna, Meister Eckhart, Martin Luther, John Calvin, John of the Cross, Theresa of Avila, John Wesley, and the list goes on.

The mystics and saints of Christianity, the theologians and the philosophers offer as profound an insight into life as any others. In contrast to most Eastern thought, Christianity is actually more down-to-earth, more concerned about life in this world, more invested in issues of justice, love, peace, and politics—all matters that burden the budding global community. The deep currents of Christian spirituality are not about pie in the sky, some supposed spiritual fulfillment in some other life. Look up the biography of any of the people whose names I just listed. None was a spaced-out mystic; each was a formidable mover and shaker who changed his or her world. After all, the central belief of Christianity is about incarnation, about a God who came to live among us on this earth. To be sure, we have taken this belief and turned it into a fairy tale about an otherworldly superman, but, surely, the notion of God-become-flesh confirms the value of humanity and this world more than it exalts God and a world to come. Christianity has to do with open-eyed, liberated, grateful living in the here and now and, then, only by implication, about hope for fulfillment in another life.

I am not trying to pit East against West, one religion against another. No way! My emphasis is the commonalities among the world's religions. I want to highlight a spiritual core that all people of goodwill could embrace. That core is in Christianity as well as in other religions. By discovering that core, we could nurture our roots in Christianity while also embracing the spiritual wisdom of other traditions.

Alienated Christians need not necessarily chuck their Christianity to find peace of soul. In their own religious tradition they can find stepping-stones that lead to spiritual fulfillment, wherever it may eventually lie.

What I propose, you see, is still in some ways a rather conservative project. The goal is not to throw off our religion but to revitalize it, and in today's global society, revitalization can only mean some kind of reconciliation of all religions at their depths. My hope is that this book will serve you, my readers, as a bridge on which to cross over to a globally viable spirituality with your Christianity intact.

THE PLAN OF THIS BOOK

I arranged the essays in this book in a particular order. As best as I could, I make the discussion progress as the chapters unfold. The topics move from very general spiritual concerns of a personal nature to more theological, social, and political concerns. Still, each essay stands as a unit and could be read on its own.

Since these essays derive from homilies (brief sermons), they use the original scripture texts to introduce each topic. The scripture readings not only set a spiritual tone for each essay but also provide a starting point within traditional Christianity. What you understand upon initially reading these scriptures will be grist for the spiritual learning mill as the essays suggest new insight and the resultant friction advances the process of spiritual growth.

I have written for people who are outgrowing their religion and struggling to find new spiritual balance. As a result, my statements are quite forthright. I support religion where religion can be of help, and I severely criticize religion where religion hinders spiritual growth. I am also supportive of people who have given up on religion altogether—as long as their exodus leads toward genuine spirituality and overflows into the betterment of our world.

This book is not for everyone. Surely, some will find it offensive, but I do not write for them. I write for the rest of us who, in today's complex world, search our souls to know the truth about life and to find a right and truly wholesome way to live. Religious tolerance makes us too respectful of anything that passes as "religion." Openness without criteria makes us hesitant to call outright nonsense what some proclaim as revealed. But in the face of widespread and deliberate misinformation campaigns, both political and religious—and frighteningly, the two are melding—highlighting the truth also requires denouncing the error. I do not shrink from this requirement. If some of what I have written seems harsh, it is only because the stakes are high.

Spiritual movements today—in the so-called culture wars—are vying for people's souls. I hope to contribute to the triumph of the good—and not just spouting rhetoric, I will say exactly what I mean by *good* so that you, dear reader, can understand and decide matters for yourself. I trust you to come to a worthy conclusion. I believe in the essential goodness of the human being. Or, to make the same point religiously, I believe that Holy Spirit speaks in our hearts, and, if we sincerely attend to our hearts in open, honest, and loving consultation with others, we can hardly go astray.

LEARNING FROM RELIGIOUS OUTCASTS

Many of the ideas expressed in these essays originally came from my preaching to gay Christians. So references to the spiritual struggles of lesbian and gay people run through these essays, and sometimes these essays address gay and lesbian Christians directly. I trust that heterosexual readers will not find this emphasis irrelevant. In many ways, homosexual religious experience is paradigmatic of today's spiritual crisis. Which other group do religious leaders so vociferously denounce while it claims inspiration from the Holy Spirit? It would be helpful if heterosexuals understood more about homosexuality, for it is one of the prime issues currently splitting the churches and, with them, society at large. The gay origins of the book should be one of its assets.

For a variety of reasons besides sexuality, many of us are religious outcasts, and as the religious battle lines are drawn more tightly, many more will find themselves cast out. In this situation, lessons from the gay Christian community, outsiders from the start, should prove enlightening as we all attempt to discern to-day's direction of genuine spiritual growth.

The irony of this state of affairs should not elude us nor should its spiritual lesson. To say it in Jesus' words, "Many who are first will be last, and the last will be first" (Mark 10:31). The publicans and the prostitutes, the homosexuals and the divorced, the women and the doubters, the outcasts of society and the sinners in the eyes of the churches, these will be entering the realm of God sooner than the self-righteous religious folk who claim to know God's will so surely and to understand God's ways so fully. From Jesus' own teaching, we should expect that those who struggle with contemporary religion would best point us to spiritual fulfillment.

Accordingly, may this book be an aid to all who seek to truly follow God's way by following the way of Jesus. May those who think they have found that way realize that, far from separating them from other people, even people of different religions or of no religion, Jesus' genuine way welcomes all God's children. May these essays, addressed to the outcasts, help us to realize that in matters of God the out-group may just turn out to be the in-group. Building on this realization and, thus, transcending the narrow limits of institutional religion, may we structure a world-view big enough to include the whole world. May we be part of the solution, not part of our world's problems. May we be positive forces in forging a global community of the twenty-first century.

TWO

Catching the Hidden Meaning of Life: Jesus Spoke in Parables

JESUS TOLD THEM many things in parables, saying: "Listen! A sower went out to sow. And as he sowed, some seeds fell on the path, and the birds came and ate them up. Other seeds fell on rocky ground, where they did not have much soil, and they sprang up quickly, since they had no depth of soil. But when the sun rose, they were scorched; and since they had no root, they withered away. Other seeds fell among thorns, and the thorns grew up and choked them. Other seeds fell on good soil and brought forth grain, some a hundred-fold, some sixty, some thirty. Let any one with ears listen."

—MATTHEW 13:3–9

SPEND AS MUCH TIME as you want explaining a symphony to a deaf person. Describe a rainbow to someone who is blind. Without the actual experience of seeing or hearing, that person will certainly make something of your attempts to communicate, but he or she will never really understand.

Or how about you? You can hear love songs and hear people talk of love. You might think you have some sense of love. You might even write papers about it, but without ever having actually been in love, you really do not know what love is. This may be your story, too, but I'm talking about *myself* in this case.

MAKING SENSE OF SUGGESTIVE WORDS

I remember being a young kid in high school. My classmates were so goo-goo eyed over the girls. Their fascination made little sense to me. I thought their infatuations were all so exaggerated. In my typical intellectual mode of that time, I rationalized their reactions on the basis of what limited data I had: My classmates were just going along with the fad. They were acting as everyone expected them to, but I was above all that; I would not play that game.

My classmates rationalized my reaction, too. They thought they understood it when I entered the seminary to become a celibate Catholic priest. Actually, so did I. But, when years later, as a priest, I accepted my sexuality, did fall in love, and allowed myself to admit that I had done so, I was overwhelmed. I said to myself, "Ah, so this is what those love songs are about! What they're saying is for real." I had never seen so beautiful a spring before that year when I fell in love. Now I was the one who was goo-goo eyed.

Some things are very difficult to put into words. Unless you have experienced them yourself, they do not make full sense when you hear talk of them. You may think you understand—like me and my teenage theory of love—but you do not. Such self-deception is especially true for matters of the heart and the soul.

When it comes to spiritual matters, often the best we can do is hint at them. We use images, metaphors, parables: "Life is like a river." "The reign of God is a sower who went out to sow." The images act like a finger pointing at the moon. The moon is the object of interest, but sometimes we get confused, and the finger is what catches our attention. Then we end up repeating empty words, for we never grasped what the sayings really mean. We had no idea what the words were pointing at.

When I was in seminary, week after week, I came out from our spiritual conferences frustrated, mumbling to myself, "Somebody must know something about this stuff!" I was certainly not hearing anything that made much sense, and in this case, I believe, it was because nobody really knew much about the subject. The conferences were empty words, formulas about distant constructs: the soul; spiritual longing; ascetic practices; sin and forgiveness; the purgative, illuminative, and unitive ways; actual and sanctifying grace; nature and the supernatural; infused and acquired contemplation; and union with God. Nobody I met could explain what these words, passed on for generations, meant.

As a result, I have spent a good part of my professional life trying to formulate a scientific account of spirituality. I want to go beyond metaphors, symbols, and merely pointing at the moon. I want to explain the spiritual in precise, technical terminology that cannot be misunderstood. Of course, most people think that mine is a misguided project. Popular and even professional "wisdom" holds that the spiritual is ineffable. Supposedly, it cannot be understood incisively nor expressed precisely.

Whether or not a scientific spirituality is possible is not the question here. The fact of the matter is that in spiritual circles people do talk about spiritual things, so talk of some kind about the spiritual is certainly possible. The catch, of course, is that when people talk about the spiritual, they do so not in precise terminology but in suggestive formulations via images, metaphors, and symbols, which all have a major weakness. Only people who somehow already have deep spiritual experiences and recognize the experiences as spiritual will understand what the metaphors and symbols mean. Only people who have risked breaking out of the prescribed religious boxes and have grappled with the reality of life will recognize themselves in the metaphors and symbols.

So, talk of spirituality is often like trying to pull yourself up by your bootstraps: Unless you already understand, the words are of little help, but once you do understand, the words are unnecessary. Yet, for the time being, at least, metaphors seem to be the best bootstraps we have with which to tug at the spiritual within us. So even Jesus spoke in parables. At the same time, until we might someday formulate spiritual things precisely, we ever run the risk of having half-cocked enthusiasts use the spiritual metaphors to fabricate religious doctrines when they haven't a clue what the metaphors really mean.

TURNING SUGGESTIVE METAPHORS INTO RIGID DOGMA

Bound by the language of his culture, Jesus preached his message in the images, metaphors, and symbols of ancient Palestine and in parables: The sower went out to sow. The kingdom (or reign) of God is like a mustard seed. Unless you become like little children. . . . The king sent out his servants. God's is already among us.

By means of parables, Jesus wanted to say that there is a power loose in this world, and it is transforming us. It is moving us toward healing and growth and often along unexpected paths. Although we may not fully understand where the paths lead, the power behind the unfolding universe is ultimately for the good. If we were to make this same point in religious terminology, we would speak of God's work among us. We would credit the goodness of the power of the universe by saying that God loves us, that God is concerned about us. And what we would really be trying to say is that the ultimate power of the universe is on our side. Life is okay, just as it is unfolding, and you are okay, just as you are currently growing. Best to trust life and flow with it.

There is certainly a sense in which those statements are absolutely true. Yet sometimes it is difficult to grasp what the words could possibly mean. Sometimes it is especially difficult to recognize their truth in our personal lives. "The power behind the uni-

verse is ultimately for the good." "Life is okay just as it is unfolding." "I am okay just as I am currently growing." "God loves us."
We might say in reply, "Oh, really! But things are crap. The world
is a mess and so is my life . . . Well, at times, at least."

We can distill the message of Jesus' parables into direct statements, but even direct statements about spiritual things are obscure. Sometimes when people hear those statements, all they get
are the words. They never really grasp the meaning. Like all of us
at times, they lead "lives of quiet desperation," as David Thoreau
so poignantly phrased it. They, we, in desperate need, cling to any
shred of hope. Those words, whatever they really mean, do be-
speak hope. So people latch onto them, repeat them, elaborate
them, preach them.

People "get religion." They become very committed to the
"spiritual," very dedicated to the proper order of things, very intent on keeping religious rules, very devoted to some power bigger than us all. At heart they, like we, are sincere and good-willed
people. We are only trying to live a satisfying life. But life is difficult. Many, most, of us may never have really been able to experience our lives to the depths: It would be too painful to actually
feel what living has been like. So we do not really experience life,
and, as a result, we really have no basis for understanding it. Talk
of deep living could mean anything, and we could not tell the difference. But having those hopeful religious teachings makes living
easier, so we cling to them.

Like me, theorizing about love out of my teenage ignorance,
people take the mere words about life that they have heard and
condense them into pat, doctrinal formulas. They tie up all the
loose ends and produce a consistent package of beliefs and morals.
Then, what is worse, filled with the new enthusiasm of their religious find or concoction, they develop a need to "share" their new
hope, to "witness" to their faith, and hardball proselytizing
begins.

From a psychological point of view, I suspect that this compul-
sion to "witness" comes from a hidden inner sense that there is

still something missing in such prepackaged faith. To keep the lack from showing, the true believers fill their worlds with words. They keep themselves preoccupied with set formulas, with many and long religious services, with the task of making converts, and with crusades against the "godless." Thus, they never really have to dwell in the silence of their hearts, and they really don't have time to mull over their beliefs. After all, supposedly, "An idle mind is the devil's workshop."

I know, of course, that the contemporary "Christians" —the Bible Fundamentalists—insist they are preaching out of concern to share their saving beliefs with others. Supposedly, their motives are purely altruistic. But anyone who has been subjected to the onslaught of their preaching senses the intensity, harshness, and desperation of their cause, and anyone with a sense of spirituality has a hard time believing that this preaching comes from peace-filled souls.

One Sunday morning as I exited church after an inspiring service, I and my fellow worshippers encountered a group of "Christians" picketing our church. They felt some need to protest the wickedness of Catholic belief. On other occasions, we hear of the "Reverend" Fred Phelps and his family followers picketing the *funerals* of people who died of AIDS or the funeral of Matthew Shepard, the young gay man who was pistol whipped and left to die, hung on a fence, in the cold of the Wyoming night. Their placards read things like "God hates faggots." Are we supposed to believe that these demonstrations express the love of a compassionate God?

For whatever reason, these ardent believers need to preach. They give out nice, clear formulas and nice, clear rules, and nice, clear doctrines. They have the answer for every young person's uncertainty about life, every parent's need for guidance, every spouse's marital problem, every addict's destructive habit, every medical patient's desire for a cure. Their response to the concerns of life is a one-size-fits-all solution. With infallible authority, they tell us how life is *supposed* to be, that is, how they were told it is to be, how they idealize and imagine it to be, and how they want to force it to be. How closely their version of life is linked to reality is an open question.

Such religion does, indeed, meet some human needs. People in need often find community, support, focus, and direction by "finding Jesus" in a conservative church. People who never had the benefit of discipline in their upbringing use strict religion to get their lives in order. Sociological studies have shown that, for many, fundamentalist religion takes a seven-year course. People join it, find inspiration, order their lives, develop useful habits and discipline, and then move on to a more open way of living. Certain kinds of rigid religion can benefit certain people at certain points in their lives. Like any fiction, the inspiring reassurance of unquestioned religion is often helpful.

Unfortunately this helpfulness is not universal and not permanent. When the formulas of rigid religion are taken as unquestioned truth, they can also be crippling. They limit life and put boundaries on experience, thought, wonder, and delight. They actually shut down the curiosity and unbounded openness of the human spirit. They corrode the soul's very potential for deep experience of God.

Such religion is like an overstuffed suitcase: You push down on one side, and things pop out the other side. If you insist on closing the thing, nonetheless, you end up either breaking it or crushing everything in it.

Life never fits into nice, neat, little packages. People never fit into nice, neat patterns. Life goes its own way; there are "the slings and arrows of outrageous fortune," as Shakespeare noted. Such is life: It continues to grow and to change and to move. A job, a relationship, a circle of friends, a political era—how long do these last? Five, ten, twenty years? They all eventually change or pass and more quickly than ever in our crazy-making, fast-paced, contemporary society. Life has its ups and downs; it cannot be embalmed and preserved. Besides, people are all different. That is the beauty of people. They will never all fit into predefined categories. They even change the categories by which they define themselves.

Yet some religious folk attempt to rationalize and systematize everything. They want to make everything fit. When someone doesn't fit, they conclude that there must be something wrong with that person, something inherently wrong, something intrinsically evil. Conveniently, they write off whatever or whoever does not fit into the prefab plan that religion worked out in an ideal world that exists only in the imagination. Whatever wisdom might actually be in their beliefs gets lost: They are too out of touch with the longings of the human heart to recognize such wisdom.

Some time ago, I spoke with an old and wise priest. He was in his seventies, a marvelous, wonderful man, talented, beautiful. He was telling me about some of the converts he made in the days when converting people was the thing to do. He did a good job, and he really did know what he was doing. He was open to people. He liked people. He let them be who they were.

We got talking about homosexuality, and on this topic he hit a snag. "That's the one thing I can't figure out yet," he said. "I talk to these people, and I listen really hard, but I can't quite put my finger on something in their lives that I could use to show them that they are wrong. I just can't find the example I need. I can't find anything wrong."

That was his way. He was a clever man. He would listen closely to people and find the flaw in their thinking. And then he would gently point it out to them. And they would say, "Oh, I never thought of that. Thank you for telling me that." And they would realize that he was right, that his heart was in the right place. He really did speak for God, which is to say, he guided people toward healing and growth, toward all that is right and good. But regarding homosexuality he frankly reported, "I can't quite get it on this one." Sadly, because of his religious beliefs, it never occurred to him that maybe there was nothing to get!

How long must we go on trying to make sense of a religious doctrine when nothing in reality seems to square with it? What does it take to finally conclude that the doctrine must be wrong? How much experience do we need before we understand that our preformed ideas are out of sync with life? Twenty years? Thirty years? Forty years? How long do we have to live before we realize that this is it? What we see is what we get. We already have enough experience to know how life works. Hope and believe as hard as we might, the process of life won't become anything other than what it is. But dogmatic religion, repeated by rote and out of touch with real-life experience, makes it hard to connect the dots and come to the obvious conclusion.

I understand where that old priest was coming from—and the Biblical Fundamentalists whom I encounter. I was there myself. I remember that, once in my first parish assignment, I ran an intellectual bulldozer over the parish youth minister. He mentioned that the kids brought up the topic of masturbation, and he encouraged them to just forget about it, to stop worrying about this absolutely natural thing.

Still ill at ease with my own sexuality, and so, too, with sexuality in general, I went into pastoral mode. Gently but firmly I convinced this youth minister of the error of his ways. I talked about the role of sex in marriage, the sacramental meaning of orgasm, the psychological implications of masturbation, and the danger of becoming a social misfit by finding pleasure in oneself. (In fact, repeated studies show that people who enjoy solo sex—people who are comfortable with themselves—also tend to be more socially outgoing than those who do not.) I dredged up all the arguments I knew to show why solo sex is a grave wrong. (I really was a naïve, sincere, and obedient Catholic priest at that time, and, devoid of personal experience, I only knew the party line I had been taught.)

Better educated and wielding the power of ordination, I easily convinced the youth minister. He went away shaking his head, pondering the wisdom I had revealed, repenting his ignorance, and hoping he had not led the parish youth astray. Or, at least, that is what I supposed his parting attitude to be. Perhaps, actually wiser than I and wanting to keep his job, he just put on a good show for me, seeming to bow obediently and respectfully to the authority of the priest. I actually hope it happened this way.

Not really knowing what I was talking about and hiding from my own insecurities, I parroted the party line. I reaffirmed all the myths about masturbation that I had learned. I buttressed the sagging edifice of religion's unrealistic, uninformed, and outdated sexual morality. I furthered the religious cause of guilt and shame. I myself was caught up in dogmatic, out-of-touch religion.

As I recall those early years, my only consolation is that former parishioners tell me they remember no nonsense coming from my lips. Evidently, they were not as blind as I imagined. They saw through my words to the intentions of my heart. They remembered my sincerity, goodwill, and desire for the things of God. Thankfully, what they remember was inspiration. Obviously, our personal impact, more than the words we say, is often what people take away with them. So, because of forces deeper than religious authority, the voice of dogmatic religion sometimes helps people despite itself. Being in touch with the depths of their hearts allows people to hear the truth and goodwill that may lie behind even misguided statements.

DARING TO STEP OUTSIDE THE BOX

In fact, none of us is totally or irreparably blind when it comes to the things of the heart. In the depths of our being, we are in touch with more than our conscious mind knows. Unless, in pride and self-righteousness, we deliberately shut ourselves down—the "sin against the Holy Spirit" for which there can be no forgiveness (Matthew 12:31–32; Mark 3:28; Luke 12:10)—our inner wisdom will eventually come to the fore and challenge our petrified religion: "Ask, and it will be given to you; search, and you will find; knock, and the door will be opened for you" (Matthew 7:7). With open-mindedness and goodwill, eventually we recognize and admit that, if repeatedly we "don't get it," probably there is nothing there to get. We realize that our religious beliefs just do not square with life's reality.

Talk about spiritual things is difficult to understand in any case. If you haven't opened yourself to life and experienced the spiritual firsthand, it is hard to know what the religious words are supposed to mean. Worse than that, it is challenging to let yourself experience the depths of life in the first place. Personally you have to let go of too much, and socially you have to buck the tide of the know-it-all religionists who continually want to push you back into the box.

Each of us is unique in our individual situation. Words can never tell us exactly what we have to do to find our way. No one can give us permission to be ourselves. Indeed, nobody knows what we are to be. You, I, he, she—we never happened before. We are, each one of us, unique occurrences. There may be hints in the parables and stipulations in the teachings, but for you and me to find ourselves, we inevitably have to step out beyond what is already defined. We have to embrace our uniqueness. This is risky and scary. Few will dare to attempt it. "The gate is narrow and the road is hard that leads to life," Jesus said, "and there are few who find it" (Matthew 7:14). Yet only those who have dared pass through that gate for themselves will understand the parables, spiritual metaphors, and religious doctrines whose real topic is profound life.

The many who turn from that narrow gate and avoid that hard road do so for lack of experience. It's not that life has not offered sufficient experience but, rather, that we are not alert to the experience we are having. According to one wise saying, "Life is what happens to us while we're making plans." Intent on other things, we let life pass us by. When we don't fully experience what's going on in our lives, the religious words we hear do not mean life, hope, and joy. Rather, we make of the words whatever our narrow experience allows them to mean. Our conscious minds need to make sense of things, to tie up loose ends. We cannot live without some vision of life and some meaningful plan. So we make the pieces fit together, whatever bits of the pieces we have. The result is usually some form of suffocating religion: easy answers for every occasion, ready advice for every need, a finely honed set of rules for every situation, deadly reliance on "willpower," excessive use of guilt, repentance, and resolve, and an ongoing effort to make everything fit into an undersized suitcase.

The spiritual traditions themselves are cautious about trying to box life in. Some emphasis on open-mindedness runs through them all. Even the pop versions of spiritual teachings convey this message. Remember *Star Wars* and young Luke Skywalker. When Yoda was teaching him to do the tricks of an adept, Luke had to learn to trust himself more, and not even Yoda could tell him exactly how to do so. Luke had to learn for himself how to go with the flow. He had to find within himself what it means to trust the Force. In some way or other, all the religious traditions require that each of us learn for him- or herself.

A Canadian movie about Native American culture offers another example. The story was about a young man who returned to his tribal home to undergo a traditional initiation ritual. He had been living in a modern city, but his inner call of native religion and people would not leave him at peace. While visiting his family on a long vacation, the elders instructed him in the lore of the tribe and agreed to go through the traditional initiation ceremony. In an arduous vigil he was required to stay within a circle drawn on the ground. If he were to go outside the circle, he would be vulnerable to evil forces that could be his undoing.

In a vision that night or in reality—it was hard to know which—he saw the woman he loved standing outside the circle, under attack by evil powers. Tortured in conscience but driven by love, he did a shocking thing: He dared to bound outside the sacred circle and take hold of his fiancée, and he brought her and himself back inside the boundary of safety, thereby violating the solemn rules of the initiation.

But here's the twist: With that very act of self-assertion, he confirmed his own power against evil, and in that confirmation he achieved his initiation. Only by breaking the taboos of the sacred ritual did he pass the test of the spiritual warrior and take his rightful place in his ancestral line. Though he returned to the city, he carried with him the wisdom of the age-old sages. Part of that wisdom is that the needs of the heart and the demands of changing times sometimes take precedence over ritualistic rules.

Jesus himself did similar things. He violated the Sabbath law. He associated with women. He ate with "sinners." He broke the purity taboos. Blasphemously, he claimed that God was uniquely at work in him.

Saint Paul followed suit and fought long against the ritual requirements of the Jewish Law: Circumcision is of the heart; it is symbolic, not actual (Romans 2:28). Nothing is unclean in itself (Romans 14:14). Charity is more important than visions, voices, revelations, or ecclesiastical office (I Corinthians 13). A person is not justified by performing prescribed works but by living in faith (Galatians 2:15).

Even the organizational man, Peter, pushed the envelope when he was brought face to face with reality: "I truly understand that God shows no partiality, but in every nation anyone who reveres him and does what is right is acceptable to him" (Acts 10:34–35).

In fact, as is typical of genuine spiritual advance, the early Christian movement both negated and affirmed its Jewish origins. Christianity was simultaneously an expansion beyond the bounds of Judaism and an intensification of Jewish belief: Not only is God at work in a promised land and among a chosen people; according to Christian belief, God is actually present in a human being, Jesus Christ, and through Jesus, God extends goodwill to all humankind.

This whole matter is quite peculiar. Only those who can dare to go beyond the circle of what has already been defined will understand what drawing circles means and what is actually within and beyond those circles. Only they will come to understand the message beneath the images, symbols, and words and, thus, moving beyond the pointers, be confirmed in the spiritual realities themselves.

Ironically, only those who violate religion in some way will grasp the mystery inherent in religion. Only those who break out of the box of religious formulas and regulations will personally know the spiritual that the box attempts to preserve. Thus, Jesus upbraided the religious leaders of his day, the scribes, and the Pharisees. He insisted that tax collectors and prostitutes, the religious and social outcasts of his day, would enter the reign of God before the orthodox religious leaders (Matthew 21:31). Thus, the religious and social outcasts of our day—divorcees, unmarried couples, prisoners, women having abortions, lesbians, and gays— may well have deeper insight into the meaning of life than the appointed religious leaders.

THE MEANING OF THE PARABLE

The coded message of life goes out to us again and again. In hearing the message and actually understanding it, those of us who have risked our very selves in the process of finding ourselves are blessed, indeed: "Whoever wants to save his [or her] soul will lose it, but whoever loses his [or her] soul for the sake of me and the good news will save it" [Mark 8:35 (New World Translation)]. We hear what for centuries saints have longed to hear and what prophets have wanted to know. Though the message was not formulated in scientific terms nor precisely phrased to clinch the intended meaning, though all we heard were metaphors and suggestive parables, though we risked heavy loss in trusting our intuition, having experienced in our own lives the reality about which the words speak, we have been able to hear and to understand. Our own life experience resonates with and confirms what was meant. We have ears to hear.

But not all of us. The word goes out, life continues to unfold, but some of us do not get the message. For whatever reason—the way the message was presented or our own distorting perception—the word sounds demanding, legalistic, and judgmental. We go off in our sense of failure, in our self-hatred. Far from aban-

doning religion, we might invest in religious practices, in following all the rules, intent on matching up to external standards, determined to make ourselves worthy, desperate to be "saved." On
us the Word is lost. Circumstances snatch it away. We follow the
letter of the law and miss the spirit. We may be deeply involved in
religion, but, like a small pool on a seaside rock, little by little our
lives are drying up.

For others, the Word does sprout and spring up. Some do have
a sense of the spiritual and delight in the joy of living. There is an
initial burst of freedom and hope, but the religionists come and
snatch life away. They quote inane formulas and long-standing
doctrines that neither they nor we really understand, but, seduced
into "believing," we surrender our germinal experience of God's
Spirit. We begin again to think that we are not worthwhile, that
we do not know the spiritual, that we must be "objectively disordered" (the words the Vatican uses to describe homosexual people). We distrust our own better judgment and defer to the
religious authorities. We get religion and begin to lose our souls.

Others, again, hear half of the message—that I must be okay—
but they never hear the other half—that God loves me and God is
good. That is to say, they never relate their own well-being to that
of some greater whole of which they are a part. And so they go
off, half liberated and incurably cocky, secure in their surface
selves but never tapping into the spiritual at their core. They get
lost in the spell of the flashing lights, the allure of gleaming bodies, and in all that truly is good and beautiful in life, all God's creation, but unfortunately they know it only at a shallow level. They
never break into real culture—art, philosophy, service, science—
so they are never stumped by its complexity or awed by its marvel.
They only dabble. They learn to drop the right names and to
praise the right personages. They move in all the right circles and
shift with the fads, but they themselves never make a real contribution. They never become part of the overall process of life,
growth, and wholesome change. They never produce fruit that
will last. They never sink roots into the eternal.

The seed of which Jesus speaks is life's invitation to self-transcendent experience hidden in the heart of each one of us. His parable is about the challenge of authentic living. In structuring our lives, in making hard decisions, in riding out life's ups and downs, all the while pursuing what is right, good, and true, some of us are seed eaten up by the birds, some are seed fallen on rocky ground, some are seed fallen among thorns, and some, seed planted in good soil.

Blessed are they who hear and understand. They have trusted the primordial message in their hearts. Having struggled with life, having broken out of the box, having experienced the spiritual firsthand, they know what the religious words refer to. They understand firsthand what Jesus' parables imply.

Blessed are we who can hear the word and realize God's love for us—which is to say, blessed are we who can trust that a benevolent power is at work in all the universe. Blessed are we who can move on with a sense of worth, bounty, gratitude, and ease, and rejoice in the subtle and illusive but all-pervasive beauty of life. Blessed are we who, ever following our path with courage wherever it honestly leads, are not afraid to touch, not afraid to love, not afraid to set wholesome goals and pursue worthwhile dreams, not afraid to embrace the world hand in hand with one another. Blessed are we who, having risked living deeply, hear Jesus' or anyone's words of hope and understand what it means. We are the ones who, in our turn, again bring hope to our world. We are the ones who change the world, who go out and bear fruit: one hundred-, sixty-, and thirty-fold.

THREE

THE SECRET POWER IN THE HUMAN HEART: THE MUSTARD SEED

JESUS PUT BEFORE THEM another parable: "The kingdom of heaven is like a mustard seed that someone took and sowed in his field; it is the smallest of all seeds, but when it has grown it is the greatest of shrubs and becomes a tree, so that the birds of the air come and make nests in its branches." He told them another parable: "The kingdom of heaven is like yeast that a woman took and mixed in with three measures of flour until all of it was leavened." —MATTHEW 13:31–33

THE MUSTARD SEED and the little bit of leaven—small things that become massive are a depiction of growth that actually comes from Jesus' rich imagination. How exaggerated it is! But play the game with him. Just picture it: The little mustard seed, the smallest of all the seeds—it really isn't, of course—becomes as big as the Sears Tower! Add a little bit of yeast to three tons of flour, and before you know it the whole mass fills a stadium!

A four-year-old could easily get into this fantasy, but what Jesus is talking about is not for children. In all of these images, there is the sense of growth, movement, and expansion. Something is happening. From outlandishly small beginnings something huge and imposing, something important, occurs.

THE FASCINATION OF LOVE

What could Jesus be talking about? What is there in our own lives that is like that? What is this tiny, slight, subtle, little, measly thing of which he speaks? What is this paltry thing that could take over our lives and, in fact, our world?

Perhaps you've experienced it—when you are in love or are making love. There's a dimension to love that is very subtle and fine. It's not the passion, the excitement, the rush, the pounding of the heart. No. I refer, rather, to the gentle quietness that shows itself in the mellow moments or in the moments of surrender. It is the simple awareness that you are there, very close to someone, yet what you are aware of is bigger than the two of you. It is that quiet, gentle aspect of love that passion can easily overwhelm and suppress. Yet if we allow it, we sense that it is immovably there.

Sometimes it surfaces when you are away from the one you love. Maybe you're missing your lover, though you talked only a short while ago. There comes a feeling of belonging, of being together, and yet there is the feeling of not belonging. You feel you are a part of something wonderful, yet you wonder if you aren't going to be torn apart. Indeed, sometimes you feel yourself being shredded, strand by strand. You and your world are unraveling. Still, there is a sense of something bigger there, and you want it. You want to belong to it, to be a part of it, and you know that somehow you already are but, at the same time, you are not yet. You are caught in between. You are there, and you're not. You belong, and you don't. You have it, and you are still empty.

Sometimes it occurs when you catch sight of some particularly stunning person—that Venus, that Adonis—and all of a sudden you are riveted through to your soul. Ah, to die for! And you would, for this magnificent, beautiful creature whom you don't even know. Somehow his or her image touches your depths, and you find yourself caught up in something overwhelming. You want to reach out. You need to touch. You know full well that this cannot be all that you dream it is. (At least you should have learned this lesson by now!) In fact, it is not just the beauty of that person for which you are longing. Somehow that beauty has rocked your soul and opened your heart. You are feeling something that is much more profound, something that goes much further than the mere mortal you see: "Heaven must be missing an angel." But no, not an angel; that beauty, that person, that mortal, has become a symbol of the unattained fullness that haunts your soul. It is that having and not having. It is that already being a part and yet still always longing to connect.

Psychologists might apply names to that thing like "fusion" or "attachment hunger" or "oceanic feeling." And sexologists and psychiatrists of the Freudian persuasion might say that this experience harks back to childhood. Supposedly, it is the lingering desire to be one with mother again or to return to the womb. And the male-biased sexual allusion should not be overlooked; it is deliberate.

Provocatively, the gay and lesbian experience wreaks havoc with that psychoanalytic theory. The biological supposition, the male-female configuration, is too simplistic. For lesbians and gays the biological parts just do not fit the way "they're supposed to." Sex is not of the prescribed form. Yet even for them—something that antigay religion just will not believe—that fuller dimension, that haunting, that poignancy is there!

Of course, the remembrance of childhood's fantasies may well be part of the picture and, even more so, adult emotion and sexual bonding. After all, we are physical and emotional creatures. But we are also spiritual. That thing I am talking about is different from the psychoanalyst's projections. When you are gripped by it, you sense that you will never become totally one with it: We are always in process. You delight in the union and know you are it, yet you are aware that the beauty and joy there exceed your reach. There is always something else calling you from beyond, as in *South Pacific's* "Bali Ha'i." There is a completeness, a richness, a massiveness that is you but that somehow you are never going to have. This is no fusion, no attachment; this is no infantile symbiosis.

In fact, with sex you can suppress that thing. A little lust goes a long way to shut down the longing of the soul. A surge of passion can easily overwhelm the outreach of the human spirit. Go out and do some cruising, go catting around some night, and the excitement will dull your soul and fill your mind with other things. Any kind of chase after excitement—alcohol, drugs, money, power, fame—all the things preachers traditionally rail against will work as well. Distract yourself, and pretty soon you won't be feeling that quiet, inner aching anymore. You will be free of it, But you will also have suppressed one of your most precious assets. You will have dampened your own soul. You will have smothered the longing of your spirit. You will be on the way to losing the real meaning of love and life.

That quiet yearning, that longing that will not be fulfilled, is very small and subtle. It is easily covered over, easily suppressed; it is there nevertheless, and it stays there. It hangs out "on the backroads of our memories," "ever gentle on our minds." It is a glow on the fringe of our awareness. It haunts us at the end of the day. It comes upon us when we are unexpectedly alone. It is only a wispy, cloudlike thing, but it is there.

If only we would nurture it and allow it to grow, it would become massive and dominant. It would take over the whole of our hearts. It would open our lives to rare beauty, unexpected joy, childlike magic. It would snatch us up into the universe and make us one with the stars . . . and also exact its periodic price: the poignant experience of unbounded potential, inner void that would contain the cosmos.

THE OPENING TO THE DIVINE

Perhaps that is the kind of thing that Jesus was talking about: the little mustard seed that, with a small bit of yeast, grows to unheard-of proportions. We often talk about that thing in religious terms, but I hate to bring God into this picture. All too easily we bring in God, and then everything goes fuzzy and gray. Everything becomes mystery, and we are only left baffled, put down, silenced, proven ignorant. After all, who can say anything in the face of God? Yet we know more about that thing than we want to admit. Not God, it is part of us. It is within our own selves. We experience it. We live with it. We are it. We certainly know something about it.

In the introduction to his famous *Confessions*, Saint Augustine spoke of it this way: "Lord, you have made us for yourself, and our hearts are restless till they rest in You." Now, it may be true that in the final analysis only God will satisfy our longing, for in God we are to have everything else. But do not be distracted by this talk of God. We do not know what "God" is. We get lost in pure speculation, mere ideas, when we talk about God. Attend rather to Augustine's clue: It is our very own hearts that are restless. Built into our very selves is the *opening* about which Augustine speaks—so that thing around which people build religion, when it is true religion, is that very thing that hangs on in our hearts and aches to be fulfilled.

It is not in God that we know that thing. The process works the other way around. We know that thing in our lovers and friends. We know that thing when we miss someone we adore. We know that thing when we are riveted by a Venus or an Adonis. Then, knowing that thing through these very human loves; we have a possible doorway to the Divine. Then we have an intuition of a Fullness that would actually fulfill us. And then we have reason to risk resting in that thing; it leads us to something beyond.

It is the Venuses and Adonises of our lives, our own human loves, who plant the mustard seeds and stir up the leaven in our hearts. Of course, we make a mistake in wanting to possess our loves, to get hold of Adonis, to have Venus. Venus and Adonis cannot be had. The finite will never satisfy that longing within us, for the reach of our spirits is infinite: "You have made us for yourself, and our hearts are restless until they rest in You."

But neither does that fact mean that we should not touch or embrace or make love. You wouldn't know what I—or Jesus—am talking about if you did not do these things. So love, by all means, and touch and embrace. But do not clutch; do not cling; do not try to possess. What we can hold on to is always smaller than ourselves, and that is not what our hearts *really* want.

THE SPIRITUAL IN OUR HEARTS

There is some picayune thing that can grow and reach out to the whole universe. It is in us; it is with us; it is a part of our deepest selves.

Actually, we can experience that thing everywhere, not just in interpersonal relationships. Being out by the beach and beholding the sea can open the unbounded in us. At the ocean we know beauty, vastness, and rapture as well as a smallness, separation, and distance. We want to be all that it is. Somehow we know that we can, yet obviously and achingly we are not.

I once heard a five-year-old child who was watching fireworks cry out, "Mommy, Mommy, I want to shoot up into the sky and pop." And don't we all actually want to *be* the very wonder of it all?

There is something magnificent about fireworks: They just keep opening and opening and opening. No wonder they speak to the depths of our being, as do the ocean, the mountains, and the stars at night. There's that belonging and not belonging and that exquisite pain: the heart cut open and dying, yet knowing its fulfillment. Watching children at play. Listening to a symphony. Enjoying art, surveying a sculpture, cheering a hard-won victory—there's a fullness that sometimes overflows in bittersweet tears. That thing! It is there. It surfaces whenever given a chance.

Prayer is about that same thing, taking time just to be for a while. And so is gathering for worship about the same thing, though here that thing might have a more emotional tinge. In every case, the key is that it requires quiet. It takes slowing down a little bit. It takes tuning your ears and sensitizing your touch because that thing is tiny. It is a gentle, diminutive whisper. Unless we are quiet and listen closely, we miss it. But it can grow and get powerful. At times it can be overwhelming. It is central to what people are about in forming a community of love.

Of course, these experiences I'm talking about are spiritual. They are actually experiences of our own human spirit. That elusive thing is our human spirit. Our spiritual nature calls us to move ever beyond ourselves. Such is the nature of spirit. The technical term is *self-transcendence*. Its movement points toward absolute transcendence. And here is where God can come in for those who believe in God. Christians would go even further and recall that the Holy Spirit is an added, God-given urge that powers our human spirits to follow their natural self-transcending course. So a Christian could say that, in experiencing that thing, what one actually experiences is also God alive in our hearts. But that experience is something all people know, regardless of how they name or conceptualize it.

OUR NEED TO KNOW OF THAT THING

Of all people, however, we in the lesbian and gay community must know, should know, of that thing, the spiritual dimension of our being. People simplistically identify gays and lesbians as sexual. That's what they know about us—we're the homosexuals—and all they know of homosexuality is sex. Well, then, if we play our part and keep them all happy, we should at least know something about sex. We wouldn't want to disappoint them. We ought to know what sex is about, where it leads, what all it actually involves. More than others, we ought to know the depth of sex—that thing! We, of all people, ought to know about the spiritual that lurks in each of us.

We need to leave space in our lives so we can get in touch with it. We need to allow our deep loves to grow so we can experience its pull. We need to get away from petty lusts that suppress true poignant love. We need to know about that thing, we homosexuals, of all people.

Of course, that's just a joke: "We homosexuals, of all people." The very same lesson must apply to everybody else. Husbands and wives, of all people! Parents raising children, of all people! Teenagers trying to figure out life, of all people! Singles struggling with loneliness! Fathers fretting over the payments for life! Alcoholics and drug abusers in recovery! The elderly with a whole life's experience behind them! The sick and the dying! In fact, we all, all of us, of all people!

Imagine what would happen if we could get in touch with that thing, that tiny, quiet, gentle spirit inside us. If we would just give it space and time, it would begin to grow. It would begin to take over our lives, bigger and bigger, stronger and stronger, from so small a beginning. We would become new people. We would know love to its depths. We would become solid and whole. We would become good through and through. We would be set on a course of unendingly unfolding fulfillment. We would be people of sound spirituality, those rare people who become guides for others, those unusual people whose very presence changes for the good every situation they enter.

JESUS' MESSAGE IN SECULAR FORM

When Jesus spoke about a mustard seed and a bit of yeast, he was speaking about something that is in each of us, something, I think, that all who have ever dreamed, loved, or delighted know. Do not let religious jargon baffle you. Do not think the gospels are not about you. Do not miss the spiritual in your life because you think you are so secular. That drive toward unbounded unfolding is there. With a moment's attention, you could identify it.

We are called to let that thing grow. Our very being wants that thing to expand. At our core we are spiritual. We reach out to the universe. In each of us is a mustard seed that could grow into a stately tree so that others could come and lean on us, climb up on our branches, rest in our limbs, thank God for our presence. In ourselves is the yeast that could rise and transform the whole mass of society. All it takes is a beginning, a little beginning.

FOUR

No Pain, No Gain: Take Up Your Cross and Follow Me

ONCE, when Jesus was praying alone with only the disciples near him, he asked them, "Who do the crowds say that I am?" They answered, "John the Baptist; but others, Elijah; and still others, that one of the ancient prophets has arisen." He said to them, "But who do you say that I am?" Peter answered, "The Messiah of God."

He sternly ordered and commanded them not to tell anyone, saying "The Son of Man must undergo great suffering, and be rejected by the elders, chief priests, and scribes, and be killed, and on the third day be raised." Then he said to them all, "If any want to become my followers, let them deny themselves and take up their cross daily and follow me. For those who want to save their life will lose it, and those who lose their life for my sake will save it." —LUKE 9:18–24

"THERE IS NO FREE LUNCH." This is a sad fact of life. You never get anything for nothing. Of course, this saying is not completely true: The sun shines; you do not pay for it, but it is one of life's beauties. The sun sets every evening, producing a light show that puts lasers to shame. Flowers bloom, thunder rumbles, mountains tower, waves roll, children hug, and people smile. Sometimes the best things in life *are* free.

Still, for most of the things in the human world, you do have to pay. We have set up our world this way, and the result is often cruel, especially for the poor, underprivileged, and disadvantaged. But even in Nature, the "no pain/no gain" principle often holds. It holds for building up muscles. It holds for study and learning. It holds for artistic and athletic achievement. It holds for successful relationships. It holds for having a baby. It holds for growing up. In many ways, it is a cardinal principle of life. Most things in life worth having do cost.

This very same principle applies in the case of Jesus' life, death, and resurrection. In a sinful world, goodness always costs. In Jesus' case, bringing about good actually cost him his life. Theology may put a technical label on the matter and speak of "redemption," but at stake is a common fact of life: no pain, no gain.

For this reason Jesus tells us that we must all take up our cross daily. It is not a question simply of following Jesus. It is not a matter of piously calling ourselves Christian or of somehow having an inside track on life's race or of secretly believing that we are better than others. Such things are not what taking up one's cross means. Rather, this principle is a matter simply of living a worthwhile and productive life. Good living is the issue, not piety or religion, and good living has a cost.

THE NEVER-ENDING STORY

The civil rights movement started with people living in impoverished ghettos, studying at low-level schools, working only menial jobs, drinking at separate water fountains, sitting in the back of buses, and being refused service at lunch counters. Those who first objected were ousted and beaten. Even the law was against them. The struggle was horrific. Then Martin Luther King, Jr., was assassinated. This senseless murder was a turning point. Until the hatred took tragic form in the killing of a peacemaker, widespread change of heart would not happen.

Though church burnings and racial harassment have persisted, only now are people willing to admit that racism is alive and well (recall the resignation of Senator Trent Lott and the despicable discussion that ensued about how to retain racist white votes without losing black votes!), and there is again some flicker of motivation to address the racial injustice in our country. It takes death and destruction to get good things to happen.

There was the assassination of Bishop Oscar Romero in El Salvador. For decades civil war had run on. People were disappearing. Justice was only a word. Romero dared to speak out against the political regime, and he was shot dead while saying Mass at the altar. His death became a rallying point. The martyr's blood watered the cause of reform. The struggle still goes on, and many continue to pay the price.

Something similar can be said about the nuclear energy industry. Critics have opposed nuclear energy all along. We moved too fast. We did not know what we were dealing with. The accident at Three Mile Island gave us reason to pause. Indeed, to me the whole atomic energy industry seems patently insane. We continue to produce radioactive wastes that will be dangerous for tens of thousands of years to come. We do not know where we will put the wastes, and the radioactivity is corrupting their containers, but we go on.

Then came the accident at Chernobyl: people killed, land polluted, radiation spewed around the globe. We still do not know the full effects of the meltdown, but this human and ecological catastrophe raised global awareness of the dangers of nuclear energy. At least for one brief moment the world stopped to think, but the price of getting that attention was awfully high. Yet again, the prospect of diminishing oil reserves and the increasing need for energy are driving a new wave in construction of atomic reactors around the globe; safer models, to be sure—but in the end, suicidal.

The explosion of the Challenger space shuttle tells a similar story. Because of nuclear irresponsibility and destruction of the environment, many people had lost faith in science. The NASA space program still seemed to maintain the ideal: science as an unbiased, honest, and good-willed study of the natural world. But investigation into the Challenger explosion showed otherwise. The graft, corruption, and cutting of corners that were revealed to be part of this "scientific" picture probably played a part in the Challenger disaster. It took the nationally televised death of seven innocent people in a ball of fire to get the NASA program back on track again. Then we witnessed the same tragic display in the breakup of the Columbia.

And then there is the gay liberation movement. The murder of Harvey Milk, the San Francisco superintendent, comes to mind immediately as does the murder of Matthew Shepard, the slight young man who was beaten and left to die, hanging on a country fence in Wyoming. These well-known cases are only the tip of the iceberg. Statistics suggest that, at some time in their lives, about half of all gay men are physically assaulted for being gay, and about a third of all lesbians. Too numerous to count must be the jobs that are lost and the family ties that are broken, all because of homosexuality, all for people's desire to be allowed simply to be how they are.

The history of AIDS adds another sad example to this list. It took almost 50,000 deaths (as many as in Vietnam) before the American government really acknowledged the epidemic and began an all-out response. President Reagan refused ever to mention AIDS in public. Antigay prejudice is a hard nut to crack. For many, the death of gay men is a negligible event.

The price of justice is high, as all these examples show. Getting something good to happen inevitably costs somebody dearly, and that somebody is usually innocent of any crime.

THERE'S NO FREE LUNCH

Consider that lesson. First, there is always a price to be paid if justice is to prevail. Somebody is going to have to bear a cross. Somebody is going to have to lose a job, to plod through the court system, to contribute money, to give up free time. There are always price tags attached to changes in the social system, and the changes will not happen unless somebody pays the price.

Sometimes the price is high. Sometimes it is somebody's life. Sometimes it takes the murder of an innocent person before people stop and say, "Good God, what are we doing? How far have we let things go?"

The typical case is the stop sign placed at a busy residential corner only after a child has been hit by a car. And, as it so often turns out, the residents had been begging for the sign for years. So a child gets killed, and the neighborhood is up in arms, and the news media publicize the story, and finally the authorities act. The tearful parents of the child appear on TV. They say they are grateful that at least another needless death will be prevented. They take some comfort in believing the death of their child has not been in vain. Some good comes from it—other parents will not have to suffer the same tragedy—but then, of course, the death of the child never should have happened in the first place. A human life was the price of the change.

Sometimes only innocent death will bring us to our senses. And in faith we attribute this change of heart to the grace of God. Thus, Zachariah 12:10 has God saying: "I will pour out a spirit of compassion and supplication . . . so that, when they look on the one whom they have pierced, they shall mourn for him, as one mourns for an only child." The Christian scriptures apply this passage to the death of Jesus. The notion is that it took the horrible death of an innocent person to affect a change of heart in people.

Only when our wrongdoing reaches a point of shocking excess do we finally get hold of ourselves and recognize our evil. Otherwise, we go on and on, one small step at a time, deeper and deeper into the mire, never recognizing our decline because it comes, oh, so slowly. As Ricky Martin sings of infatuation for Maria, "*Es como un pecado mortal que te condena poco a poco.* [It's like a mortal sin that condemns you little by little.]" It takes a jarring shock to snap us back to reality, like the slap on the face of a hysterical person.

But someone must absorb that slap. Someone must give his or her life. Someone must pay the price of making the change happen. There is always a price to be paid.

THE INNOCENT PAY

The second point of the lesson is this: It is always the innocent who end up paying the price. The innocent lose their jobs. The victim must plod through the courts. The generous souls support the worthy causes. The people of goodwill volunteer their time. How could it be otherwise? The people who are doing the damage do not care. They are not going to pay for it. They are not going to contribute their money. They are not going to put in their time. They are the wicked, the evil, the perverse. Their concern is not the common good. They are only out for themselves. Only those who care will do what is needed. Only the innocent will pay the price.

This state of affairs makes you wonder: "Who set this whole thing up? It's a pretty rotten show." And our immediate thought is that the culprit is God. Couldn't God have made a different kind of world? Why is everything so costly? Why is life so unfair? Why must good people always take up the slack for the corrupt?

These thoughts bring us close to Jesus. He is hanging on a cross. What is he doing there, anyway? Some people suggest that God demanded that the debt of sin be paid. So Jesus had to give his life in return for our sin. What an atrocious way of understanding Jesus' death! This interpretation not only misreads the scriptures, but it also makes God out to be a monster.

Look at it another way. Here is this man who is living a good life, who is out doing good. People think he is some kind of a prophet, some kind of saint. But, of course, anybody who is just, honest, fair, and good, and especially if he or she is challenging the authorities by disturbing the corrupt status quo, is going to run into trouble. Honesty and goodwill threaten the crooked powers that be. Unfortunately, in many ways we have made our world a den of thieves. God did not create the world this way. This state of affairs was not God's doing. The authorities, not God, took Jesus in.

What would it have taken for him to get himself off the hook? Just a few compromising words: "Hold on, you guys. I didn't really mean what I said. You misunderstand me. Don't take everything so seriously. Hey, lighten up." Just a few words, and he would have been free. He would also have been discredited, but at least he would have been alive.

But alive for what? To live out his now petty life, always afraid of the authorities, never able to face himself honestly again. That experience in itself would have killed Jesus. A man deeply in touch with his heart, he could not have lived with himself. So he willingly bowed to the inevitable. He freely gave up his life. Better to die on a cross than to live with self-betrayal.

Jesus could easily have saved his skin, but, oh, at what a price! The reason he died was, ultimately, because he was an honest man. It was his goodness that brought him to death. He maintained his integrity even at the cost of his life. He stood for what he stood for. Was it not he who said, "Let your Yes be Yes, and your No be No" (Matthew 5:37)? He knew what was right, just, and good, and he would not back down. His is the same story as that of so many innocent others. Their story lines parallel point for point.

So, it was not Jesus' death that saved us. That notion is a misconception. Death in itself is useless. Pain in itself is a waste. In themselves pain and death don't do anybody any good. God does not want people to suffer. God did not want Jesus' death. On the contrary, God wants us to live and thrive. God would have wanted Jesus to live. Expressed in less religious terms, what the universe is about is life. The Power behind it is positive and creative. This is the meaning of evolution. The Force of the Universe hardly guides things in a path of destruction.

To be on the godward path is to foster growth, development, joyful living. Jesus was on that godward path. His whole life was an expression of the positive thrust of life that courses through the universe, and that thrust is what is saving. His human virtue is what is redeeming. Goodness is what saves us, goodness firm and strong even in the face of death. It is not death that saves.

We pray each day: "Thy will be done." What do we make of this prayer? Too often we think that we are voluntarily committing ourselves to suffering, but suffering is not at all what God's will is about. To pray "Thy will be done," is to long for a beautiful world, to ache for justice, to delight in peace and goodwill. God's will is for joy and peace and abundant, buoyant life.

God did not create a world in which pain and death have a positive value. Suffering and waste are not what life is about. Truth, love, honesty, justice, and goodwill—these tell another story. These are saving. These are of benefit to everyone. These are the positive values, and they are worth dying for. To stand for justice even in the face of death is the ultimate contribution, not because death is valuable or because God wants blood but because solid virtue is valuable and goodness is what godliness means.

What God wishes is virtue. God does not want death. Human corruption, not God, is the source of death in our system. Is this not the lesson of Genesis? Is this not the meaning of "the sin of Adam and Eve"? Our own wickedness makes life miserable. Our own dishonesty puts the burden on the innocent. It is we human beings who make the system stink. We are only undoing a human mess when we innocently pay the price for someone else's wrongdoing.

Of course, in strict justice the innocent should not be paying the price of the cleanup, but run on strict justice, the world would simply not work, nor would it be a very pleasant place to live. It is not that altruism is the supreme virtue. Away with such simplistic thinking! Rather, as Saint Augustine argued, it is simply that every so often it takes a dose of selfless charity to restore balance. Someone has to go out of his or her way to set things right again.

Besides, we could never get the culprits to make good on their deeds. Often, they simply could not, even if they wanted to. Who can restore a life? Or unbreak a heart? Or unpollute the environment? Or readjust the economy after the Enron and WorldCom debacles and restore investors' trust in government and business? These evils are beyond price. Were the innocent to hunt down the culprits, nonetheless, and try to squeeze every penny from their filthy hands, the innocent themselves would become cruel and mean. Now they would be part of the problem instead of part of the solution.

Only mercy can redeem the system. Only charity can reset the balance. Only a change of heart can make things better. But changes of heart cost dearly. And only the good are willing to pay the price, precisely because they are good and they are the ones who love.

THE MISTAKE OF SELF-IMPOSED PENANCES

To be willing to pay some share of that price—this is what Jesus means when he says, "Take up your cross and follow me." He does not mean that we are supposed to fast on bread and water. Or crawl down the isle of a church on our bare knees. Or put pebbles in our shoes so that we can feel miserable. Or lash ourselves and think that "sin" will go away. Or continue to live with an abusive spouse out of respect for the "holy" institution of marriage. Or live a lonely life in the closet so as not to offend others' prudishness.

These are very strange religious notions, and they are downright dangerous interpretations of the cross. These activities only distract us from the important matters of life and allow us to feel self-righteous. After all, we are "doing penance." We are "making up for sin." We are "saving the world."

Such warped spirituality is just another form of dogmatism and fundamentalism. It is unthinking, otherworldly, and humanly irresponsible religion. This is the religion of the Publican who prays in the front of the synagogue: "O God, I thank you that I am not like other people: thieves, rogues, adulterers" (Luke 18:11). This is the out-of-touch religion that teaches people to be moral robots and to feel good when others poke fun at them. "Persecuted," they cherish the delusion that they are actually suffering for Christ's sake.

Christ was not into suffering. Neither is God. If you would take up your cross in the style of Jesus, commit yourself to something worthwhile: Begin working for justice. Find shelter for the homeless. Get medical coverage for all citizens. Revitalize our school system. Renew our urban ghettos. Effect a fair distribution of profits in our industries and corporations. Discover meaning in life that will compete with the high of drugs. Bring fairness to our police forces and justice to our courtrooms. Change corporate policy so that our environment can be preserved. Refocus global priorities so that resources are shared fairly. Or just start doing your daily job conscientiously. Be concerned for your family and neighbors. Work on your friendships and love relationships.

Begin doing anything well in the real world, and you will find out what the cross of Christ means. It is not something we impose on ourselves. It is not something in the pious realm of religion. It is something that comes with the territory, with the territory of a just world or, in religious terms, the reign of God.

Begin being open to what is happening in your life and in the lives of those around you. Start being honest about it, and don't get cynical. Then you will inherit a cross. Then you will be following Jesus. The cross will not be of your making. You will probably find that you would have preferred to design your own cross, but, then, to choose your own cross would not be to follow Jesus, would it?

The truth is that many of us do design our own crosses. We cause problems for ourselves, and then we go around lamenting how hard life is. We place unnecessary burdens on ourselves in the name of religion, or God's will, or family responsibility, or the demands of friendship, or social expectation, or personal ambition, or job requirements. We buy into games in which we do not really believe, and as a result we bear self-made burdens.

Sometimes we even bear the burden of actually being corrupt. It takes effort to manipulate and take advantage of people. It is hard work to cheat without getting caught or to swindle an employer or customer. You have to worry over these activities. And even if these little challenges can be fun, especially when you win, there is also the burden of having to face yourself in the mirror. Those little pangs of conscience can become a drag. They tend to eat away at your self-esteem. You have to stifle the music of your soul to be able to go on. You have to desensitize yourself to emotions. You have to shut down your inner self. You end up disgruntled and sour, and you have to go through your life with a cloud hanging over you.

PAY ONLY THE PRICE OF THE GOOD

In the end, there really is no way of getting away from pain. Life has its costs. In one way or another, everybody carries a cross. Or as Bob Dylan used to sing in provocative double entendre: "Everybody must get stoned." So, if paying some price is unavoidable, why not pay the price for something worth having? You can be miserable caught up in the petty things of life, or you can shoulder the burden of something that matters. You will have your share of hardships one way or the other. Why not invest in something worthwhile?

Worthwhile things have a price that includes a cross to be borne. Only when someone carries that cross and pays that price will justice and peace come to this world. The suggestion is not that you have to become a martyr. You do not have to go out this minute and put your life on the line. Part of the challenge of working for good is being prudent and wise. You have to know when to move forward and when to stand in place. The goal is not to make a big show and then go down in a blaze of short-lived glory. The goal is to get good things done, and sometimes this calls for compromise. Effectiveness always calls for good sense and balanced judgment.

There's a line in the gospels that activists and do-gooders need to take to heart: "Be cunning as serpents and innocent as doves" (Matthew 10:16). This is Jesus' own advice. You need to be shrewd to do God's work. It is not enough to be sincere but naïve like Charlie Brown. Sincerity alone does not get things done. One need not play the fool in being a fool for Christ (1 Corinthians 3:8).

SHOULDERING THE CAUSE OF JUSTICE

These thoughts are very relevant to gay liberation, and the relevance carries a universal message. Not everybody has to be "out" in every situation. Not every battle has to be fought just now. President Clinton's attempt to change policy on gays in the military was evidently ill prepared. It did not get very far, though it certainly opened up discussion. The push for legalization of gay marriages also seems badly timed. Strategy, planning, and timing are all part of the task of building a world worthy of both God and humankind. The French have a proverb that says as much: "*Tout se commence dans la mystique et se termine dans la politique.* [Everything starts with mysticism and ends up in politics.]"—just like this book.

The gay liberation movement is indeed a mission of justice and peace. It really is a part of Jesus' work. It is a facet of the kingdom of God. So, too, are women's liberation, environmental activism, school and political reform, universal medical care, corporate responsibility, and racial equality, and the hardships associated with these activities—these covert ministries—are a part of Christ's cross. They are the price that some must pay so that others can live. Those who suffer innocently and contribute generously to these and other causes are carrying forward the redemptive work of Christ. We need to remember that fact. We need to keep things in perspective. We need to know that our Christian faith is relevant to our life in this world. Our faith is actually about real life in this real world.

When we gather as Christians and read the scriptures and celebrate in Eucharist the death and resurrection of Jesus, we also celebrate our own lives and deaths in Christ. We are all in this thing together. All of us, not just Christians, but the whole human race. "Christ" means all humanity gathered into one body. Thus, Christ lives in us, and we live in Christ. Together we find strength, insight, and courage. In our fellowship we have the support we need to go out and do as Jesus did. As we carry our *redeeming* crosses, each in our own small way, we bring peace, love, and joy to this world that demands, "No pain, no gain."

FIVE

Finding Your Niche in Life: Jesus' Call to Follow Him

NOW AFTER JOHN [the Baptist] was arrested, Jesus came to Galilee, proclaiming the good news of God, and saying: "The time is fulfilled, and the kingdom of God has come near; repent, and believe in the good news."

As Jesus passed along the sea of Galilee, he saw Simon and his brother Andrew casting a net into the sea, for they were fishermen. And Jesus said to them: "Follow me and I will make you fish for people." And immediately they left their nets and followed him. As he went a little farther, he saw James, son of Zebedee, and his brother, John, who were in the boat mending the nets. Immediately he called them, and they left their father Zebedee in the boat with the hired men, and followed him.

—MARK 1:14–20

JESUS CALLED THE DISCIPLES, and they followed him. Luke's account is even more striking. It says: "They left everything and followed him" (5:11).

The gospel is not just a recounting of things that happened in the past. The gospel is also addressed to us in the present. If the disciples were called to follow Jesus, this means that we, too, as today's disciples, are also called to follow him. The gospel puts out a general call to all disciples. It is an all points bulletin, if you will.

The gospel's call is also specific. It is directed to each individual and each group particularly. If Jesus is calling us in particular to follow him, he must be calling us to something specific and particular. One of the challenges of life is "to find our niche," or, in religious terms, to discover our specific and particular vocation.

THE MEANING OF DISCIPLESHIP

Let's get clear what it means to say that Jesus is calling us. The matter has become quite confusing. We hear so many appeals to "Jesus" from so many different sources these days that we can never be sure just what "Jesus" stands for. "Jesus" is like religion; it means whatever people want it to mean.

The other day I saw three young well-built guys come into my gym wearing JESUS SAVES in bold white lettering on black T-shirts. The three, exuding equal measures of confidence and testosterone, projected the conviction that, already at twenty-two, they had it all figured out and would be very happy, indeed, to share their wisdom with anyone. After all, they were advertising their religious message on their backs. Evidently, some new Bible campaign had just hit the city. I shuddered.

These days I get scared when I see people proclaiming "Jesus." I've been duped too often by their bait-and-switch "evangelization" tactics. I don't trust them. My suspicion is that they belong to some high-powered preaching group that is out to convert the world to its particular—and usually very narrow—worldview.

I also get scared now when I hear people say they are "Christian." I cringe. I'm afraid of the simple-minded and domineering propaganda they may be pushing. I get angry thinking of the power religion wields to manipulate people's thinking. And I feel sad to realize how Biblical Fundamentalism has deformed the religion I hold dear. For fear of being identified with them, I must now hesitate to mention Jesus or to admit I am Christian. Their self-righteous and secretly arrogant attitude—like the wolves in sheep's clothing about whom Jesus warned—has an effect that is the opposite of what they profess in words. Out to preach Jesus, they turn people off. Nowadays, I believe, most thinking people tune out when they hear talk of "Jesus." The Bible thumpers' simplistic and rote spiels have convinced everybody that "Jesus" has nothing relevant to offer. So there is need to clarify what it means to be "called by Jesus."

In bygone years, this call was interpreted narrowly. In Protestant circles "to be called" meant that you are to be a preacher. Similarly, for Catholics, to be called by Jesus was taken to mean that the priesthood or religious life was your vocation.

In contrast, Jesus' call is something much more general. The gospels say it is a call to *discipleship*. That is, we are to become followers of Jesus. To be his disciple does not necessarily mean that you become a minister or join a religious order; it means simply that you live your life according to the example of Jesus. We are to make him our master. We are to let his way of living become ours. The matter is as simple as that.

CHOOSING A MASTER TO FOLLOW

To talk of following Jesus is just the Christian way of talking about being a good person. It is to do what is right. It is to seek always to do the best we can. I can use another religious expression to make the same point: It is to act as God would want; it is to do God's will.

Speaking of Christian discipleship or of doing God's will are just religious ways of talking about something that applies to every human being whether you are religious or not; whether you are Christian, Jew, Hindu, Buddhist, or Muslim; and even

whether you believe in God or not. As a topic of practical concern, goodness is first and foremost a human thing, not necessarily a theological thing.

There is a spiritual dimension to the human mind, and it is this
dimension that makes us human. It is our capacity for wonder,
marvel, and awe. It is self-aware, and it is the source of self-
transcendence. It is the miniature mustard seed or small bit of
yeast that leads to great things. It generates in us incessant questions. It prods us with an unquenchable desire for love. Because of
it, we would want to be open to all things, to understand everything about everything, to reach out and embrace the universe,
and to somehow become one with it all. The spiritual is that dimension of our human minds that makes us open in wonder and
awe to all that is.

But this spiritual thrust in us, like all other things in nature, has
built-in requirements for proper functioning. It can only approach its goal of embracing the universe to the extent that we are
open, honest, and good willed. Dishonesty and ill will inevitably
lead to a dead end. Falsehood and evil eventually self-destruct.

Therefore, the very makeup of our human nature demands
that every human being live honestly and justly, openly and lovingly, with tolerance and repentance, forgiveness and mercy.
These or similar requirements are part of all the religions of the
world. In fact, these requirements embody the spiritual thrust of
our human nature.

Thus, talk of following Jesus may be a Christian way of talking,
but in practice this talk implies nothing peculiar or unique. If Jesus
was of God and if God stands for all that is right and good, following Jesus and living for God simply mean doing what is right and
good. Adding talk of Jesus, Christianity, and God to the matter
does not change those basic, human, spiritual requirements.

The same point can be made negatively. We must not make
the mistake of thinking that we have some privileged perspective
on life just because we are following Jesus. We may believe that
Jesus was God and may be correct in this belief, but even this fact

does not necessarily make our position any better, more certain, or more correct than somebody else's. We and they and anybody of goodwill are all striving to live as we ought. The fact that we look to Jesus for our lead makes us no different from others who look elsewhere for their lead. All of us are looking for a lead, and all of us still need to interpret that lead and to apply it to our own circumstances.

Following some great religious figure from the past never gives us automatic answers to the questions of today. Besides, given the many great religious figures in human history, we are forced to make a personal choice to follow this one or that one or some combination of many. So our choosing to act as this or that figure taught ultimately depends on our own decision to follow this or that figure. We can no longer brush off the responsibility for our religious beliefs by saying that they were "revealed by God" or that we were "gifted with faith."

We need to be honest about this fact: We ourselves decide to accept our religious beliefs as "revealed" in the first place. If we had not chosen to accept those beliefs, we would not be claiming that they are revealed. The choice is our own, and the responsibility for our beliefs is our own. The fact that one's "call" or "revelation" may have come during a powerful emotional or "religious" experience does not cancel our responsibility for choosing to act on that "call." The claim "God revealed it" or "Jesus touched me" or "the Holy Spirit overcame me" or "the Bible tells me so" or "the pope requires it" is as simplistic and irresponsible as the opposite claim, "The devil made me do it." What we believe is our own choice and what we do our own decision. It is foolish and infantile to try to pass off our own responsibility on "God." Regardless of which religious figure we are following, we are all still left trying to discern what is the best thing to do here and now and to follow through and do it. From this point of view, Christian or not, we humans are all in the same boat.

Insofar as following Jesus means living according to God's way and insofar as living according to God's way means doing what is right and good, anybody doing what is right and good is engaged in the very same enterprise as we who are following Jesus. Adding talk of Jesus to talk of what is right and good adds nothing except Christian vocabulary. "To follow Jesus" is just a Christian symbol for talk about living as we ought.

We may continue to use Christian language, which is all well and good. For many of us, it is the only language we have to talk about the right and the good. Better to use it than to give up talk of the right and the good altogether. However, nowadays we must also be aware of what we are doing when we use Christian language, and we must not use Christian language to drive wedges between us and other people of goodwill. For the most part, our Christian language is simply a way of talking about the very same things that other people and other religions talk about in their own ways. Never realizing this point, many believers think that the only way they can help other people to be good is to preach Jesus at them. This well-intentioned strategy is not only ill conceived but also counterproductive: it turns people off.

JESUS, THE DIVINE MASTER

Of course, traditional Christian belief insists that Jesus was unique: He was literally God become flesh among us. No other religion makes the same claim for any religious figure. So Christians hold up Jesus as the ultimate religious figure before whom all others must give way.

I would not dispute the basic belief of Christian faith that Jesus was God. I gave a full account of this belief in my book *The Same Jesus*. This belief can be shown to be fully reasonable. There is nothing self-contradictory in it. It is a fully plausible belief. However, in the last analysis, there is no way to prove this belief one way or the other. There is no way to show that the historical figure Jesus of Nazareth actually was the divine figure in human form that orthodox Christian faith proclaims him to be. The historical evidence is simply insufficient to counter all reasonable doubt about such a claim. So argument over it will ultimately get us nowhere, and making it the focus of discussion merely distracts from the more pressing concerns about wholesome human living.

Debate about Jesus' divinity—or the inspiration of the Bible, the Bible's inerrancy, divine revelation, the persons in the Trinity, salvation in Christ, the distribution of grace, and the like—all too conveniently takes the focus off our need to make responsible decisions. Theological debate fills up the time that we ought to be spending on loving one another and making the world a fit place to live. Preaching Jesus at people can allow us to feel good about ourselves while neglecting the real injustices in our world. These injustices Jesus himself would decry to high heaven: widespread poverty and hunger, poor schools, inadequate medical care, insufficient housing, low wages, drug abuse, corrupt government, obscenely opulent living, a growing gap between rich and poor, environmental pollution, and so on.

Neither affirming nor denying the divinity of Jesus, I suggest here that the matter is irrelevant. While the debate goes on, the world goes to hell in a handbasket, and conservative "Christians" have become today's legendary Nero, who fiddles while Rome burns.

Jesus' being the Son of God does not relieve us of our responsibility to honestly and lovingly decide how we will live our lives. In today's world, it is impossible to claim revelation without ourselves taking responsibility for the claim. We cannot pretend that our own choice to believe in a particular way is an act of God. Our choice is our own act. This state of affairs makes the divinity of Jesus a moot point.

WAYS OF CONCEIVING GOD'S WILL

So the question before us is this: To what does Jesus call us? What would God want of us? Expressed in nonreligious terms, what is the right and good thing for us to do? If Jesus were in our shoes, a godly human being in our present situation, what would he do? In fact, the Christian tradition has offered a number of ways to express what it means to do good, to follow Jesus, and, thus, do God's will.

Most obviously, there are the Ten Commandments. We should revere God—respect the Power behind the universe. We should pray regularly—take time to attend to that power. We should be respectful of those who deserve our respect. We should not abuse or harm other people. We should be responsible in our sexual behavior. We should not cheat or steal or lie. So if we ask what are we to do, the answer is: Follow the Ten Commandments.

The focus on the commandments might also point to the double commandment that Jesus gave us: Love the Lord your God with your whole heart and your whole soul and your whole strength; and love your neighbor as yourself.

There are other pointers from Jesus. To the negative Thou-shalt-nots of the Ten Commandments, we could add the positive and open-ended requirements of Jesus' teaching in the Sermon on the Mount. Matthew (5:1–11) summarizes the core of this teaching in what has been called the eight beatitudes, eight statements about who is to be considered lucky. In Latin, *beatitudo* means "blessedness" or "happiness."

"Blessed are the poor in spirit, for theirs is the kingdom of heaven. Blessed are those who mourn, for they will be comforted . . ." We should give ourselves over to being poor of spirit. We should live in simplicity. We should be sensitive to the needs of others. We should be merciful and forgiving. We should fix our hearts on what is right and good. We should be dedicated to justice. We should be willing to suffer for what is right. "Living according to the beatitudes" is another way of saying what it means to follow Jesus.

VIRTUES AND VICES

Still another approach has played a major role in Christian history, though this approach has recently been neglected. It is the emphasis on virtues. In the classic formulations, there were the three theological virtues: faith, hope, and charity. They are called "theological" because they focus on our relationship with God. There were also the four cardinal, or principal, virtues: justice, fortitude (or courage), temperance, and prudence. The cardinal virtues refer to our relationships with other people. They are said to be the principal virtues because they are supposed to be the foundation of all other virtues and are thought to characterize all virtuous behavior.

The list of the cardinal virtues was inherited from the Greeks and Romans. The great twentieth-century Roman Catholic moralist, Bernard Haring, would make humility a fifth virtue to be added to this list. He suggests that attention to humility is an original contribution of the Christian tradition. Friedrich Nietzsche had made this point earlier and ridiculed Christianity for its supposed "slave morality."

But, as Saint Benedict spelled out in his famous *Rule* for monasticism, humility must be understood correctly. It does not mean being a patsy, playing the fool, or bungling one's affairs. Being humble means having an accurate appraisal of our particular role in the sweep of things. It means having a realistic view of our limited place in the cosmos. The positive side of humility is recognition of our talents and abilities. Far from requiring us to be modest about our accomplishments, humility requires that we acknowledge our talents and use them to do what needs to be done. The humble person is not the one who sits meekly on the sidelines while others perform a task that he or she could do better. Such behavior is not humility but rather cowardice and laziness. The humble person knows his or her abilities and volunteers to serve as needed. The humble person does a superb job and may even know that he or she is the best but without getting big-headed over it. Humility does not mean putting oneself down; rather it means being honest about what one actually is, both positively and negatively.

The Christian tradition also acknowledges that the virtues have negative counterparts, which form the list of the seven capital or deadly sins. These are the ones from which all other sins are said to flow. They are pride, envy, gluttony, sloth, greed, anger, and lust. The movie *Seven* cleverly—and brutally—played off the list of the deadly sins. However, this movie, like so many others, just came and went. Public concern about virtue in our society seems to do the same. Attention to virtue serves only ulterior motives: to provide quaint themes for stories or to criticize opposing public figures. Then we hear of virtue no more. Our sick society has subordinated even virtue to petty, self-serving goals.

CHARACTER EDUCATION

Rather than foster virtues or develop good character, our society tends to insist on keeping the law. We are a commandment-oriented people, not a beatitude-oriented or virtue-oriented or character-oriented people. Does anyone even know what "good character" means any more? In a recent conversation with my brother, I was impressed by something he said. He lamented the decline of a man he knows who was overcome by emotional distress. A machinist and a genius with his hands, my brother has had no advanced formal education, yet he thinks deeply about things and his heart is pure gold. He speculated aloud one day that this man had not made an effort over the years to correct his character flaws—impatience, anger, paranoia, domination—so, under stress and compounded over the years, the flaws eventually got the better of this man. I was impressed that my brother just took it for granted that one should work to discover and correct character flaws. My brother just presumes that such a project of self-perfection is the task of life. We all need to work on ourselves so that we become good, virtuous people, people of good character.

Unfortunately, goaded on by the religious right, we wrong-headedly pin our hopes for a just society on legalities. Laws can never spell out every detail of what should be done or avoided. Therefore, incessant suits and countersuits characterize our litigious society, and interminable trials, entangled in technicalities, clog our judicial system. Laws cannot make a people or a society just. Only noble, worthy people can create a just society. The best of laws cannot guarantee justice unless there are virtuous people to apply the laws. Not law, which is administered externally, but virtue, which goes to the heart, is the sound basis for a just society. Having law-abiding citizens is only a shaky beginning. What we need is honest, respectful, just—virtuous—citizens, people of good character who will do what is right with or without a law.

The character education movement in the schools has resurrected emphasis on virtue and, in doing so, may be a positive force in reorienting society toward the good. This movement emphasizes virtues like honesty, respectfulness, trustworthiness, loyalty, helpfulness, fairness, thoughtfulness, responsibility, and good citizenship. This movement is dedicated to teaching these virtues in the public schools.

Character education is a clever way to address ethics in a pluralistic society. Whereas insistence on specific behaviors—"Obey your elders, including big brothers and sisters" or "Always tell the truth"—might not apply in different cultures or in every situation, virtues always apply. Virtues are general standards, so they don't tell you exactly what to do. Rather, they imply that you yourself find the right thing to do in any situation.

The emphasis on character may well be our best option for reviving a concern for ethics in our secularized and pluralistic society. My emphasis on goodness again and again in this book follows the same strategy. I don't claim to know the solutions to all our world's problems, but I do know we will find the solutions more effectively if people are committed to doing good and make an effort to discern what the good means in every particular case.

Justifiably sensitive to our need to build a more ethical society, the religious right is solidly behind the character education movement, but there is danger that the religious right, with powerful backing from the White House, will hijack this movement and use it to impose its own particular views on our schoolchildren and our society. In denial about the fact that there can be valid non-religious approaches to ethics, the religious right insists that the Bible be the basis for living or, to be more precise, the religious right's particular interpretation of the Bible. Still, the character education movement is a hopeful sign; only the totalitarian agenda of the religious right is a problem.

Of course, both virtues and laws are needed, and they play off one another: Good laws guide people in virtuous living, and virtuous people make good laws. The Ten Commandments, Jesus' two great commandments, the eight beatitudes, the three theological virtues, the four cardinal virtues, the seven capital sins—in their own way they are all attempts to express the same thing: God's will for us, the calling of a Christian, the right way to live, the built-in ethical requirements of human nature.

Western tradition, secular and religious, has expressed the same teaching in many ways. In fact, all people are called to the same thing: We are all to live virtuously. We are all to do what is right and good, and, doing so, wouldn't we, then, also be doing the will of God? Then, loving one another, whether baptized or not, wouldn't we, in fact if not in name, be followers of Jesus?

THE CONVERGENCE OF EASTERN AND WESTERN SPIRITUAL WISDOM

As I consider those aspects of the Christian tradition, I also remember other Christian mnemonics for good living. As a child, I learned to enumerate the seven corporal works of mercy and the seven spiritual works of mercy, which derive from Jesus' teachings and from other sources in the Bible. The corporal works of mercy, those concerned about people's physical well-being, are these: to feed the hungry, to give drink to the thirsty, to clothe the naked, to shelter the homeless, to attend to the sick, to visit the imprisoned, and to bury the dead. The spiritual works of mercy, those concerned with people's soul or spirit, are these: to instruct the ignorant, to counsel the doubtful, to admonish the sinner, to comfort the sorrowful, to bear wrongs patiently, to forgive all injuries, and to pray for the living and the dead. It strikes me that Christianity has many useful lists for helping us remember what "good living" means.

There are similar lists in the Eastern religions. Buddhism, for example, has its four pillars: All life is suffering; the cause of suffering is striving or desirousness (what the Christian tradition would call "concupiscence"); there is an end to striving; the end comes in following the way of the Buddha. To follow the Buddha, there is the Noble Eightfold Path: right faith, right resolve, right speech, right action, right livelihood, right effort, right thought, and right concentration. There are also the three jewels: the teaching (dharma), the community (sangha), and the spiritual leader (guru). Then, there are the six perfections of the bodhisattva's practice. A bodhisattva is one who withholds his or her own enlightenment in order to dedicate him- or herself to the enlightenment of all people. In this respect, the Buddhist bodhisattva could be said, in Western terms, to be a Christ figure. The six perfections are giving or charity, ethics, forbearance or patience, effort, concentration, and wisdom. Don't all these religious lists, Eastern and Western, seem to add up to more or less the same thing?

In addition, my Catholic tradition proposed many saints as examples of godly living, like Mary, the Mother of Jesus, a model of obedience to God; St. Francis of Assisi, the patron of poverty, simplicity, and the love of animals; St. Albert the Great, the patron of scientists; St. Joan of Arc, the patron of conscience; and St. Theresa of Avila and St. John of the Cross, teachers of the mystical way. And, once again, the Eastern religions also have their lists of greats, whose stories serve as models for contemporary seekers. A favorite of mine is the self-sacrificing Jesus-like figure Avalokitesvara, who advocates the delay of one's personal enlightenment, and thus one's freedom from reincarnation, until all sentient creatures are enlightened.

THE UNCHARTED DEPTHS OF THE WESTERN SPIRITUAL TRADITION

My comparison of Eastern and Western religion carries an important lesson: The religions of the world teach much the same thing about good living. However, many of us have missed this lesson.

Ironically, as people in the West today hunger for spiritual guidance, they are more likely to study the Eastern traditions and their spiritual wisdom than those of the West. It is chic to go Eastern, and there are reasons for this trend. We are so close to our own traditions that we see only the flaws in them, but we know nothing of the disputes and schisms within the Eastern religions. Again, we read only the best of the Eastern traditions that merited translation, and we compare these Eastern classics to the productions of second- and third-rate Christian writers and preachers that dominate our everyday Western world. Moreover, bombarded by uneducated preaching and too aware of ongoing bickering among and within the churches, we identify Christianity with narrow moralism, unthinking literalism, and petty sectarianism, and we miss the spiritual treasures in our own tradition.

How sad is this state of affairs! Those second- and third-rate Christian thinkers have entranced us with some notion of a magic religion. Inoculated with this mentality, we go off to find an elusive "salvation" in the East when we have not been able to find it among its own proponents in the West. Believing that there is some secret formula that will make the challenge of life go away, we keep searching for "enlightenment." Disillusioned with our own religious upbringing, having failed to tap the core of our own tradition, we believe that some other religious tradition will show us that magical way.

Of course, to be fair, looking into other traditions can help us grasp the lessons we have overlooked in our own tradition. I, for example, am immensely grateful for the time I spent meditating in a Buddhist monastery and for the Buddhists texts I read. I am humbled by the generosity of those Buddhist communities, which welcomed me and shared with me their sacred practices. These experiences helped me ferret out the spiritual wisdom in my own Christianity. But far from having me leave one religion to find elusive salvation in another, my Buddhist experience enabled me to appreciate my own tradition and, what is more, to realize that no tradition holds the supposed answers to life. Rather than providing answers, authentic religion "merely" helps us to productively face the great unknowns of life.

As far as I can see, the Western tradition contains much the same wisdom as the Eastern. Of course, the philosophical or theological beliefs of the various traditions do differ, and it is wrong to suggest simply that all religions believe and teach the same thing. But doctrines are not the same thing as the spiritual wisdom that the doctrines attempt to express, and often doctrines obscure the more valuable wisdom contained within them. Just like the West, the East also has its peculiar doctrines: karma, reincarnation, the caste system, the unreality of the physical world, a multiplicity of gods, the essential spiritual nature of all reality, the identity of good and evil or truth and falsehood. Misunderstood or taken too literally, these doctrines produce as bizarre an understanding of life as do any simplistically understood Western dogmas. Yet, the spiritual wisdom underlying the various doctrines is universally very similar.

There need be no competition between Eastern and Western spirituality. In-depth experience of any one religious tradition will open onto every other, and to the extent that such experience does not, I would venture to say, the tradition must be off track. All the great religious traditions are the product of the human spirit. Religion results from open-minded, insightful, honest, and good-willed people striving to live this human life well. All the religions arise from and address the same human condition. If they are on track, their resultant spiritual teachings should be similar. So, in practice, to be a follower of Jesus should look more or less the same as being a faithful believer in any religion.

HOMOSEXUALITY AS A TEST CASE

The calling to follow Jesus applies not just to ministers, priests, and vowed religious but to all Christians. Then, let's look at a specific case. What would it mean for someone to follow Jesus?

I propose to use the example of gay and lesbian people. In many ways, opposition to homosexuality is the last bastion of Biblical Fundamentalism. Biblical Literalism has lost the debates on slavery and, in the big picture, has already lost on divorce and the role of women in society. The conservative opinion on sex is the last battle line. No wonder the religious right is opposing homosexuality so ferociously! So this topic is well worth considering; if the Biblical Literalists lose on this one, they obviously have no ground left on which to stand. What I want to suggest here is that, in fact, they do not.

What is the calling of lesbian and gay people? Their very makeup, different from that of other people, must shape their Christian discipleship in some distinctive way. What would it mean for lesbians and gays to leave all and follow Jesus?

That question is only one version of the universal Christian question, so the lessons derived from it apply to everyone. The lessons apply especially to anyone who is living on the fringes of the church, who is at odds with official religious teaching, or who feels estranged from her or his spiritual roots. The specific answer to the question of each individual may be different, but the basic approach is the same overall. Therefore, looking into the gay issue can be instructive.

Some people would answer that question about gays and Jesus quite bluntly and succinctly: "Just don't do it! Lesbian and gays are supposed to give up their homosexuality and proclaim Jesus as Lord and Savior! This is how they are to follow Jesus."

Certainly, one could not go wrong in taking Jesus as one's Lord and Savior, but that little bit of advice has a barb in it. Swallow the whole thing, and you get hooked on narrow-minded religion. This advice uses Jesus as bait to capture and imprison people's souls. The catch is that this advice unthinkingly presumes to know what following Jesus would mean—in this case, giving up one's homosexuality—but such advice does not make sense.

THE IMPOSSIBILITY OF CHANGING SEXUAL ORIENTATION

Everything we know about homosexuality shows that you cannot change your sexual orientation. It is already permanently fixed probably by about the time you get to second or third grade. No credible long-term studies show that anyone has changed their homosexuality—or their heterosexuality. People might restrict or change their sexual behavior, but their sexual orientation does not change. What is worse, attempts to change it usually end up harming people by leading them to discouragement, depression, despair, self-loathing, and sometimes suicide.

The claims of successful change generally involve people who were bisexual to start with or people who have been induced to hate themselves for being gay, so they have good reason to want to be heterosexual or to pretend to be. In the end, these people do not change their internal inclinations. They only learn to control and channel their external behavior. They can stop having gay sex, just as, given sufficient motivation, anyone can stop having sex, but they cannot reverse their spontaneous sexual inclinations; they cannot stop being homosexual.

The proof is in the pudding, and this pudding is really messy. The most notorious case of supposed religious healing of homosexuality—and relapse! —is that of John Paulk. Chair of the National American Board of Exodus International, one of the first and the nation's largest "ex-gay ministry," and poster boy for the religious right's claim to change sexual orientation through faith in Jesus, he was featured with his wife, an "ex-lesbian," on the cover of *Newsweek* magazine, August 17, 1998. Then, on September 19, 2000, he was spotted in Mr. P's, a gay bar in Washington, D.C. There for some forty minutes and with a cocktail in his hand, he claimed that he was only looking for a restroom. One of my college students explained that, as her minister told her, Paulk was actually in the bar doing ministry to gays—and she believed it. The naïveté and denial of reality that control the ex-gay movement are astounding!

Other cases support the same conclusion. For example, in 1976, Michael Busse and Gary Cooper were instrumental in founding Exodus International. They professed to be "ex-gay" themselves. However, often working and traveling together, they fell in love.

They had never known so powerful a bond. They quit the Exodus "ministry" three years after founding it, denounced it as ineffective, and stated that, in their experience, it had not really changed one person. Out of hundreds of people who had gone through the Exodus program by that time, Exodus had declared only eleven truly changed. Busse and Cooper were among the eleven.

There is also the case of David Caligiuri, who founded the Phoenix chapter of Homosexuals Anonymous and was founder and director of the national "ex-gay ministry" Free Indeed. In 1991, he resigned from that work. He had been having gay sex for years and reported the same to be true for other leaders of the "ex-gay" movement. "We'd go to conferences in other cities, and we'd be paired up in hotel rooms," he reported. "Everybody was sleeping with everybody else."

All the evidence, even that smuggled out from the "Christian" antigay industry, suggests that one's sexual orientation cannot be changed. Wayne Besen's *Anything But Straight* reveals all the lurid details. The scandal of the ex-gay industry is ongoing. Add in the 2006 resignations of the Reverends Ted Haggard and Paul Barnes. Haggard was the prestigious president of the National Association of Evangelicals and founder and pastor of New Life Church in Colorado Springs. Accused by a gay prostitute, Mike Jones, of three years of gay sex and drug use, Haggard admitted, "I am guilty of sexual immorality." Barnes was pastor of the megacongregation Grace Church in Denver. Also reported to be having gay sex, he pitiably lamented, "I have struggled with homosexuality since I was a five-year-old boy . . . I can't tell you the number of nights I have cried myself to sleep, begging God to take this away."

Are we to suppose that following Jesus requires people to dedicate their lives to the impossible? Are we supposed to build our lives around the expectation of a miracle? There must be more responsible ways to spend one's days.

The advice to give up one's homosexuality and follow Jesus is dishonest and self-destructive. Would Jesus want us to go about hiding and denying the deep movements of our hearts? Would Jesus build on guilt and fear to make people change their ways? Would Jesus call us to a life of self-imposed solitary confinement? From all I know about theology, psychology, and spiritual growth, the answer is clearly no. Sincere sharing is a pathway to freedom of the soul. The experience of emotional intimacy, which often includes physical intimacy, is the starting point for responsible decisions regarding wholesome living across the board. Truly following Jesus could certainly not mean cutting off a God-given and natural path to love, connection with others, and service.

THE SUPPOSED EVIL OF HOMOSEXUALITY

There is also a more moderate answer to that question about lesbians and gays following Jesus. Having accepted that sexual orientation cannot be changed, the moderate religionist's advice is to become celibate, to abstain from all sexual involvement. But again, there is a catch in this advice; it presumes that there is something wrong with lesbian and gay love in the first place. Why else would one want to avoid it for the sake of Jesus?

And. once again, the evidence simply does not support the presumption. I have never heard a coherent argument to the effect that gay and lesbian sex is wrong. Neither biblical studies nor historical scholarship nor philosophical reasoning nor scientific explanation nor Christian homosexual experience supports this claim. So why presume something is wrong when no one can show you why it is and when your own honest experience suggests that it is not?

The only authority the conservative religionists can mount is their own insistence that homosexuality is wrong. They claim God revealed the matter, but nothing we know apart from their claim supports this notion.

I presume that my book, *What the Bible Really Says about Homosexuality*, shows conclusively that the Bible does not condemn same-sex love or, at the very least, that current scholarship raises so many questions about the matter that one could not fairly invoke the Bible to condemn homosexuality. Why should we accept the Fundamentalists' opinion when it relies on faulty biblical studies?

Are we to think that God requires things that, from everything we honestly know of the matter, do not make sense? How foolish God would be if God decreed things without reason but merely on whim! How foolish we would be to believe in such a capricious God! Who knows, we might wake up tomorrow to be told that, just as a test, God had reversed all the commandments: What was wrong is now right, and what was right is now wrong. God has spoken! "Ours is not to wonder why. Ours is but to do and die." Such an attitude is theological, religious, and spiritual nonsense.

What, then, if we were to give the benefit of the doubt to the antigay religionists? Perhaps their advice simply means that gays and lesbians are supposed to stop living promiscuous, irresponsible sexual lives. But if so, was there ever any question about it? The commandments, the beatitudes, and the virtues—as well as the Buddhist Sevenfold Path—already cover this matter. Nobody should be living an irresponsible sex life. So the advice to avoid irresponsible sex has nothing to do with being gay or lesbian. Besides, if those conservative religionists think promiscuity is what homosexuality is about—any more so than heterosexuality—they obviously know nothing of the matter.

Sometimes—when I'm feeling optimistic—I think that ignorance is the biggest hurdle in the current debate over homosexuality and so many other topics of contemporary debate. In fact, sex is a relatively new topic of scientific research. Solid information on it is even newer. Many people still know little about sex beyond the innuendos they hear on the streets and the jokes they see on TV and in the movies. No wonder people are so uptight about homosexuality! Granted what they know, their response is understandable. Still, at this point in history, ignorance is no longer excusable and certainly not among religious and political leaders.

The conservative "Christian" opinion against gay love is coming from out of left field. The people voicing it really do not know what they are talking about. I do not believe they really understand what sexual orientation is, and I do not believe they really know Jesus. Oh, yes, they have their opinions, and they proclaim them loudly and clearly, but, to put it simply, I think they are wrong. All the evidence suggests as much.

The words they speak have no connection with the real world. They justify this shortcoming by saying that they speak for God. They claim a message that comes from another world. But if that otherworldly message is completely out of sync with this world, how is anybody supposed to make any sense of it? They would say that you are not supposed to make sense of it; you are just supposed to believe it—or go to hell. Then why did God give us minds that ask questions? Why should anyone who is really committed to the truth have to shun questions? And why should anyone automatically believe the Fundamentalists rather than other, more positive religions?

Notice how again and again I rest my case on the evidence. My argument is that good religion is about good living in this world: "By this will they know that you are my disciples, that you love one another" (John 13:35). "I was hungry and you gave me food, I was thirsty and you gave me drink" (Matthew 25:35). "Who was neighbor to the man who fell among thieves? The one who took compassion on him" (Luke 10:36–37). What does not make good sense for good living in this world cannot be of God—unless God is some irrational ogre making demands like some power-crazed terrorist. I am proposing a strong argument against all magical religion and its appeal to intangibles to cower people into submission. I am arguing that Jesus stands for sane living in this world. Following Jesus simply means living in this world the best way we are able.

Therefore, the conservative religious opinion about gays following Jesus is sheer nonsense. Some other approach is needed. And the same must be said about a lot of other contemporary questions for which religion has quick and easy answers, such as women's rights, abortion, divorce, stem-cell research, genetic engineering. When the religious arguments ignore the evidence and the moralizing claims make no sense, the godly thing to do is to ignore the religious teachings and to search out a more responsible approach.

"GOD"—THE SOURCE OF IT ALL

From all that we now know about homosexuality, anybody who believes in God would have to say that God makes people homosexual. Homosexuality is just like so many other things about which we could ask: Why were you born where you were? God arranged that. Why do you have the parents you have? That was part of God's plan for me. Why do you have the talents you have? They were God's gifts to me. Why are you left-handed? God made me that way. Why are you so tall? That is how God made me. How did you happen to meet this person you so happily married? God let it happen. Why are you homosexual? God wanted me to be this way.

Of course, let's be clear what we mean when we start saying all those things about God. We tend to speak as if we really knew what God is and really understood how God works. In fact, to speak of "God" is just to express a basic, optimistic belief, namely, that there is a good and loving power behind the universe and in one way or another this power is working through everything.

This belief is certainly correct, but most of the time we imagine that power as if we were still five years old. When we speak of God, we tend to imagine some mighty miracle worker in the sky who steps in every so often and makes things turn out okay, just as Mommy or Daddy used to "miraculously" appear to catch us when we were about to fall or to kiss our boo-boo and make it better, but that image is just infantile, magical thinking. It is not authentic belief in God.

I have a colleague who works with drug and alcohol addicts. He tells them that there are only three things you need to know about God: (1) God exists; (2) you are not God; and (3) God is not Santa Claus.

As it is, the forces of the universe have their own laws, and things work out according to these laws. So, given the right circumstances, a seed will grow into a plant, and, given the right circumstances again, the plant will produce more seeds. This cycle of life is built into the universe, and this cycle allows for variety. Some plants grow large, and others are small. Some produce flowers of one color, and others, flowers of another color. Studying the outcomes, we can predict how many are likely to be of each kind. In part, the functioning of the universe depends on statistical probabilities.

Just as we can predict how many flowers will be red, white, or pink, we know that a certain percentage of the population will be left-handed. Another certain percentage will have blue eyes. A little more than half of those born in the USA will be female; most of the remainder will be male; and a rarely acknowledged few will be of indeterminable sex. Depending on how you measure it and on how you define the thing, about 10 percent of the population will be more or less homosexual.

These outcomes depend simply on the luck of the draw. For anything you name, there is a certain chance that things will go one way or the other. Things turn out as they do on the basis of probabilities. These probabilities are built into the ordinary functioning of the universe. The laws of physics, chemistry, biology, and psychology formulate the probabilistic regularities that we have discovered thus far. But God is the author of these laws. God set up the universe as it is. God is the one who decided that things should unfold in this probabilistic way. This point is important, so it should be stated more accurately: Whatever it is that set up the universe, this we call "God."

I say that this is a more accurate way of stating the matter because we really do not know what "God" is. "God" is only the name we give to whatever (or whoever) it is that explains the universe. I say "whatever" or "whoever" because, again, we really do not understand the ultimate explanation of the universe. We imagine God to be a person—a He or a She—somebody to whom we can relate, but what could it actually mean to say that God is a person? If "God" is the Force behind all things, then It certainly does not seem very personal. Nonetheless, if this Force is behind all things, It must be intelligent and freely acting, and, if so, It must be a person, someone who set the whole shebang in motion and keeps it in existence. On the other hand, if this intelligent and freely acting Force is the ultimate explanation of the universe, He/She/It could not be a person in the same way that we are persons. He/She/It must transcend anything we know to be a person. Therefore, people could legitimately quibble about applying to Him/Her/It the term *person*, and this discussion does not come to a simple conclusion. In the last analysis, either way, person or force, or both, "God" remains an unknown. Whoever or whatever He/She/It is, we really do not understand "God," and the matter is not worth debating. Like debate about the divinity of Jesus, such debate about God just distracts us from the more pressing task of honest living.

The best we can do is say that *God* is a word we use to name the ultimate explanation of all things. We know He/She/It must exist, but we do not comprehend Him/Her/It. Like a subatomic particle that is itself never seen but that leaves tracks that can only be explained by positing the existence of such a particle, so "God" is affirmed but never directly experienced or known in Him-/Her-/Itself. Putting the name "God" on Him/Her/It should not delude us into thinking that we know what we are talking about. To believe in God is to believe in an unknown. Believing in God is to believe in something that surely must be there—all reason points that way—but believing in God is to believe in something that we really do not understand.

Religion talks about that fact by saying that God is a Mystery or by saying that God surpasses all understanding. But, I suspect, few religious leaders really understand what this mysteriousness of God means. So they turn it into a club and beat people over the head with it. God's "mysteriousness" becomes an excuse for whatever they want to proclaim. In the name of God and the Mystery, they preach things that are unreasonable, unrealistic, and even silly. They buffalo people by appealing to a God who is beyond understanding. In the face of the unknown, they scare people into obedience by threatening them with the fires of hell. In this way, they maintain control over the masses even while these same leaders refuse to address the deplorable injustices of the day.

Nonetheless, to affirm a God who challenges our understanding is a reasonable thing to do. There certainly must be some power behind the universe that we know, and we certainly do not understand what that power is.

THE MEANING OF DIVINE PROVIDENCE

To affirm God is also to believe that God is good. Anything else would be unreasonable. If God were ultimately evil, why would anything at all come to be? How would the universe come to be a thing of marvel, excitement, and beauty? And it really is such a thing despite the fact that its probabilistic way of unfolding also brings us a good dose of heartache and pain.

We believe that God is good, so we trust the workings of the universe or, more accurately, the other way around: We trust the workings of the universe, we are grateful for the opportunity of being alive, so we profess that "God," the Source of it all, is good. What other option have we? To buck the natural system? To swim constantly against the current? To affirm nonexistence as preferable to any existence at all? To despair in hardship and to surrender to meaninglessness? Not at all. Rather, we learn to live in accordance with the laws of the universe and to be grateful for what there is. We affirm the life we have. We call it good, and we work to make the best of things—that is what belief in God means. To believe in God is to believe in life, and to believe in life is to always seek the good in whatever life brings and to make the best of it. To believe in God is to enjoy the game regardless of what cards you have been dealt.

I remember once talking with a young seminarian at the end of the school year. This seminarian was going his way, and I was going mine, and it was unlikely that we would ever see each other again. In fact, we never did. We shook hands, and I, the priest, said to him, "Good luck."

He was really an insightful guy. In the short time we had known each other, he had already picked up on my thinking. In fact, he had already been thinking that way himself. He was going to dedicate his life to making this world a better place to live, but he was dropping out of seminary. He decided that the priesthood was not for him. He would do his "ministry" in some secular mode, and I was glad to hear of his decision.

He looked at me and smiled and said, "Thank you. And good luck to you, too. And, oh, by the way, I know what you mean. 'Good luck' is the secular way of saying 'God bless you.'"

I remember those words to this day. I was struck by his response. He actually got it! And he could say it back in his own words. So few people ever come to understand these things. So few free themselves from the servile bonds of religion while still being able to hold onto its spiritual core. This young man realized that there is no magic in believing in God. To believe in God is simply to recognize that there is a good power at work behind the sometimes-seeming chaos of our lives.

What the unbeliever calls "luck," the believer calls "Providence." It's a matter of viewing the same thing through a wider lens. Without expecting magic, we who believe in God see God's good hand in everything, so we embrace life fully and make the best of whatever comes our way. We know that, in one way or another, everything that happens is God's doing because God is at work in each and every ordinary happening in the universe. After all, the universe is God's creation and a work in progress.

GOD'S WAY AND THE "SECRET OF LIFE"

Now, let's return to our example. When asked why she or he is homosexual, any lesbian or gay must respond: "It's just the luck of the draw." But a homosexual Christian could also respond: "God wanted me to be this way. I am this way because this is how the natural processes of human conception, birth, and rearing led me to be. God has been at work in my life. Divine Providence decreed that I should be gay."

If that's the case, then, following Jesus' call must include accepting one's homosexuality—or whatever else. Not to accept it is to resist God's call. Not to accept it is to reject the divine plan for us. This same lesson applies to anybody: the man "born" irresistibly heterosexual and unable not to think of marriage, the woman born with awesome and burdensome intelligence, the family struggling against poverty, the spouse who simply cannot make the marriage work, the parent grieving over the death of a child, the couple who just cannot have a child, the gifted employee out of work because the economy went bad, the person living in too small a town who has no way out, the artist hard-pressed to make a living without silencing the music of his or her soul, the stunningly beautiful guy or girl trying to be just one of the crowd, the scientist or entrepreneur or athlete or politician who just happened to be at the right place—or the wrong place—at the right time. In these and other cases, religion tells us to accept God's will, to trust in Divine Providence. This advice does not mean to give up and succumb to mediocrity or to get puffed up and lord it over others; it means to realistically face the facts and to do whatever we can to make the best of them. When we cultivate such a positive attitude, sometimes surprisingly good and totally unexpected outcomes result. Grappling with reality forces us to come up with creative alternatives.

I find no other way to understand things. Life must be lived as it comes. There is no privileged way out. Belief in God does not take the challenge of living away. Religion and spirituality do not provide an inside track on life. Prayer to God does not merit miracles that remove life's difficulties. On the contrary, authentic religion and mature spirituality lead us to look life in the eye, to embrace it for what it is, and, with our best wits, our best intentions, and what like-minded companionship we can find, to make the most of it for ourselves and for everyone else.

People are always wondering, "What is the secret of life?" Well, there it is. I have just written it. After a long and arduous search, I know no other wisdom, nor do I believe there is any other. Authentic spirituality is not about achieving some supposed comprehensive insight or experiencing some blissful, altered state of consciousness. What life actually offers us leaves us living in unknowing, in trust, in faith. And to live joyfully in such faith is, I believe, what it means in practice to be a Christian. This same is also what it means to be enlightened or to be a mystic. And it is what it means to be like Jesus and to follow Jesus' call.

As far as I know, there is no other way. To seek another way means inevitably to indulge in some kind of idolatry. Idolatry is substituting some more palpable and convenient "god" for the Unknown in which we live. We make many things into idols: money, houses, clothes, cars, careers, beauty, friends, romance, drugs, political causes. We expect them to keep us secure and make us feel good. Even religion—simplistic fundamentalism, reliance on miracles, a literal Bible, the teachings of my church, the word of the pope—is liable to become an idol. It was for good reason that Jesus condemned his religious contemporaries for being too invested in their religion and too negligent of the things of God. The difficulty is that to attend to the things of God is to live in ultimate uncertainty, surrounded by a cloud of unknowing.

THE UNIVERSAL VOCATION

Understanding faith as I portray it here turns many things upside down. As Jesus said, the first will be last, and the last will be first. So the sinners, the publicans, the outcasts become examples of godly living, and the self-professed "Christians" become the Scribes and Pharisees to whom Jesus' word was: "Woe unto you!" (Luke 11:39–52)

Jesus says we are supposed to reform our lives. We are supposed to repent. What does this call to repentance mean? Most fundamentally, to repent and reform means to stop demeaning ourselves. We need to stop condemning ourselves, stop rejecting ourselves, stop repressing ourselves. We are to repent precisely of refusing God's doing in our lives.

We should acknowledge the feelings we actually have, the gifts and propensities that make us uniquely ourselves. We should embrace and encourage our affections, our curiosity, our delight. Affections enable us to love. We should thank the Power behind the universe for the capacity to love. Curiosity opens us to the marvels of the universe. Fascination makes us grateful for being alive. Delight moves us out of ourselves and into spaces in which we can grow. Delighting in beauty, innocence, simplicity, and achievement makes us come alive. What we need to repent of is ignoring our life-giving qualities or even suppressing them.

Jesus says to repent. Yes, indeed, do repent. Repent of your denials of yourself. Repent of the harm that your negative outlook has caused you and others. Repent of your doubt, and believe in the possibilities for good that life has to offer.

Jesus also said that the reign of God is at hand. What does belief in the reign of God mean? The reign of God is a symbol for universal justice and blessing in the world. So we should not give up working for justice, justice for ourselves and for everyone else. We should not give up. Success is guaranteed, and this guarantee is what it means to say that God's reign is at hand.

Justice will not come soon, to be sure, certainly not in our lifetimes, and, to be honest about it, justice will probably never come in final form. There will always be corrupt, deceitful, selfish, and ill-willed people to undermine justice again and again. Still, the victory of justice is assured at least in this sense: Injustice will never be able to stand supreme. You cannot build a lasting society on evil and dishonesty; their very nature is eventually to self-destruct. The unjust system is doomed from the start; it carries its own undoing in its guts. Of course, it is tragic that, until unjust regimes fall, so many resources and so many human lives will be wasted, including some of our own. So that some can get their kicks, others are assigned to languish. Thus has it always been. But the negative factors can only hang on because they lean on the positive. The negatives must inevitably fall away; they have no substance in themselves. The positives alone have a future. Honesty, truth, goodwill, mutual concern—only these are lasting. The "of God" will ultimately prevail.

Recall the hymn about Christian vocation: "I have decided to follow Jesus, / No turning back, / No turning back." This should be our song. We should follow Jesus without turning back, but we must be careful about what "following Jesus" means. Jesus' call is directed to each of us individually and specifically. He calls each of us by name. God's will, the plan of the universe, is different for every one of us, but the differences do not exclude any of us. The interplay of differences results in the overall, positive unfolding of the universe. Each and every one of us has a calling, and our particular place and time in history determine what that calling is. The challenge is for each of us to recognize what we are and to make the best of the present situation, to draw the good out of whatever is our lot. Such calling is necessarily different for each one.

Still, in the big picture, the calling is the same for everyone. The future of the cosmos requires that each of us be committed to the good. That is to say, Jesus calls us to be good, wholesome, loving people. Each of us has to figure out how to be that way realistically and in our own particular circumstances. To be a loving person in every aspect of our lives is to follow Jesus. Following Jesus is as simple—and challenging—as that. There is not much more to it. Jesus calls us to be ourselves and, together with one another, to promote the good of our world as best we can. His call is to be good-willed and full of hope. From such a calling there is never need for turning back.

SIX

FORCES FOR POSITIVE CHANGE: THE REIGN OF GOD AMONG US

JESUS ALSO SAID, "The kingdom of God is as if someone would scatter seed on the ground, and would sleep and rise night and day, and the seed would sprout and grow, he does not know how. The earth produces of itself, first the stalk, then the head, then the full grain in the head. But when the grain is ripe, at once he goes in with his sickle, because the harvest has come." He also said, "With what can we compare the kingdom of God, or what parable will we use for it? It is like a mustard seed, which, when sown upon the ground, is the smallest of all the seeds on earth; yet when it is sown it grows up and becomes the greatest of all shrubs, and puts forth large branches, so that the birds of the air can make nests in its shade." —MARK 4:26–32

THE SEED GROWS BY ITSELF. There's not a word about what makes it do that. This plot would fit a science fiction movie: A pod falls down from the sky and begins to grow. No one knows where it came from or why. It gets bigger and bigger, and it starts to take over the world . . .

Jesus' parable does convey a sense of something alien, peculiar, unusual. There is something eerie there, something mysterious. Given our current knowledge, we might pooh-pooh the mystery in Jesus' parable. It's just about a growing plant, and we know about plant growth. Water softens the seed and stimulates growth. The cells begin to multiply. They live on nutrients included in the seed, and later the plant absorbs nutrients from the soil and forms its own food. DNA programs the process. It's a matter of protein formation in predetermined forms and of energy production through the metabolic decomposition of carbohydrates. No big deal. We know a lot more about biology than Jesus or anybody in his day.

Nonetheless, we must admit, we still do not understand what "life" is. Why do the DNA molecules function as they do, initiate their processes, differentiate tissue development, guide long-term growth, eventually break down? What are the switches and triggers in this process? What makes it all happen? Why did it develop in the first place? We can describe the process in remarkable detail, but we really do not know what the process actually is. Indeed, botanical growth might seem even more remarkable today than it did in Jesus' day. Our very insight into the complexity of the process makes the unknown dimensions more fascinating than ever. The whole thing is really awe-inspiring.

Jesus' second parable is of the same kind. It, too, is weird and strange. Again the reign of God is like a seed. This time it is a specific seed, a mustard seed. Jesus exaggerates and says that it is the smallest of all the seeds. Then he exaggerates again and says that strangely, it becomes the biggest of all the shrubs—which it certainly is not. There is something funny going on here: The mustard seed is growing, and it starts taking over, and before you know it, it overwhelms you. Very peculiar.

CONTEMPORARY PARABLES ABOUT THE REIGN OF GOD

Jesus says he is talking about the "reign of God" (also sometimes referred to as "kingdom of God"), which also sounds mysterious. But this time the mysteriousness might be that "reign of God" sounds distant, unknown, and maybe even irrelevant. It is mysterious in the sense that we do not understand it, and, well, frankly we don't much care about it. It is not a part of our lives. It belongs to another universe.

To the contrary, I would suggest that Jesus' parables about the reign of God are talking precisely about us and our world, the social and political developments in the early twenty-first century: the movement for racial equality, the demand for women's rights, the emergence of sexual minorities, the openness to diversity and pluralism, the beginnings of a global society. These parables are about people who, in one way or another, are coming out or breaking out or taking charge or finding themselves. These parables are about our human lives and how they unfold and about how the end result is bigger than we would ever expect. Rather than talking about the growth of seeds, Jesus could have cited many other examples. This peculiarity is everywhere.

We like to believe that we are in charge of our lives, and to a large extent we are, but another unavoidable aspect of life is that things happen *to* us. We wake up one day, and suddenly we feel awkward, restless. We go through the day pensive, inexplicably discontented, searching for a way to feel settled. Nothing is as it was. Or we turn on the TV, and there's been a shooting or a traffic accident or an earthquake or a strike or a political uprising or a violent death, and our world is suddenly precarious, off kilter, ominously unsafe. Or we turn on the radio and hear a particular song. Suddenly we are somewhere else. Memories and hidden longings reemerge. We become nostalgic, and our mood and our day suddenly take a different direction.

We do not know what causes these shifts of focus. New things just happen, and once they've happened, they cannot be undone. Their effect begins to spread like ripples in a pond. We and our world are not the same any more. People meet. Coincidences happen. Accidents occur. Secrets become public. Ideas break through. Feelings rise up. Passions stir. People change their minds. Attachments form. Movements start. We sing about such things. On a whimsical trip to the city, the young couple in *Hello Dolly* fall in love. They sing: "It only takes a moment to be loved your whole life through." Similarly, in *West Side Story*, Maria and Tony meet, and soon families and neighborhoods are in turmoil; the streets are alive with fighting; and love and tragedy ensue. Likewise, in "Some Enchanted Evening" from *The King and I*, "you may see a stranger across a crowded room." Later, you agree to a dance, on "the clear understanding" that one dance could change your lives: "That sort of thing can happen." Indeed!

Falling in love may be the most obvious transformative moment in life. For most of us, finding one special someone is perhaps life's most powerful experience. But just growing up —puberty, maturity, old age—is itself an amazing experience beyond our own control. It just happens, and we are left to grapple with the results. And the same kind of discombobulating turn of events can befall us in other situations: a trip to a new city, a riveting and transforming book, the failure to get the job you wanted and expected, the death of a loved one, stunning success in a project, an illness and long recuperation, a thrilling role in a play, participation in a political rally, a chance to help out in a disaster, a near-death experience. Many unexpected and transformative events happen to us in the course of life.

Once such a thing has happened, there is not much you can do about it. Have you ever been in an auto accident—or just missed having one—and wondered how one split second could make such a difference? If only you could go back and relive that moment. If only you had left the house one minute earlier or later. Had you made that phone call, had you polished your shoes, had you taken your usual route, had you actually come to a full stop at that stop sign. . . . If only thinking about it could change what happened. You rethink it over and over, but it has happened. It is done. It cannot be undone, and the experience begins to unfold. The event takes its own shape. The natural consequences fall into place. The event takes on a life of its own. It begins to push in certain directions. There is no holding it back. Pretty soon amazing things—or horrible things—are happening, and you get caught up in them. They begin to overshadow everything else. Your life will never be the same again.

A LESSON FROM THE GAY EXPERIENCE

"Coming out" is a good example of how small, unexpected beginnings can lead to great things. By "coming out" I mean consciously realizing that one is homosexual, acknowledging the fact, and working with it. But coming out applies to any need to actually face the facts, such as eventually getting that divorce or quitting that job or finishing that project.

Coming out can occur in many ways; different people have different stories. Some are now coming out without any difficulty whatsoever. They grow up knowing that the shape of life has many natural variations, and they are able to size up their own situation rather easily. They may even have family and friends who are supportive.

For many others, coming out is as long and difficult a process as it was in former years. Until recently, there was precious little information available on the topic, and what was available was hardly helpful. There were no role models: No one was publicly gay or divorced or in an interracial marriage or female and educated. There was no way to categorize the homosexual experience. Most notions were derogatory and did not fit people's beliefs about themselves, so people could not identify themselves as gay. They were left grappling virtually alone with a disturbing inner feeling. Nonetheless, eventually they came out.

Then and now, people come out. In one way or another, their homosexuality asserts itself, and there is little they can do about it. Facts do not go away. So somewhere along the line some feelings or thoughts or fascinations begin to crop up. There are hints; there are clues; and they may get ignored or even denied. Then perhaps a friendship develops. Words come surprisingly easily. Intimacy is established for the first time since childhood. Bit by bit the relationship blossoms. Indeed, to say the least, this relationship becomes a very deep and emotional bonding.

Some may pass the experience off with a comment like "I'm just a very sensitive and artistic type. That's why I get so emotionally involved with my friends," but eventually, irreversibly, irresistibly, the truth begins to show itself: This is not just an emotional bond; it is also sexual. And people begin to realize: "Yes, I am homosexual." "Oh, so that is what *homosexual* means. No wonder my friendships were so close and my feelings so deep."

There is a process that kicks in, and it will express itself. It comes up all by itself; it acts on its own; and it cannot be suppressed. Gradually, slowly, it happens. There is no way of avoiding it. Reality will have its say. The process is irreversible; once it begins, it takes its course.

To be sure, there are stories of people avoiding their sexuality or some other unwanted fact of their lives. They succeed at bottling it up for years, at hiding it behind elaborate schemes. They throw themselves into school or work. They get involved in projects, even community service and church work. They say, "This is what life is about: making a contribution," and they accustom themselves to living under a dark cloud with a nagging dissatisfaction: "Oh, that's just a part of life. Everyone feels blue now and then. You just have to trust in God and go on." They act this way in good faith. They really could not do otherwise; they are not yet psychologically equipped to face their reality. (I speak from experience.) Besides, good-intentioned but ignorant people tell them: "Just hang in there. You're okay. Things will work out. Just trust in God. You'll see. It will be fine."

But it won't be fine, and they are not fine. They are fleeing from themselves, and they take themselves with them wherever they go. Whatever the issue is, it will not just disappear growing.

Besides, their religion is wrong. It should have taught them that God does not want dishonesty and so-called heroic self-sacrifice, both of which work against the very forces of life's unfolding. Such artificial virtue, such an iron-willed sense of duty, or such repressive obedience to God is not what sanctity means. But too few people know better. Most do not want to know. In the name of God, "holy" religion fosters blissful ignorance.

Eventually, reality wins out. We cannot repress what we are. We cannot go on ignoring the facts of our situation. Core facets of our personality—like creative talent, certain career inclinations, buoyant or even-keeled or melancholic moods, core compatibility or incompatibility with another person, or sexual orientation—cannot be kept at bay. They eventually surface and play their role. They are not ours to pick and choose; they are the cards that we've been dealt. We can choose only to pick up our cards and play the game or else piddle our lives away.

Over the years we learn that it is not we who set the schedules. It is not we who plan our lives all the time. As the Scottish poet Robbie Burns put it: "The best laid schemes o' mice an' men / Gang aft a-gley." There are forces at work in our lives, strange, uncanny forces. We can but work with them and creatively make the best of things.

RELIGIOUS INTERPRETATION OF THE UNCANNY

Religion expresses the matter otherwise: "Man [or woman] proposes; God disposes." Believers speak of life's happenings in terms of "Divine Providence." They understand that God is working in all those processes of life. Of course *God* is the name we put on the mysterious, eerie, and curious forces that set up the universe and govern its unfolding. So God is indeed the power behind those things, and the way things unfold is, indeed, God's doing. Religion is right on this score: In one way or another, God's good guidance, Divine Providence, is behind all things.

Nonetheless, naming that uncanny power "God" does not change the situation or make its resolution more obvious or actually help us to deal with it better. Oh, putting unexpected events into the context of our religious faith can make these things easier to face. Believing in God can give us a psychological benefit when we grapple with life's challenges. But religious faith does not really make the resolution of the problem itself any easier. We still need to live with the situation for a while, size it up, confer with knowledgeable others, mull it over, "pray over it" (which means to open ourselves to broader possibilities), and, then, finally on our own, decide what needs to be done and do it.

Religious faith does not remove the challenge or magically provide us with a solution. In fact, to go on coping creatively and positively with the unexpected is precisely what belief in God means in practice. Religious faith does not resolve life's problems for us. To be accurate, it's the other way around: We have faith to the extent that we courageously and insightfully resolve those problems ourselves. When we give up, we must say that we've lost our faith, that we no longer trust in God. Religious faith is "just" the broader context in which we can securely situate the happenings of life. Naming the whole process "Divine Providence" is the little bit of sugar that helps the medicine go down, but the sugar itself is not part of the cure.

Besides, religion also has its dark side. Naming the mysterious forces of life "God" often obscures the reality about which I am talking. Religion can just complicate things. Religion often leaves us caught in a web of mythical and magical thinking that prevents us from living our lives. Anyone who has spent years trying to overcome religiously induced guilt or any visionary who has dared to express a unique and provocative idea or any generous and charitable soul who has suffered disillusionment over the failure of an ambitious charitable project will know what I mean. Anyone honest enough to open his or her eyes to life will know how religion, besides helping us get through, can also blind us to reality and keep us "faithful" to flawed commitments and the status quo.

Religion can paint dishonest living in the color of virtue: self-sacrifice, obedience, loyalty, commitment, duty, love of God. We need to be wary even of our religious faith, for it can sometimes camouflage the uncanny power at work in our lives. Religion can dull that very mystery and awesomeness that religion is supposed to foster.

ISOLATED EVENTS AND HISTORICAL MOVEMENTS

The forces of life eventually have their way. An individual's coming out as gay is one powerful example, but there is more to the matter. As a social movement, gay liberation takes the mysterious process of life to another level and casts even further light on the tiny seed that mushrooms into the reign of God. Coming out is a huge personal challenge but it's a mere pixel in the whole picture. It does, however, grow. A little understanding, a little honesty, a little acknowledgment, and all of a sudden you find yourself in a new place in life, and things start happening around you. You begin by cautiously sharing your new self-awareness with one person, and then two or three, and the whole family, and your circle of friends. While you are nurturing that tiny seed, others are doing the same. So one by one and then in groups, you find yourselves meeting and planning and forming organizations. Soon you have a national movement on your hands.

Every year in late June, the gay liberation movement celebrates gay pride. The demonstrations, even those in smaller cities, are impressive. The fact that these demonstrations occur at all is a wonder; they were just never supposed to happen. Similar things have happened with other liberation movements, but gay liberation is remarkable in that its members were invisible at the start, and it is profound in that its concerns touch civilization's core concepts: man and woman, marriage and family, friendship and social intercourse. Much of what modern psychology has come to understand about inner human experience, information that was simply unavailable before the twentieth century, comes to bear and is at stake in gay liberation.

It is as if the gay liberation movement arose from nothing. Whereas before, there was nobody who was gay or lesbian, nobody seen or known as such, nobody calling themselves by these names, now there is a movement of international proportions. This phenomenon shook even the pope when, in 2000, world pride was celebrated in Rome. John Paul II—in a disgraceful and most un-Christ-like reaction—announced that he was "offended" that "these people" had come to "his city" during the "Holy Year." And, of course, debate over gay marriage has religion and politics churning.

The civil rights movement for racial equality and women's liberation began among people who have long been obviously present—people of color and women—and their requests have been for rights that others have already enjoyed. In striking contrast, gay liberation represents something completely new: a new group of people demanding a new way of living. It's no wonder that gay liberation threatens people! No wonder that lesbian and gay Christians claim the Holy Spirit is at work among them! Are there not echoes in this movement of the scripture's declarations: "Everything has become new!" (2 Corinthians 5:17), "See, I am making all things new" (Revelation 21:5)? It's no wonder, then, that religious gay liberation can offer so powerful a lesson for all people who, for whatever reason, are grappling with facts of life that don't quite square with their religion!

What is happening among gay and lesbian religious folk is like that mustard seed. Starting small, it begins to grow and eventually becomes an imposing presence. The writing is on the wall. The train has already left the station. There is no turning back now. Inevitably, all the churches will allow homosexual expressions of sexuality, and all will bless lesbian and gay relationships. A totally unforeseen shift is taking place.

Of course, when Jesus spoke about seeds that grow on their own, he hadn't a clue about coming out and gay liberation. Not that Jesus was oblivious to same-sex behavior; it was a standard part of the Roman world, and the Romans were occupying the country during Jesus' time. He certainly knew the Romans and their sexual practices. In fact, recent scholarship suggests that he actually met a Roman who was in a sexual relationship with another man—the centurion of Matthew 8 and Luke 7—who asked Jesus to heal his ailing servant. (Indeed, in the first *credible* argument that I've ever seen, in *The Man Jesus Loved,* Theodore Jennings suggests that Jesus may actually have been gay. Perhaps for this reason Jesus' perspective was so countercultural. Think about it? Why would a Roman officer, who was wealthy enough to build a synagogue, be worried about losing a slave who was dying? Perhaps it's just that the centurion was a kind man, but this suggestion does not fit the harsh reality of ancient slavery. Besides, as is obvious in the original Greek, the centurion uses one word to refer to his slaves in general and another word, a term of endearment, to speak of his sick servant. It is not far-fetched to conclude that the centurion and the slave were lovers and for this reason the centurion was so concerned about him. Neither Jesus nor Matthew nor Luke said a word about the matter. The evangelists only reported that Jesus healed the servant, restored him to his lover, and commended the centurion's faith.

Jesus certainly knew about same-sex relationships and, evidently, was not concerned about them. Sex was not something that preoccupied him. His concern was something bigger: the reign of God. The Man of Galilee was not concerned about gay liberation. How could he be? He knew nothing of it, although, were he here on earth today, he would certainly be supportive of it as well as racial equality, women's liberation, environmental responsibility, universal health care, adequate education, and all the other justice concerns of our day.

NEGATIVE ASPECTS OF
GAY LIBERATION

When Jesus spoke of the reign of God, what he did intend may well have outright excluded aspects of "coming out" and "gay liberation." This may be the case because coming out is not always as rosy as what I just described. Nor is gay liberation. Sometimes coming out is an excuse for people to break loose and do whatever they want. If coming out means finally realizing that you're gay, fine. But since there are no specific rules regarding it, some people take being gay to mean that questions of right or wrong no longer apply. After all, when you've broken one of society's most fearsome taboos, why should any rules restrict you? If gay love is supposed to be such a god-awful thing and you rightly realize that it is not, do religion and society really know what's right and wrong? Thanks to religion, some people have been made to believe that by coming out they are automatically destined for hell, so why shouldn't they have as much fun as they can before they get there?

There are others who, having been so often rejected and emotionally wounded, are unable to love themselves and cannot believe that anyone really cares about them. Indeed, society at large gives reason to think that "faggots" are utterly worthless. So, if nobody really cares, why not just do whatever you please? Nothing matters anyway. Your life does not really count.

Some people think that finally coming out should make up for all life's disappointments. Because they are out, they think that the world now owes them every happiness. They reason that, if they have to live with this curse, they at least have a right to as much fun as possible.

In all these cases, gay liberation has nothing to do with the positive unfolding of the universe. Put into a religious context, it has nothing to do with God's liberating action among us. On the contrary, it has to do with shutting down the process and eliminating healthy discourse. Surely, this was not what Jesus meant when he spoke of the reign of God.

There are wrong and destructive dimensions to gay liberation. However, to a large extent, misguided and oppressive religion is the cause of those negative realities. We reap what we sow, and religion has sown irrational guilt and vile self-hatred in many people. Religion has broken people's spirits and warped their souls. The natural result is dysfunctional and destructive living and a distorted understanding of ethical responsibility. There's no need to call on God, to quote the Bible, or to cite the pope to understand these things. Ordinary psychology explains them perfectly well.

While the religions would like to blame those negative developments on people's "sinfulness and wickedness," oppressive religion is itself the culprit. Clearly in the case of homosexuality, by offering no spiritual guidance, religion has done a massive disservice to present-day society. Like the physically abused child who bullies his classmates and later abuses his own children, people spiritually abused by religion grow up ethically dysfunctional. They are hard pressed to act responsibly.

A religion that is unreasonable and disrespectful of people in the name of God destroys their inborn moral compass. When elders insistently teach their young that certain things are unethical, yet the young cannot reasonably accept such teaching, the conflict between external and inner authority short-circuits the whole moral system. Neither the authorities nor one's conscience can be trusted, so both are neutralized. Both the wishy-washy conscience and the devil-may-care attitude are the product of religion and a society that are morally bankrupt.

In this regard, the religious gay liberation movement has an important lesson to offer. All those who have been wrongfully condemned by the church and society—women seeking equality, couples seeking divorce, singles having responsible sex, intellectuals questioning traditional beliefs—can benefit from this lesson: Do not reject your own soul when you reject the established caretakers of souls. Do not reject all ethics along with the flawed teachers of ethics.

Organized religion has traditionally been the keeper of spirituality, and this arrangement served well enough in the past. But this arrangement is not absolute. Spirituality is not essentially a matter of established, organized religion. Spirituality is, first of all, a matter of the human heart. While religious institutions may come and go, the heart and its spiritual sensitivities—the human hunger for truth, goodness, and beauty—must ever be respected. Our own spiritual growth may require that we break the yoke of our religion's spiritual oppression, but in the process we must not claim to be liberated if, actually, we have only dulled our spiritual capacity.

If we focus on gay liberation in its immoral and socially destructive expressions, obviously, we are not speaking of the reign of God. To be sure, we are still speaking of the mysterious and powerful forces that can issue from small beginnings, but in this case, we speak of the demonic, not the divine.

Demonic implies fundamental disorientation in the life system. Through disorientation, our physical and emotional forces are cut off from our spiritual drive toward wholeness and broad-based fulfillment. These forces, like affection, sexual desire, and the love of fun, are powerful goods in themselves; they bring substance and joy to life. But spun out of control, unresponsive to the spirit, split off from the rest of the person, they lack the direction that points them toward the open-ended unfolding of life. This disorientation is demonic because it is utterly destructive. It shuts down cosmic process. It stops growth. It uproots the plant. It kills the seed. It destroys people's souls. It is the core meaning of *evil*.

LIBERATION AS THE IN-BREAKING OF THE REIGN OF GOD

If the thrust of a movement is positive, it is an expression of the reign of God because the movement in question is life giving. It is a matter of people's basic civil, human, and moral rights; a matter of justice, mutual responsibility, equal opportunity, and social contribution. It is a matter of people's finding themselves and being happy to be alive, of bonding deeply with others and entering into rich and supportive relationships, of finding a worthwhile reason for living and creating a wholesome life that benefits everyone.

In this case, liberation would have to entail honesty, justice, goodwill, and love, virtues that traditionally have been considered the responsibility of religion, the "things of God." Therefore, when we acknowledge God's wondrous work in the secular movements of our day, we are speaking even as Jesus spoke. The liberation movements about which we speak are an expression of God's movement in the world. Talking about human liberation, we are talking about the reign of God.

Those who work for the basic human rights of women, immigrants, people of color, and the poor; for the care of children, the mentally ill, the elderly, the sick, and the infirm; and for the dignity of gay, lesbian, bisexual, transgender, and intersex people—those who champion any of the oppressed—are the ones who "hunger and thirst for justice" (Matthew 5:6). And Jesus said they would be satisfied. They who are committed to these causes are the ones who mourn over the injustice they see, and Jesus said they would be comforted. They will be satisfied and comforted because they are involved in the force that moves the universe. Their success as well as their open-ended future are ultimately assured.

If we would only recognize the fact, we could confidently say that in the liberation movements we are actually experiencing the emergence of the reign of God. God's reign is certainly not any one of the liberation movements, but every liberation movement is certainly part of God's reign. Just by being honest and goodwilled in what we experience and do, we are involved in God's reign; we are engaged in a monumental endeavor. From small and unlikely beginnings, great achievements can result. Acting with informed goodwill, we flow with the cosmic currents that Jesus symbolized as the reign of God's breaking into the world.

CAUGHT UP IN THE FLOW
OF THE UNIVERSE

Merely by attending to our own lives, we can understand what Jesus was speaking about, though it is a mysterious thing, to be sure. What is happening among us is not really completely our own. No one of us, on our own, started the process of coming out—or civil rights or women's liberation or the green movement or prison reform or the forgiveness of international debt or the protest against unneeded war. Rather, a force pushing up from inside of us began calling for attention. No one of us singly put any of these social movements in motion. Rather, they began as a number of like-minded individuals emerged and gravitated toward one another. Elements from a common process began to coalesce. From the very beginning, unbeknown to ourselves, we were part of a larger process. Throughout, something bigger than any one of us, and even bigger than all of us together, has been afoot. That something is the power of life — truth, honesty, justice. Release these in a tiny quantity, and they begin to grow.

Give an honest response to one small, honest question, and the response provokes still other questions. Pursue the questions with honest answers, and the answers begin to fall together until a whole new vision emerges. The ongoing re-visioning that results from question and answer moves toward a coherent understanding of everything about everything. The process is geared toward the ultimate coherence of all things. As long as the process is open, honest, and good-willed, it will keep moving, shifting, adjusting, until it reaches its fulfillment. It will take over and eventually encompass the universe.

Perform a small act of love, and your heart and the heart of another are touched and opened. This opening, if allowed with goodwill, leads to yet more love. Wave a "thank you" to someone who let you change lanes during rush-hour, and you set out a ripple of goodwill that brightens people's drive time. A deliberate good deed triggers a process. It begins to spread and grow. In the ideal, it will take over the world. Its goal is to affirm and enhance everyone and everything, all that is worthwhile, beautiful, and lovable. The process is geared toward the ultimate unity of all things. It will spontaneously embrace the universe.

Openness, honesty, love, and goodwill are the stuff of the reign of God. Nonbelievers might not recognize this stuff as actually pertaining to God, but if they are good people, they will be dedicated to it, nonetheless. Whether they recognize it as God's or not does not matter. Whether they live it or not, that is what counts.

Believers, of course, will recognize this stuff as belonging to God. In it they will see an opening onto a fulfillment that echoes in the words of Jesus. In it they will join the quest of good and holy men and women throughout the centuries and across the continents.

It is a strange and weird-sounding matter that Jesus broached—until you begin to understand it for what it is. It is like a small seed that, once set to growing, begins to take over the world. It will take over because its nature is that of the very Power that governs the universe. It sets the unique path along which all constructive processes move. By definition, it is positive and good. It defines what *good* and *positive* mean. In contrast, what is built on dishonesty cannot have a future. What is evil eventually implodes upon itself. Such is the essential nature of the "negative" and the "wicked."

The reign of God, the coming fulfillment about which Jesus spoke, is made of the positive stuff. Once released among us, it provokes and prods and urges its own expansion. Whereas, by nature, the negative must come to a dead end, the positive opens up to infinite expansion. From our own experience we can know what the reign of God means. It is at work within us, and we are a part of it.

Albeit, disconcerting to admit, we are caught up in a process that could take us over. A strange and weird force is loose among us. But no menacing pod ominously fallen from space, no destructive robotic creature rising up from below, happily, this thing is the power of life among us. Jesus called it the reign of God, the dominion of the forces of goodness. It lies and works within the expanse of the universe. Absolutely primordial, it grows on its own. It ever resurrects. It is uncanny and eerie. With eyes open to see it, we delight in its working even as we tremble at its awesomeness.

SEVEN

PREPARING FOR CHRISTMAS: A VOICE CRYING IN THE WILDERNESS

THE WORD OF GOD came to John son of Zechariah in the wilderness. He went into all the region around the Jordan, proclaiming a baptism of repentance for the forgiveness of sins, as it is written in the book of the prophet Isaiah: "The voice of one crying in the wilderness: 'Prepare the way of the Lord, make his paths straight. Every valley shall be filled, and every mountain and hill shall be made low . . . and all flesh shall see the salvation of God.'" —LUKE 3:2–6

AND PEOPLE FROM the whole Judean countryside and all the people of Jerusalem were going out to him, and were baptized by him in the river Jordan, confessing their sins. Now John was clothed with camel's hair, with a leather belt around his waist, and he ate locusts and wild honey. —MARK 1:5–6

[THEY] SENT PRIESTS and Levites from Jerusalem to ask him, "Who are you?" He confessed and did not deny it, but confessed, "I am not the Messiah." And they asked him, "What then? Are you Elijah?" He said, "I am not." "Are you the prophet?" He answered, "No." Then they said to him, "Who are you? Let us have an answer for those who sent us. What do you say about yourself?" He said, "I am the voice of one crying in the wilderness, 'Make straight the way of the Lord.'" —JOHN 1:19–23

ADVENT IS THE FOUR-WEEK preparation period prior to Christmas. Now that's a quaint idea. It is downright medieval. Preparation for Christmas really starts in July, doesn't it? For merchandisers, of course it does, and long before July. And for consumers, Christmas preparation starts by September or October at the latest.

Thanksgiving used to be the traditional day for starting the secular Christmas season. That date squared pretty well with the liturgical calendar, so the church celebration of Advent and the secular preparation for Christmas kicked off at about the same time.

Nonetheless, perhaps the sales season always did overshadow the spiritual meaning of Christmas. Even back in those "good old days," Santa Claus was the main figure. He brings presents, and someone needs to buy them. But the church celebration of Advent begins with a focus on John the Baptist. His stark presentation brings stern words, and he's expecting you to give something that can't be bought with money. What an unlikely figure to associate with Christmas! Of course, that depends on what you think Christmas means.

JOHN THE BAPTIST
VERSUS SANTA CLAUS

In the Christian tradition, John the Baptist is a typical Advent figure. He is the one who "makes ready the way of the Lord," but he is a strange, haunting figure. Not wearing soft, furry clothes like Santa, not sporting a come-hither twinkle in his eye and a dimple on his chin, John is usually pictured stripped down in a brawny way. He has animal skins draped over his shoulders and a leather belt around his waste. He holds a long, thick staff and looks with penetrating eyes. He's a loner, living in the wilderness, surviving on locusts and wild honey.

John the Baptist is a counterculture figure: He does not quite fit in. He stands up against the trends of his times and calls upon others to see things differently. He wants things to change. He intends to get things back on track. He speaks in terms of repentance. He shows the threatening side of Santa Claus: "making a list and checking it twice, gonna find out who's naughty or nice." Up against the social currents, John the Baptist is a figure like us, like any of us who are both Christians and religious outcasts, on the sidelines of respectable society and the fringe of the churches, often loners, people who don't quite fit in. And like John the Baptist, in some ways we are also making ready the way of the Lord. We are calling for a new order and working to make it happen. We are revolutionary people.

"To prepare the way of the Lord" does not refer to a religious thing, unless we want to think about this revolution in religious terms. The phrase is a religious way of talking about working for a world of fairness, justice, honesty, and goodwill, a world where all are welcome and all are respected. The point is that such a world would be one worthy of God. Such a world would stand for the things about which God is concerned. In this sense, building such a world would be arranging circumstances for God, leveling out God's path, preparing the way of the Lord.

Building such a world is not something that you particularly do in church. Indeed, many churches would not want to be associated with something so political or, even worse, something that challenges the system so profoundly, but such subversive activity is exactly what preparing the way of the Lord is about. This "way of the Lord" is not so much about God in heaven as about people on earth and treatment of each other and our structuring our society. It's about justice and peace. So we can see this revolutionary project as a religious one if we want to, but we can also be involved in it even if we are not religious. Indeed, many a religion is very far from it.

CHRISTMAS CHARITY IN A SECULAR SOCIETY

The secular celebration of Christmas may actually be "preparing the way of the Lord" even more than some churches do. People do a lot of good in the name of the secular holiday season: contributions for the poor, toys for needy children, Christmas dinner for the homeless. Were it not for the secular holiday of Christmas, most people would not be doing these good deeds.

These charitable gestures are often mere tokens, isolated actions with no long-term effects. The good deeds we do at Christmastime may make us feel better rather than really changing someone's life for the better. These good deeds may even serve to blind us to the real needs of our society and let us comfortably believe that somebody is actually taking care of the needs of the poor.

At Christmastime we collect toys and old coats for needy children, but our well-established economic system rolls on all the same, keeping them in poverty year after year and systematically ignoring their plight. How is it even thinkable that there be so much malnutrition and homelessness in the wealthiest nation ever to exist on the face of the earth? About 20 percent of the children in our fair nation live in poverty.

We like to think of America as the biggest and the best, so we are blind to the inequities in our social system, and the sanitized news we receive keeps us deluded. In comparison with other industrialized nations, we have more child poverty by far, more infant mortality, more high school dropouts, more violent crime among youth by far, more youth suicide, more teen pregnancies, more abortions, more elderly poverty, more medically uninsured citizens, lower average wages, longer working hours, less vacation, lower life expectancy, and the widest gap in income between the rich and the poor. (See Marc and Marque-Luisa Miringoff's *The Social Health of the Nation* for some sobering statistics.) And we spew out more than our share of toxins into the air and, likewise, consume more than our fair share of natural resources.

Our celebration of the holidays does include good deeds, but these deeds may serve as a cover-up for a highly corrupt social system. In addition, our secular celebration also does a lot of outright harm: overindulgence, waste, physical exhaustion, spending on unnecessary luxuries, accumulation of debt, unscrupulous advertising gimmicks, Scrooge-like preoccupation with profits, unfair upper-management bonuses, and obliviousness to the common good. The holidays, like anything else, can be a real mix of good and evil. The trick is to sort out the two and to balance the comfort of Santa Claus with the sternness of John the Baptist.

THE PROPHETS OF OUR DAY

Many of us—including many in the churches, synagogues and ashrams—who are on the fringe of society or the outcasts of the religion, really are working to make a better world. We are preparing the way of the Lord. Or, if we are not yet actually doing much, at least we are wishing and hoping and aching for a better world. We are dreaming about good things to come. Dreaming the dream is the first step in making it come true. Even Jesus said that those who hunger and thirst for justice will be satisfied some day, because our hungering will eventually drive us to act.

Outsiders are often more able than insiders to see the problems in a system. So those of us whose lives don't match up to the official religious and social standards have insights that can be a valuable contribution. Women in inferior positions, alternative families viewed with suspicion, racial minorities with second-class citizenship, sexual minorities condemned out of hand—such people as we are able to see through the social façade and name the systemic injustices. Living on the fringes, knowing inequity first-hand, we are not taken in by the smooth words of religion and politics. We question the rosy picture of the status quo and reject the condemnation of our "deviant" lifestyles. Like the African Americans who refused any longer to sit in the back of the bus, like women who refused lesser pay for the same work, like gays who took to the streets over harassing police raids in Greenwich Village, we outsiders can recognize "the way of the Lord" along unbeaten paths. We know in our hearts that the common good requires challenging the establishment. We know what justice requires because we experience the lack of it.

When we finally see through the propaganda that supports the party line, we actually take a giant step forward. We break out of the stereotypes that surround us. We hear a different music, and we march to a different drummer. We experience the loving and life-oriented drive that is at work in all creation. We let it, and not the naysayers, take possession of our souls. We affirm ourselves. We speak out. We protest. We stand up as loved by God. We take a powerful and revolutionary stand. In so doing, we have heard a message; we have seen a vision; we have had new insight into an old problem. In religious words, we have received "a revelation from God."

Isn't *revelation* the appropriate term? The power for life that is at work in the universe expresses itself everywhere, above all, in our minds and hearts. In the depths of our own soul, we experience a dawning, a realization. We grasp an intuition, and from it we form a new message, we configure a new vision. It comes from the source of all goodness. It emerges out of the Life Force that is working in and through us all. Our vision or message points toward a more wholesome life for everybody.

Isn't this what "revelation from God" is about? Isn't this what "hearing the word of the Lord" means? But we picture revelation in more dramatic terms: flashes of lightning, claps of thunder, audible words shaking the ground, palpable images rising up before us, like R2D2's projected hologram image of Princess Leia in the opening scenes of *Star Wars*. Such drama is the stuff of Hollywood, not the stuff of real life or the real God.

The lesson of Elijah is to this very effect: God was not in the rushing wind; God was not in the earthquake; God was not in the devouring fire. Rather, Elijah encountered God in "a tiny whispering sound" (1 Kings 19:11–13).

The work of God manifests itself in our world in everyday, ordinary ways. The cycle of the planets, the birth of new stars, the evolution of species, the change of the seasons, the ordinariness of ongoing life—these *are* the work of God. A notion that emerges unexpectedly in the mind, pointing the way to a richer life, setting the course for positive growth, opening onto the unbounded unfolding of the universe—this *is* the expression of God's creative wisdom breaking through to our world in human thoughts and words.

You can legitimately put the religious name on this process and call it "revelation," if you like. Or you can just have the experience and act on it without ever thinking of it as religious. Still, what happens is the same in either case, is it not? The substance of the experience is the same. This substance is what "revelation" is about.

Religion likes to save the word *revelation* to glorify important spiritual insights from the past, and religion likes to make such moments of insight into extraordinary or even miraculous events. Yet, surely, the process of past revelation is the same as that of our gaining new insight today. And, surely, the major contributions of gifted leaders from the past are of the same kind as those of gifted leaders today.

Insight always comes as a gift. You can prepare for it and desire it, but you cannot make it happen. It is thrust upon you, like a bolt out of the blue. It always comes, if you will, as "an act of God." It is part of the surprising, delightful, and ever ongoing expression of the life of the universe.

Once insight comes, everything looks different. Finally solve a puzzle, and you wonder what took you so long. Once the solution comes to mind, the elements of the puzzle are blatantly obvious in their coherence. How could you ever have missed the solution? It was there staring you in the face from the beginning. Now everything is different; yet nothing has changed. All things are made new.

Is this very process not the substance of religious revelation? You object, "Oh, but revelation comes from *God*." The objection carries no weight because God is acting in every event in the universe. In some way or other, everything comes from God. You insist, "Oh, but revelation is a *special* intervention of God." The insistence carries no weight. It leaves us wondering what qualifies as "special" and who should make this call, and we are back to debating *human* claims, and God is no longer the focus.

Calling something "revelation" is simply a religious maneuver to confer particular authority on some idea or other. Attributing an idea to God sounds so much more impressive than simply admitting that this was my or your or his or her idea. Of course, if the idea is one of ours, it is subject to scrutiny; it must be tested and proved credible, and it is subject to change when circumstances change. Attributing an idea to God makes it immune to criticism.

Taking the myth out of "revelation" can have disturbing consequences for a religion that wants to claim the authority of God. Unfortunately, really understanding what "revelation" might mean deflates that claim. Besides, at its best even religion has always insisted that no human being or human institution has the right to claim the authority of God.

Then, using the religious term and respecting its venerable heritage, could we not, with due humility and appropriate qualification, suggest that in our own way we receive revelations from God all the time? And, if they stand up to scrutiny and prove realistic and helpful, do not our "revelations" carry the same weight as any other "word of the Lord"? If so, we justifiably can say that we have received a revelation from God. Like John the Baptist, we have been inspired to proclaim hope and renewal. We are out preparing the way of the Lord. We have a message that others do not have. We see things they do not see. Like the prophets of old, we need to speak our message to the rest of the world.

When I say, "We need to," I do not mean to lay a guilt trip on anybody. I am not pushing any preachy moralism. What I mean is this: We need to, not particularly because God or anybody else commands us to, but because the message burns inside us and will not leave us at peace—even, as the prophet described his own experience in Jeremiah 20:9: "Within me there is something like a burning fire shut up in my bones; I am weary with holding it in, and I cannot." We speak out because we want to. We need to speak. We cannot be silent. Our own being impels us to speak. Here is a sense of responsibility that does not mean "toeing the line." *Responsibility* here means simply being one's own best self.

Relying on the insight that our situation as outsiders elicits, you could say that God is calling us to be prophets—if you want to use these religious words. But whether you use these words in their full religious sense or not, we do have a message to share, and it has been given to us. We are prophets in our day, just as John the Baptist was in his.

Do you think that John the Baptist was aware of the pivotal role he was playing in "salvation history"? Do you think he had any inkling of what Christianity was to make of his ministry? Do you think he had a blueprint for his "mission" from the start? Do you think he was going about his "mission" with the sense that it was precisely what God had ordained that he do? Do you think he understood fully who Jesus was and what Jesus was about? I certainly do not. Oh, the evangelists report the story that way, but they wrote the gospels after the fact. The evangelists were in the comfortable position of interpreting what had already happened. They were reading back into John's life the significance that only came to the fore once events had already unfolded. If John the Baptist was preoccupied with grandiose thoughts about his role in salvation history, he would have been distracted from his work and would have been a failure. He would not have been dealing with the concrete, then-and-there issues that were his to address. He would have been daydreaming about being a prophet, and we would never have had reason to know him as one.

The same applies to us and to the leaders of our revolutionary communities. Many of our leaders—the feminists, the Black and Hispanic politicos, gay and lesbian activists, school reformers, AIDS activists, personnel of nonprofit organizations, environmentalists, advocates for global debt forgiveness, war protestors— are not religious at all. They would not think of themselves as prophets in any religious sense, but their fully secular commitments hardly mean that they are not the prophets of our age. Those who see things through a religious lens have to learn to recognize God apart from churchy words and religious rituals. The work of transforming society is surely the work of God, and we who do that work are the prophets in our day just as surely as John the Baptist was in his.

Perhaps our problem is that we know too much about prophets, and too little. We have these grand ideas about what prophets are like. We have this solemn word *prophet* that throws us off, so we find it hard to recognize our own struggling lives as the lives of prophets. Our lives don't fit the stories in the Good Book. We forget that the day-to-day lives of the prophets of old hardly fit the grandiose stories either. Success stories always sound better after the hard victory has been won.

SCRIPTURAL TESTIMONY TO THE PROPHETS OF OUR OWN DAY

My interpretation of religious outsiders as prophets and bearers of revelation is not just spacey musing. It finds parallels in the scripture readings that the church uses for meditation on John the Baptist and the Messiah. Isaiah 61 begins: "The spirit of the Lord God is upon me, because the Lord has anointed me." Is this text not also speaking about us? Is not God's Spirit also at work among us if we are willing to see God at work in the good that goes on through seeming secular events?

"He has sent me to bring good news to the oppressed." And who are the oppressed of our day if not those who are different? The mentally ill, the physically challenged, the outré artist, the disenfranchised and disillusioned youth, the minimum-wage and undocumented worker, people of color—all are oppressed.

"To bind up the brokenhearted." Are these not our battered and abused women who are expected to stay in a marriage because "marriage is sacred and God requires obedience"? Are these not our gay youth who have been kicked out of the house and made to live on the streets? About 30 percent of street kids are there because they are lesbian or gay and their parents, often steadfast "Christians," will not have them in the house.

"To proclaim liberty to the captives, and release to the prisoners." There are prisoners all over the world. Millions were slaughtered in Nazi Germany. Thousands disappeared in Argentina and Chile. And the same story unfolded before the eyes of all the world in the former Yugoslavia. And there was also Cambodia, Tibet, and Zaire. And dare I even mention Palestine? Or Pakistan? Or Darfur?

Or even the USA? The good, ole US of A has more people in prison, proportionately, than any other nation on the face of the earth. While the rate of violent crimes decreases in this country, the rate of imprisonment continues to rise, and African Americans and Hispanics disproportionately fill our ever-expanding prison system.

In addition to imprisonment behind fences, walls, and bars, there is also emotional captivity. There are the hordes of people in bondage to their emotional and psychological states. Depression is said to affect something like 10 to 20 percent of the population.

Desperation born of isolation, loneliness, poverty, and helplessness eats away at many hearts.

Antiquated notions about human sexuality keep people's emotions locked up. For decades, lives are wasted as fear of one's own affections and sexual identity inhibit personal expression. Oftentimes, the people preaching the restrictive rules are the ones most repressed and most in need of liberation. Someone needs to save the so-called Christians. Afraid of their own selves, uncomfortable just having bodies that feel and respond, they make themselves feel normal by making everybody else uncomfortable. Rather than sexual responsibility, abstinence becomes the massively funded campaign of the day.

The psychological captivity of alcohol and drug addiction also binds many people. Current law-enforcement policy turns this psychological captivity into actual imprisonment. Our myopic and macho law-and-order society believes in prisons more than in less expensive, though more effective, treatment programs. One must wonder who is making money on expanding a prison system that is clearly ineffective in curtailing drug abuse, and one must also wonder what kind of society we have formed wherein so many people need drugs from street peddlers, drugstore counters, or pharmacists, just to get through the week.

The scriptures of old remain relevant in our own day. This fact confirms that, working for justice, we are, indeed, responding to divine revelation and functioning as true prophets. We are preparing our associates and friends, families and society, for the coming of a righteous God, for a joyous Christmas celebration.

MAKING ADULT CHRISTMAS HAPPEN

Christmas for us, as John the Baptists, differs from the standard image. We cannot afford to have Christmas be just a remembrance or a festive time: Christmas trees, gifts, gatherings, and nice things for the kids. The stakes are much too high. For us, Christmas celebrates the time when, as they say, the Lord will come and restore justice to the world. And, oh, how we know justice is needed. Christmas celebrates the time when, as they say, the Lord will come and restore love to the world. And, oh, how we know love is needed.

We are not children any more. We lost our innocence long ago. We've been through the unspeakable. We've had children "out of wedlock," we've married against parental advice, we've had gay sex, we've divorced, we've been in war and killed other human beings, we've fought for women's rights, we've been "downsized" out of a job at age fifty-five, we've had abortions, we've smoked pot, dropped acid, and danced till dawn on X.

Come to a different place because of the paths we've followed and the curves life has thrown us, we see through the party lines. We know that God is not going to step in to change anything. We will be waiting till doomsday if we wait, expecting this miracle. We may still pray to "God," but we know that nothing will happen unless we make it happen ourselves. If at all, God works though us. If at all, the Lord comes in us. With the mind of John the Baptist, "making ready the way of the Lord," we celebrate a vision that we ourselves work to actualize. We prepare for a very different kind of Christmas. We get into Advent, not just the holiday season.

Christmas changes when you've done unspeakable things or seen your dreamworld shattered. You might visit your family but not feel at home with them anymore. Family may not know; family only tolerates; or, despite the best of goodwill, family just does not understand. The outcast status is the price of breaking sacred taboos.

Christmas is just not the same, and it could not be, for Christmases past were for children, and we are not children any longer. As long as we hang onto childhood dreams of what Christmas used to be, as long as we sit by the TV and cry while watching the annual reruns, we never will find real joy in Christmas again. Somehow, bit by bit, we have to give up those childhood fantasies. We are not in Kansas anymore. We cannot have a childhood Christmas anymore. We need to take Christmas and make it into something that speaks for us now that we are grown up, street smart, "tainted," with lives and dreams of our own.

For us adults and outsiders of religion, Christmas is about more serious things than sugar plums dancing in our heads or chestnuts roasting on an open fire or even an angelic infant lying in a magic manger. If Christmas is to be meaningful, we have to make it so. Somebody has always had to make Christmas happen. When we were children, Mommy and Daddy secretly attended to that task, and we innocents actually thought that Santa Claus came. If we want Christmas to happen today, we have to make it happen ourselves. When we take up this task, we take on the role of John the Baptist.

Committed to both genuine human fulfillment and the work of God and recognizing these two as opposite sides of the same coin, we have a vision that challenges both the churches and society at large. Turning this vision into reality, we are prophets in our own day. Attuned to the actions of God, we recognize it even in secular form, and the pious façade of religion no longer hoodwinks us. Though our voices may sound like that of a lone wolf howling in the wilderness, banded together with other people of goodwill, we are a growing political force and can make a difference in our world. Together, we are actually preparing the way of the Lord.

If a four-week Advent of preparation for Christmas seems like a quaint idea, it is only quaint because, like the merchandisers, we know that our preparation must go on all year-round. Santa Claus is okay for kids, but for us the rugged guerrilla fighter John the Baptist makes Christmas real.

EIGHT

THE HASSLE OF LIFE: REDEMPTION VIA AN UNDESERVED CROSS

> THE APOSTLES GATHERED around Jesus, and told him all that they had done and taught. He said to them, "Come away to a deserted place all by ourselves and rest a while." For many were coming and going, and they had no leisure even to eat. And they went away in the boat to a deserted place by themselves. Now many saw them going and recognized them, and they hurried there on foot from all the towns and arrived ahead of them. As he went ashore, he saw a great crowd; and he had compassion for them, because they were like sheep without a shepherd; and he began to teach them many things. —MARK 6:30–33

I WAS OUT WITH SOME FRIENDS and their family the other day. The thirteen-year-old was wearing a sweatshirt that his mother had given him which read: "Thou shalt not hassle." I'm not sure if she was sending him a message by giving him the shirt or if by wearing it he was sending one to her. I think it worked both ways.

THE HASSLED AND THE HASSLERS

For most of us, life is full of hassles at work, at school, at home, and beyond: You have to pay your taxes every year. Your HMO's notices just seem to keep coming. Relentless telemarketers keep calling you despite the new laws on the books that are meant to prevent them from doing so. Even with friends and intimates, there are times when the relationship is a hassle. Someone asks for your help when you're tired or you have things to do, and you feel hassled. In every close relationship, it is easy to cross personal boundaries. You feel pressured or ignored or misunderstood. Your deep needs and those of the other don't always square. You begin to feel hassled. You wonder if the relationship is worth the trouble. Hassle is everywhere.

The other side of the coin is that we are hasslers. We have our needs. We have to rely on—or impose on?—others to get them met.

When we go to the store, we expect to get what we came for, and, like it or not, just by making a legitimate request, sometimes we're hassling the person behind the counter. You never know what that clerk has been putting up with during the whole shift. By the same token, if we're in charge of some project, we expect certain things to get done. When we prod others along, we are "hassling" them.

The same thing happens in relationships. Just when you really need somebody to care about you, the person you turn to just happens to be in the same situation: He or she also needs personal attention. Thus you turn out to be a hassler just because of bad timing.

In some ways, the hassling game is just part of being human. We all have needs. We get sick. We get discouraged. We get lonely. We have things to do, and we need people to help. We get tired, and we need rest. These are all just part of the human condition. We need each other, so we are all hassled and hasslers.

THE HASSLE OF CONTEMPORARY LIVING

The hassling game affects us on more than just a personal level; it is part of our social system. Some psychologists and sociologists say that our society is actually insane. Consider the way we live, and you might conclude the same. The pace we keep! The long hours we work! The fun bingeing we save for weekends! The high—unrealistic?—goals we set for ourselves! The constant relocation we endure! The amount of alcohol, drugs, and medications we consume! The divorce rate we experience! The number of neglected and abused kids we see! The rate of incarceration we maintain!

If the gross national product does not go up every year, we assume something is wrong. So we push, push, push. We downsize the company. We increase demands on workers. We look for new markets. We create new needs. We boost sales quotas.

Of course, it is hard to avoid all that: Our economic system is built that way. According to the system, those are the proper things to do. Stop the spinning top, and the thing topples over. The system does have its requirements. The goal is to produce, to churn out more product, to keep the top spinning. Step back and consider these matters, and the insight is obvious: The system itself is insane.

In this situation, the noblest purpose we can conceive is something like this: Educate the kids so we remain competitive in the world market and maintain our high-end way of life. Am I exaggerating? Listen to our government leaders and even our educators. When was the last time they mentioned learning for learning's sake, the joy of understanding, the value of personal enrichment, or the pursuit of wisdom?

Our collective bottom line is dollars and cents, and we have lost sight of people. When Plato and Aristotle, or Augustine and

Aquinas, for example, were asked about "the good life," their answer had to do with virtue, personal development, and community. Our TV ads define "the good life" as a bottle of beer and watching sports on a plasma TV, and our national leaders hardly tend to appeal to any loftier aspirations. Our high productivity is supposed to enhance our quality of life, and well it might, but we have lost our perspective. We equate quality of life with the availability of luxury goods, and we lack any broader view. Despite all our creature comforts, however, we remain an empty and unhappy people. Measures of happiness among the American people have steadily declined since the 1950s. Our whole system has become one big hassle. Now compounding the problem are the new "security measures" imposed in the wake of the terrorist attacks of 9/11. Rather than creatively responding to the excesses of our system—we consume 25% of the world's natural resources—that hassle us and threaten other societies around the world true to form, our leaders just ratchet up the dehumanizing demands that "the American way of life" entails.

As a requirement of survival in our crazy-making world, self-help experts tell us that we have to be assertive. We cannot let people walk all over us, which is perfectly true. Even Jesus said so. I love his line in its older translation: "Be as coy as serpents and gentle as doves" (Matthew 10:16). Jesus reminds us not to be so naïve that we let ourselves be taken. Elsewhere, Jesus commended the children of this world because they were at least shrewd enough to take care of themselves (Luke 16:8). His suggestion is that, in our own way, that is, spiritually, we ought also take care of ourselves. In John 18:23, Jesus even gave an example. In some cases, to turn the other cheek is wrong. Slapped by the temple police, Jesus protested, "If I have spoken wrongly, testify to the wrong. But if I have spoken rightly, why do you strike me?"

However, in the tug of war between assertiveness and counterassertiveness, in a system that sometimes really leaves us no time or patience for someone else's needs, insistence on assertiveness becomes just one more symptom of the deeper problem.

Learning to be assertive will not really help. Something more profound is needed. In some ways, hassling and being hassled are built into the human condition. All of us have limitations, and at some point our limitations are going to conflict. As human beings, we cannot avoid the hassling game.

THE SACRED NEED FOR RELAXATION

Hassling comes up even in the gospel story. In this case, Jesus and his disciples are the ones getting hassled. They have been working hard. They have done their good share, and they are tired. Jesus himself invites them to get away and rest. He wants a rest, too. They are going on retreat. Retreats are sacred. Retreats should not to be disturbed.

Jesus and his disciples went off on retreat, but even there the crowd tracked them down. So it's the same old story: the hasslers and the hassled.

But in the gospel story a third role emerges. It is the role of Jesus. He steps away from being either hassled or hassling. He is different. We could imagine him saying: "Oh, my God, these people! Get them out of here." Yet he looks at them, he understands their need, and he begins to teach them—and Mark adds: at great length.

Jesus' response is really striking. We could imagine that just being polite would be enough. He could speak a few words and then say something like this: "Now, y'all go home and think about that, and I'll see you again later." This is what we would expect any public figure to do: Don't be rude, don't alienate the constituents, but also do draw a line and set some limits; otherwise the public will eat you alive.

As Mark tells it, Jesus acted differently. Somewhere Jesus found the capacity to respond to the people's needs. Apparently, he did not even feel that he was being put upon, and he did not think their reaching out to him was inappropriate clutching. Where did Jesus get the ability to respond that way? Remember that in this case his situation was like many of those we face everyday. Knowing his secret could help us in dealing with life's hassle. So how did he do it? There might be a number of different answers. I can suggest three.

SENSITIVITY TO SELF AND SENSITIVITY TO OTHERS

Perhaps Jesus was more aware of his own feelings than we tend to be. In that very moment of being hassled, he knew what it is like to feel weary and needy and wanting personal attention. Knowing that experience, being in touch with his own feelings, he could identify with other people who also have needs. Thus, instead of just shoving the others away, in some way he recognized himself in them. He realized that he was dealing with himself when he dealt with them.

By showing compassion to others, in some way he was also taking care of himself. In the same way, by injecting some loving kindness into the world, we ourselves can feel more comfortable being here. And by overcoming our own disgruntlement and flashing a bright smile at others, we ourselves begin to feel better. What is more, by cultivating an attitude of compassion toward others, we form a habit of compassionate response also to ourselves in our own darker moments. We become responsive to ourselves as we are responsive to others, and vice versa: "Do unto others *as you would have them do unto you*"; "Love your neighbor *as you love yourself*." So Jesus' attending to others was also an act of self-help. If not in their hassling him, at least in his positive response to them, he was able to experience something of the togetherness that he himself needed.

After I resigned from the priesthood and while I was still trying to find my new niche, I worked for about a year as education coordinator at Consumer Credit Counseling Service. I needed a job and was really lucky to find that one. I was also blessed in the people and the learning that the job brought to my life.

One thing I learned is compassion for other people. I had never had an eight-to-five job in all my life. I had no idea what people had to tolerate just to pay the rent and put bread on the table. I remember seeing the plastic faces and sad eyes on the elevator every morning. I remember a kind African-American woman who saw my eyes watering one day and, like a mother, reassured me that I'd "get used to it." I remember the heroic effort people made to be chipper and bright with one another. The ongoing anguish of that office job and my fear of never being able again to pursue my heart's desire bore into my soul.

Those feelings are still so deep that I easily remember them, and I deliberately call them up when I see someone having a real hassle. Despite the way my own day is going, I make an effort to look that person in the eye, smile, and be congenial. I appreciate the service that that person is giving me, despite being sentenced to a cash register, customer service window, office desk, work site, or assembly line for eight clocked hours every day, regardless of feelings, personal needs, the stirrings of the heart, or the aches in the body, and I imagine what that job costs him or her. When I encounter such people, I do what I can to make their job a bit less painful.

For me, the key to the matter is to take a moment to stop and think. By pausing to register what is going on, I am not oblivious to the feelings of the people serving me. I am lucky that my feelings are still so intense that they spontaneously prompt me to stop and think. Even when I am feeling particularly hassled, the hassle triggers memories of even worse days, and I use those memories to motivate me to make someone else's day a little easier. I imagine that I communicate to them that I understand their situation and that I feel for them—when, really, I am feeling also for myself. And I believe that they catch this mutual feeling, and we are better for having shared it.

Of course, that interpretation of Jesus' response to the crowd is idealized. Taken to an extreme, it is also dangerous. It could result in what has been called "doormat theology," the supposedly Christian approach to life that says to everyone: "Just walk all over me." Such a nonassertive, self-demeaning attitude is not healthy. It not only enables us to neglect our own basic human needs, but

it also makes us accomplices in supporting other people's irresponsibility regarding their own needs. It might also enable us to
indulge in delusions of holiness. We can feel sorry for ourselves
and think we are "martyrs for Christ," or we can be full of pride
because of our supposed "exemplary charity." Such surface virtue
is inevitably deadly to the soul.

Still, there is a solid lesson for us in that idealized interpretation. It gives one an important clue for living a more peaceful
life: Be in touch with your feelings. Strange that this clue needs
to be highlighted. Our slick and efficient society does try to wipe
feelings out of the picture. Feelings complicate things too much.
We are not supposed to be moved by emotions. We are not supposed to take feelings into account. And eventually we learn that
we are not even to feel our feelings. This learning is not usually
a head thing, a lesson that we could repeat. It is not usually
something we are intellectually aware of. Rather, it is something
we have learned to do. It goes to our guts and becomes a way of
life.

Ask people "How are you?" and apart from the programmed
answer "Oh, just fine, thank you," they may really not know. They
are not sure if they are happy or sad, if they are eager or just anxious. They might have to ask that oh-so-foolish question "Are we
having fun yet?"—admitting that they do not know what they
themselves enjoy and that they are ready to let other people and
external circumstances define happiness for them. Then, rather
than experiencing whether they are happy or not, they calculate
and deduce the answer, and they factor feelings out of the equa-
tion. Then "happiness" is a conclusion, just an idea. It is no longer
a mode of experience.

Part of the problem is that it is dangerous to be aware of your
feelings. Being aware, you run the risk of feeling bad. You run the
risk of actually knowing that you are unhappy. The daily disappointments, losses, betrayals, and little hurts are all right there to
be felt. The poignancy of memories, which can be tripped at any
moment, is there to be remembered. With awareness of the feel-

ings come not only the pleasant times but also the painful ones. So, to protect ourselves from the pain, we often learn—without ever knowing it—to shut down all feelings.

This tendency to feign happiness often becomes part of religion. Since "Christians" are supposed to be ever courteous, helpful, kind, and upbeat, churchy people sometimes learn to play the role of the smiling but beleaguered servant. They wear that artificial and permanent smile on their faces and exude a sense of forced goodwill. A friend of mine used to visit a conservative church simply to develop deeper understanding of that congregation's views and greater tolerance. He reported that he was sometimes uncomfortable with those people. In his words: "They are unnaturally happy." That is, he found their positive attitude too good to be true. Again in his words: "Nobody can always be that happy." The brittleness of their surface happiness suggested that they were really out of touch with the range of their real feelings.

Our society encourages us to be unfeeling. It lives by the myth of universal happiness. We find it hard to admit that things can go wrong and that we can be unhappy: We don't want to appear unsuccessful. We need that veneer of false happiness. So we turn to alcohol, nicotine, caffeine, pills, cocaine, methamphetamine; we get hooked on compulsive sex and addictive work, anything that provides "fast relief," as the ads proclaim. We learn to run from real feelings. We learn not to feel. Out of touch with our feelings, we are also out of touch with our souls.

We can be so frantic that we do not even know that we are frantic. We are too distracted to be aware of ourselves. Running around in circles, feeling totally hassled, we do not even realize that we are having a difficult day. It doesn't register that we should expect to feel tired.

What a contrast when you come home from a busy and productive day and you are worn out! You know you are exhausted from a good day's work, and you say, "Wow, I'm exhausted! What a great day it's been!" You feel good about yourself in the very experience of feeling drained.

In counseling sessions I've been amazed how a little self-awareness can reframe everything. A person talks about being discouraged and ready to throw in the towel. After listening to his or her story, a saga of losses, disappointments, and setbacks, I could simply say, "You really have had a hard time of it. You have so much on your plate. No wonder you feel so bad. You are really going through hard times." Then, just hearing this statement, just recognizing how true it is, such clients often sit back and get a better perspective on things. They realize that they are dealing with a lot and that they haven't been aware of the mounting toll that each added hassle has taken. It is perfectly natural that they would be feeling overwhelmed. In fact, if they weren't, there would be real cause for worry. They begin to feel better just by realizing how bad they feel and that, under the circumstances, feeling bad is perfectly okay.

The paradox here is obvious. By really being in touch with our feelings and actually knowing how bad we feel, we feel better. Why? Because the human and healthy thing is to be aware of ourselves. Even if this awareness causes pain, it is a positive experience because it carries the healthy component of vivid self-awareness. Being self-aware, we realize that we are not at the mercy of changing fortunes. We are bigger than passing times. In some way we can stand outside them, even while being wholly immersed in them. We are people: Existing in part beyond the here and now, we possess an essential worth and dignity. Therefore, experiencing ourselves, we feel better. The very experience of our own sacred humanity lets us feel confirmed even while we are feeling bad.

I am suggesting that perhaps Jesus, more than most of us, was in touch with his feelings. Because he knew how he felt, he was able to respond to others in a positive way. He was not at the mercy of his feelings. They did not cloud and confuse his vision. He was tired, and he knew it, and in that very knowing he also transcended his weariness. He, the knower, was more than the tired one whom he was knowing.

I am not talking about his being God. That matter raises a whole other question. I am simply talking about Jesus as a real flesh-and-blood, deeply in-touch, highly integrated human being. What I am saying about Jesus may sound like pop psychology, but it also fits the description of enlightenment, as Eastern philosophies would name it. But enlightenment is a matter of highly developed human beings, not a matter of divinity. To be sure, the quality of which I speak, Jesus' self-awareness, is a spiritual quality, but spiritualness is a human quality. We all have a spiritual capacity. For this reason, Jesus—and Buddha—can be realistic models for us. Jesus exemplifies what living this life could be for any of us. Moreover, what Jesus exemplifies is certainly something God would want us to have. We could even say it is something god-*like*, but it is not specifically divine. I am only speaking of Jesus as an extraordinary human being.

When the crowd approached, Jesus could respond out of the fullness of his self-aware humanity rather than merely out of his weariness. With an objective awareness of those people and with a firm sense of his own being, he was able to respond to them compassionately. To him they were not a threat, not just another hassle. One key to the matter is that he was in touch with himself.

THE HUMAN NEED FOR FRIENDS AND INTIMATES

Maybe there is another reason why Jesus could respond so generously to the crowd: He had his friends. Jesus had people to support him. Jesus had his disciples, his intimates, with whom he shared. In that sharing he was strengthened and nourished. With them he found the relaxation and renewal that let him reach out to the others.

It's the same with us. We are grounded and can be more stable, more unflappable when we feel we belong with others. Social support is one of the most important facets of life. When we are feeling alone and isolated, we become defensive. We become protective of what little sense of self we have. We easily get caught up in our own minds and our own little worlds. We lose touch with the bigger reality of life. Acquaintances, colleagues, friends, families, and life partners are vital to our mental and spiritual health.

Religions talk of weekly services in terms of worshiping God, but our weekly "worship" is more for ourselves than it is for God. Saint Augustine was clear on this point. It is we who need these regular gatherings, not God. We speak of them in terms of "worship" because they are, indeed, directed to God, but it is our own spiritual needs that our worship serves. We cannot thrive without regular attention to the meaning of our lives and the values we hold dear. And we cannot be true to those meanings and values without kindred spirits with whom we share, and from whom we gain, support.

In no area of life does isolation work. No one makes it alone. The studies are conclusive. Increased heart disease, high blood pressure, weakened immune response—all kinds of medical conditions result from social isolation. The stark fact is that people who live with others survive longer than people who live alone, especially men. Ironically, men, more than women, tend to opt for the strong and silent, rugged individualist role, yet men need other people most of all. We are only killing ourselves when we try to go it alone. Just as many hands make for light work, the support of other people dilutes the stress and hassles of life. The Bible is clear on this point: "It is not good that the man should be alone"—nor woman (Genesis 2:18).

Unfortunately, that Bible teaching cannot just stand on its own without a defense of all types of relationships. There is no reason to believe that, in making this statement, God or the author of Genesis had sexual orientation in mind. The Bible was not making heterosexual relationships a universal requirement. The Bible was simply approving as God-given the fact that humans are social and, lacking our current knowledge, took for granted that people are heterosexual. However, if people do not find intimacy with the opposite sex, they are still being true to human nature and God's design by at least having someone with whom to share their lives.

The same must be said of people whose marriages fail. Surely, God does not want them to remain in a destructive relationship, doomed to a life of misery. Surely, God wants them to blossom in a new relationship that is responsibly established. A prime reason that Jesus forbade divorce was concern for the wife. In his day, a woman literally could not survive without a man: a father, brother, or husband. A man could divorce his wife simply by handing her a statement to that effect; she had no say in the matter. In this case her only option was prostitution, the option that many women throughout the centuries have had to choose to survive. So Jesus condemned divorce. In our day, however, when women can more easily support themselves, Jesus would undoubtedly encourage women to get out of an abusive marriage.

We are social by nature. Sharing deeply with others allows us to shrug our shoulders at life's hassles. So maybe Jesus was able to deal with the hassle of the crowd because he had the support of his disciples, his friends. He must have been a very good friend, not just a friend to others but also one who allowed others to be a friend to him, for real friendship is a two-way street. So Jesus must have opened his heart to others and expressed his mind to them. He must have let people in and shared the secrets of his heart. In that friendship he found the strength to deal patiently with the hassle of the crowds.

THE POWER OF PRAYER

Perhaps there was still another reason why Jesus could react so kindly to the crowd. At the beginning of his gospel, Mark notes forcefully that Jesus often went out to be alone and pray. Jesus got strength not just from the support of his friends and not just by being in touch with his emotions. He also attended to the spiritual dimension of his being. He spent time "in prayer."

I do not mean to suggest that our emotional or social lives have nothing to do with our spiritual life. We each have a body, and thus we are physical. We have a psyche and are emotional. But we also have a spirit; so we are self-transcending. By virtue of our human spirit, we are open to wonder, marvel and awe, to unending pondering, to far-reaching imaginations, to unbounded longing and desire. We reach out to the universe. This spiritual, transcendent dimension is the essence of our humanity. So we are physical, emotional, and also spiritual, but we cannot cut ourselves up into pieces.

The whole of our being is involved in all we are and do. Every facet of our lives relates to our spirituality. Nonetheless, just as we are always using our bodies but sometimes still need to focus on physical exercise, so, too, at times we also need to focus on spiritual exercise. To do so, we can go off by ourselves, calm our bodies and still our emotions, and settle into awareness of this transcendent dimension of our being. Long quiet moments allow awareness of the spiritual to emerge. By attending to it, we can develop and strengthen it; it can lead us to the grand, beautiful, and lasting fulfillment toward which it tends.

Such attention to the transcendent dimension of our being is what we achieve in prayer. Of course, we usually think of prayer as communing with God, but I have been talking about accessing the spiritual dimension of our being, not necessarily about reaching out to God. Just like physical exercise, the "spiritual exercise" to which I refer applies to us all as human beings, whether we believe in God or not. So I want to leave room for the fact that, though I am using the word *prayer*, I am speaking about a practice that need not necessarily involve belief in God—like the meditation found in many Eastern philosophies. But even in prayer that is conceptualized as a relationship to God, if you analyze the matter, it is clear that opening ourselves to God has the psychological effect of loosening the transcendent dimension of our own being. Prayer to God is a way of enhancing the power of our own spirits. Thus, prayer—or, better, meditation, contemplation, quiet attention to the spirit—is a practice that broadens our perspective and situates the elements of life in their proper place.

Most people think of prayer as talking with God, and such talk is, indeed, a legitimate form of prayer. Yet there are other more mature and more effective forms of prayer. If we conceive prayer only as conversation with God, the atheist's criticism of prayer is often on target: We are just talking to ourselves. Indeed, even believers must admit that this talking kind of prayer often results in our just going round and round on some topic in our heads. Until I learned more "quiet" ways of praying, prayer without words or thoughts, I used to get frustrated on retreats. Locked up for days in my own thinking mind, tied up in a tangle of repeated thoughts, memories, emotions, and wishes. Such mental gyrations or inner conversation is not what prayer is about.

A more rewarding form of prayer involves what some call, rather, listening to God. In this sense, prayer is a matter of quieting our thoughts, stilling our emotions, and leaving ourselves open to transcendent experience. It is a matter of letting ourselves be aware of our own ever-active awareness. Then words, thoughts, and feelings may fall away, and we may rest in a silent moment. But this "just being there" is active; it is an uncluttered openness to all that is. What I am describing is usually called meditation.

This process can be understood psychologically; there is nothing specifically religious or mystical about it. Through the use of various techniques, like repeating a word—called a *mantra*—in your mind, focusing on an object or sound, attending to your heartbeat or breathing, or simply dismissing thoughts and feelings that arise within yourself, you still your mind's constant hopping from topic to topic and become aware of the very process of being aware. You heighten your awareness of your own awareness as well as your creative capacity. You attend to the pure function of the human, open to the self-transcending or spiritual dimension of the human mind.

In such pure awareness, in openness to the present moment, we are present to the very fact of our existence or our being. Insofar as God is the source and sustainer of all existence, we are, then, also open to the very presence of God. Thus, openness to our own spiritual capacity is closely linked to openness to God. For this reason, the spiritual giants speak of prayer, not so much as talking with God, but as communing with God or resting in the divine presence or abiding in the awareness of God. In this case, words, thoughts, and feelings directed *toward God* actually become distractions from a more substantive and immediate experience *of God*. I have in mind this more substantive form of prayer when I speak of gaining strength for living and of achieving a healthy perspective on life through prayer. I have written about this matter in more detail in my book *Meditation Without Myth*.

Luke 10:38–42 tells the story of Jesus' visit to the home of Martha and Mary. While Martha busies herself with preparations, Mary sits and listens at Jesus' feet. Martha objected that her sister ought to help with the work. Jesus responded with words that are famous in the Western spiritual tradition, words that are really addressed to all of us: "Martha, Martha, you are worried and distracted by many things; there is need of only one thing." That one thing, of course, is to be attentive to the presence of God in our midst.

Perhaps more than the rest of us, Jesus attended to the one thing that really matters. His attention to the things of the spirit and, thus, to the things of God, allowed him to see that much of the rest is needless worry and distraction. Perhaps, then, for this reason, he was able to respond with kindness when the crowd intruded on his retreat. His heart was well centered. He spent ample time in prayer, easily able to keep the crowd's intrusion in perspective.

THE PRICE OF REDEMPTION AND THE DOCTRINE OF THE CROSS

Surely, we could offer many reasons why Jesus was able to respond with compassion to the intruding crowd. (I just made three suggestions.) And to ponder those reasons is all well and good. Nonetheless, in the end, those suggestions do not answer the question. Jesus was going off to get some rest so that he could be in touch with himself, but he never got there. He was going to relax with his friends, but the crowds never gave him the chance. He would often get strength and perspective from prayer, but the crowd allowed him no time for prayer.

Those are all nice suggestions, and in general they are valid, but in this particular situation they just do not seem to fit. Oh, they would fit if we idealized the matter, if we turned Jesus into some superman. Then we would expect him—and in pathological imitation, ourselves—to find calm, strength, and courage when the interior source was simply exhausted.

We idealize Jesus as did Mark. That idealization is not always bad. The gospels are meant to inspire us. Jesus' response to the crowd who followed him is inspiring, and inspiration is good. It makes us think. It motivates us to do heroic things. But I am not sure we should take those suggestions about Jesus' behavior uncritically. The fact is that there is only so much a person can do. We have our limits. We need our rest. We cannot go on giving forever without periodically being recharged. There do come times when the solutions I've offered just do not work. There come times when the very thing you need is precisely to get away—and you can't. Then what? The situation with Jesus and the crowd was just that kind of situation. Facing this fact makes us stop and think. What is life all about, and how does it actually work?

When you look at the story, you have to admit that Jesus got a bum deal. He had already done his share, and the crowd was asking for more. And he gave it! That fact often seems to be the key difference between Jesus and the rest of us. He was willing to do more than his share. He was willing to go the extra mile, to give his tunic as well as his cloak. In this, he gave us a lesson. There come times in life when giving only what's fair is just not enough. If you are concerned about people, if you want people to grow, if you want people to feel loved, if you want life to move in a noble and wholesome way, someone has to pay the price. Setting up a loving world costs.

Who is going to pay the cost? Not the people who cause the trouble: They don't care. If they cared, they wouldn't be causing trouble. So the people who care must pay the price. There is no one else to do it. There is no other way out.

This world is corrupt—not because God set it up that way. It is corrupt because we make it that way. This is the lesson of Genesis: God created the world, and it was good. But the sin of human beings disrupted the order, destroyed paradise, and made things go bad. You don't have to take the story of Adam and Eve literally to preserve the truth of the Bible. This story is as true as any ever told: The corruption of the world is the work of corrupt human beings. In a corrupt world the innocent end up paying for the wrongs of the wicked. This system is not fair, but that is the way it is.

Recall the S&L scandal following the Reagan years. Financial institutions all over the country went bust for billions of dollars. Unless those institutions were bailed out, the whole economy was liable to collapse. So money had to be funneled in. And from where do you think it came? Certainly not from the scoundrels who masterminded the scams. They had gone broke or else were too slick to get caught. But someone had to pay, and it turned out to be Joe and Mary Taxpayer. Of course, the Taxpayers were completely innocent of the affair, but unless somebody paid, the situation would have been far worse for everybody. And there have been more recent busts of similar kinds: retirement plans cancelled, legally, after a lifetime of work. The results are always the same: The innocent suffer the losses, and the perpetrators cleverly slip through the cracks in the "justice" system. If ever there were an example that legality is not the same thing as morality, this is it: The innocent pay for the wicked. The virtuous take up the slack for criminals. Those who care have to put in enough to make up for those who do not. Redemption of a corrupt world comes only through the suffering of the innocent.

This is no religious matter about which I am talking. It is not a matter necessarily of being "a good Christian" or "a follower of

Jesus." It is simply a matter of the way this world works, whether you are Christian, religious, or not. To some extent, concerned and responsible people will always end up paying the price for the doings of the irresponsible and the unjust.

If there is someone you love and if you really care, you will give of yourself, even more than your fair share. People in relationships talk about giving 150 percent each. If you really want an important project to go forward, you will put out more than your due. If you want the world to be better, you are going to have to invest. If the concerned do not make the extra effort, who will? Inevitably, the innocent and generous end up getting the short end of the stick. Things go that way in a world where some people are corrupt and uncaring.

There comes a point when we need to stop being assertive. There comes a point when, knowingly and willingly, we need to stop insisting on our rights. In such cases we really do know that the situation is unfair—and we accept it. We accept it because it is the only way to make things better. By not accepting it, we would only make things worse. We would become as petty and self-serving as those we are calling culprits. We would betray our own personal integrity. We would surrender our commitment to the common good. Thus, when Jesus went off with his disciples to get a little rest and the crowd tracked them down, Jesus responded with compassion, though the crowd was really being unfair. This assessment does not suggest that the crowd was necessarily evil or wicked, though it seems that the people were, indeed, thoughtless and inconsiderate. But who knows what was going through their minds? And who knows if this incident actually happened as Mark wrote it up?

And what does it matter? In life, the bottom line never is a matter of computing who, in fact, is guilty or not. Bigger things are at stake. Our litigious and law-and-order society would do well to realize this fact. The budding trend toward mediation is encouraging in this regard. What Mark presents is simply a case for Jesus to give more than his share. The lesson is that Jesus understood the principle of innocent suffering, and he acted on it willingly. The hard lesson for us is that sometimes we are called on to do the same.

There are rules in life, and one rule is, "Thou shalt not hassle." You can even display this rule on a sweatshirt and hope that others will note and heed it. A complementary rule: "Thou shalt not allow thyself to be hassled." But these rules do not cover all the cases. Jesus added some principles of his own: "Blessed are the peacemakers"; "Blessed are those who suffer persecution for justice sake." These principles are not always easy to accept, but the picture is incomplete without them.

NINE

ANGUISH AND HOPE AT OUR PASSING LIVES: THE MYSTICAL MARRIAGE AT CANA

ON THE THIRD DAY there was a wedding in Cana of Galilee, and the mother of Jesus was there. Jesus and his disciples had also been invited to the wedding. When the wine gave out, the mother of Jesus said to him, "They have no wine." And Jesus said to her, "Woman, what concern is that to you and to me? My hour has not yet come." His mother said to the servants, "Do whatever he tells you." Now standing there were six stone water jars for the Jewish rites of purification, each holding twenty or thirty gallons. Jesus said to them, "Fill the jars with water." And they filled them up to the brim. He said to them, "Now draw some out, and take it to the chief steward." So they took it. When the steward tasted the water that had become wine, and did not know where it came from (though the servants who had drawn the water knew), the steward called the bridegroom and said to him, "Everyone serves the good wine first, and then the inferior wine after the guests have become drunk. But you have kept the good wine until now." Jesus did this, the first of his signs, in Cana of Galilee, and revealed his glory; and his disciples believed in him. —JOHN 2:1–11

THAT READING IS ABOUT a wedding, but the wedding is not the wedding of a man and a woman. In fact, the bride and groom's names are never mentioned. The wedding in that gospel reading is really our own.

THE SYMBOLISM IN JOHN'S GOSPEL

John's gospel is overlaid with symbolism, layer upon layer. The story of the wedding at Cana is the beginning of the second chapter of John's gospel. If you look back through the first chapter, you will find that there are a number of sections leading up to this one, and three of them are introduced with the words "The next day . . ." If you count all those days, the wedding feast should be taking place on the fifth day. But this passage starts with the words, "On the third day."

Remember that three is a mystical number in the Hebrew mind. Jonah was in the belly of the whale for three days. Jesus rose from the dead on the third day. Here Jesus performs his first sign . . .on the third day. In the biblical mind, the third day is the day of fulfillment. It is the day of the Lord. It is the awaited day. So already we get the sense that there is something extraordinary about to take place.

The way Jesus talked to his mother is also unusual. He called her "Woman." To address a woman with that term was nothing extraordinary in Jesus' day. But in Jesus society, one would never address one's own mother that way. Likewise, Jesus' response to his mother—"What concern is that to you and me?"—is unusual. This whole exchange suggests a distance between Jesus and his mother. The gospel is highlighting the fact that Mary and the rest of us are in one realm, and Jesus is in another. Again, we have an indication that something extraordinary is going on.

Then there were those water jars. They were available for use in a Jewish purification ritual. Jesus takes that very water and changes it into wine. The implication is that the old has been done away with and something new has arrived on the scene. Again, a divide appears. Again, we sense the symbolism and mystery in John's gospel.

Also note how much wine Jesus made. There were six jugs, each holding twenty to thirty gallons. So after the guests had already quite drunk their fill, Jesus sets out about one hundred fifty more gallons of wine! He certainly knew how to throw a party. And when the head steward tastes the wine, he notes that it is the best, by far. Clearly, John's exaggeration means to say something. The new wine that has come—that is, what is happening in Jesus—surpasses anything that was seen in the past.

Finally, notice what John says when he comments on this event: Jesus revealed his glory. The first chapter of John speaks about glory: "In the beginning was the Word, and the Word was with God, and the Word was God. . . . And the Word became flesh and lived among us, and we have seen his glory, the glory as of a father's only son, full of grace and truth." Here at Cana we get the sense that now this mystery, the divine mystery of Jesus, is beginning to be revealed. At the wedding at Cana we see the first of the signs that showed the glory of Jesus.

So many facets of the story of Cana have deep religious meaning. How easily we could miss all that! We ourselves do not tend to express ourselves in such subtle symbolism. We tend to come right out and say a thing. This difference between the gospel mentality and our own should teach us a lesson. We should realize that there really is such a difference. Then, we should not go around reading the scriptures as if they were written yesterday, in our times, in our language, in our mind-set. Such literal reading—the Fundamentalist approach—leads us to miss the real meaning of the scriptures and leads us to impose our own personal views on the word of God. Then we can end up claiming—and how convenient it is!—that our opinions are really those of the Bible.

THE MARRIAGE OF GOD
AND HUMANITY

Without ever saying it outright, John portrays Jesus at Cana as the fulfillment of Jewish expectations. In Jesus the third day has come, the glory of God is revealed, a bridge between God's realm and our own is opened. So a wedding is certainly being celebrated at Cana. But the center of John's concern is not the marriage of that anonymous man and woman. John's concern is the wedding of God with humankind. Our own wedding with God is the focus of attention. In Jesus marvelous and new things are happening.

The prophets announced such a wedding centuries before. Isaiah 54:4–6 speaks of God's taking God's people back: "Do not fear, for you will not be ashamed. . . . The disgrace of your widowhood you will remember no more. For your Maker is your husband, the Lord of hosts is his name, the Holy One of Israel is your Redeemer, the God of the whole earth he is called. For the Lord has called you like a wife." At stake here is the union of God and God's people, the joining of humankind with God.

OVERWHELMED BY
THE BEAUTY OF LIFE

I recall a beautiful Sunday afternoon in May in Austin, Texas. The sun was shining. The sky was clear. I took my bicycle for a ride along the river trail. I got back home, sprawled on the couch, and turned on the classical music station. They were playing Strauss waltzes. I just love that music. So the whole scene, the whole afternoon, was just heavenly for me. As the music continued, the famous "Blue Danube" began to play. It's a tune we all know. In fact, we know it so well that it sometimes becomes trite and is made much too common: da-dum, da-dum, da-dum, da-dum . . .as in one of those squealing electronic "music" devices sandwiched into a greeting card, and as a result many consider it trite.

I was thinking to myself, Johann Strauss. Early nineteenth century. Where did he get the inspiration? Where did this music come from? In some ways his waltz is a simple ditty, yet when orchestrated, when filled in with its crescendos, diminuendos, and allegros, it is just a magnificently beautiful piece of music—all come out of that man's mind! Isn't it strange that he is gone. He is dead. He produced this beautiful creation. It is here. It is still being played and enjoyed. It is part of this marvelous, wonderful world in which we live. His music must be among the most beautiful creative works that we have, and yet he himself is gone. Does it make sense to think that he just lived his life, and that's the end of him? That he gave us this exquisite music and then disappeared? It just does not seem possible that he would have stopped existing eternally, that his death would be the end: gone, disappeared, nonexistent. What he was involved with—the darting melodies, the stunning playfulness, the enthralling rhythms, the timelessness of beauty—this is all just too precious, too transcendent, too godlike. Could he himself have just stopped being? He who produced all that? He who created it: that mind, that spirit, that being? Could he now be simply dead and gone?

It's the same for all of us. Just look at your own life, your home, the things and people that are dear to you: the artwork, the outfits, the little tricks you play, the sentimental lines you write, the memories you cherish. There is so much beauty and marvel all around us. Perhaps we are not great composers, but we all make our little contributions: a hello here, a smile there, a secret wink or a nod, a pet project completed, a hobby pursued, a relationship cherished, a friend supported, a neighbor visited, a dream trip completed. We all know longing and loving and giving. We are all gripped at times by profound movements of the heart. Is it possible that we, who are capable of such things, we for whom such things are the most precious core of our being—is it possible that we could one day suddenly just stop existing? Could we routinely touch what seems eternal and most sublime and then just cease to be?

COULD LIFE JUST END WITH DEATH?

While I was thinking I became deeply disturbed by these thoughts, and this conclusion occurred to me: We simply must affirm that life goes on! It would seem that the only alternative is to opt for absurdity.

I have a friend who appreciates life at least as deeply as I do, yet he no longer believes in God or life after death. For him, it is not absurd to think that, once we die, we simply pass away and lose all that we have known and been in our human lives. For him, it is important to be grateful for what there is and never to take it for granted. And, he would suggest, it is only arrogant of us to think we should live forever. Everything else in the universe comes and goes. Why not also we?

Most Jewish people are of that same mind. They do not believe in life after death. Rather, they are grateful for those who have passed before us and celebrate their contributions, and they keep those dead loved ones alive through a loving and appreciative memory of them.

Some people say that, without life after death, we would really have nothing to live for and all morality would go by the board. Supposedly, only belief in a life to come keeps us honest in this life. I disagree. I would go so far as to say this: If our belief in an afterlife changes how we live this life, we are not living authentically. Authentic living means that, regardless of what might or might not come in some supposed afterlife, we live our life as best we can. We honestly and lovingly meet the demands of living here and now. If we live only for a life to come—which we really do not know—we are not living this life but some projected fantasy. If we are good only out of concern for an afterlife and not because of commitment to goodness itself in this world, we are not really good people at all.

My friend would basically agree with my point of view and would even take it a step further. He suggests that, because people are so focused on a life to come, they ignore, devalue, and miss the life we are now living. He himself is as committed to justice and is as honest, noble, and sensitive as anyone I know. He argues that, precisely because we have only this life, every moment is precious and every individual must be reverenced. The worst of all atrocities is to deprive someone of the beauty and marvel of life because, as he insists, this is all he or she can ever have. So we must be committed to justice for all.

Everyone deserves a basic foundation—education, medical care, adequate housing, personal understanding and support, access to music and the arts—every offense or hurt against another is a grave and serious matter. The waste of lives, the abuses, the caste systems, the poverty, the built-in inequities, the enslavements, indeed, the genocides, with which human history is shamefully replete to in our own day, are beyond comprehension. Every injustice we suffer makes us feel less grateful for life. For my friend, belief in an afterlife excuses us from making this life worthy of every human being.

My friend came to this position because he came face-to-face with death. By coming to grips with death, he says, he learned how to live. The irony of the matter is that, after years of treatment for a fatal illness and after long preparation for death, his diagnosis turned out to be a mistake. He was not destined for an early death at all. Then he had to face the challenge of living again.

Thus, my friend's opinion is not frivolous speculation. He speaks with authority. His experience taught him that it is not absurd to believe that life could come to a complete end in death. He sees death as a simple matter of fact, and, facing this fact in the goodness of his heart, he goes on to conceive a world of reverence and dignity for all. In light of the wonder and frailty of life, he imagines how things in this world ought to be, and, even more importantly, what he imagines is no different in practice from what sincere religious believers propose. With or without God and an afterlife, the core of honest living remains the same.

HUMAN PARTICIPATION IN DIVINITY

Such an absolute finality in death is hard to face. So, do we just fool ourselves? Are we just driven to believe that life goes on? Should we give up that hope . . . ?

Still, there is more to the picture. What we experience in our present life—the wonder, the marvel, the sheer beauty at times—does seem to reflect some greater and even more magnificent reality. At times, we seem to be glimpsing, if only glimpsing, some of infinity. And we are already a part of it or, at least, so it would seem. In some ways we appear to be in sync with the forces of the universe. The sheen of the sun on the river and the beauty of the waltzes of Strauss have something in common. And when we touch it, we participate in it. In some intangible but undeniable way, we belong to the universe.

Profound thoughts of this nature, such musings on the meaning of life—these same concerns lie behind the writings of John. He, too, was pondering the heart of the matter, the ultimate meaning of life. He suggested that Jesus took that meaning and radically transformed it. Jesus drew the human into the divine. In Jesus, the longings of our hearts become signs of the presence of God. The fleeting beauty and marvel that we now enjoy anticipate the fulfillment that we are promised. That common something of the universe that we only touch now and then becomes the doorway to eternal, divine life. We are united with God. A wonderful wedding has taken place.

In the Roman Catholic Mass there is a one-line prayer that speaks to these issues. As the priest mixes a few drops of water with wine in preparation for the Eucharist, the priest says, "By the mystery of this water and wine, may we come to share in the divinity of Christ, who humbled himself to share in our humanity." This prayer summarizes a pervasive theme in the writings of both the Greek and Latin Fathers of the church, those early Christian thinkers who lived from the second to sixth centuries. The Greek Fathers even had a word for this thing, *theosis*, the process of become godlike. We translate that word in English as *deification*.

What might that transformation mean? Consider, for example, that we humans have insatiable curiosity. We want to know everything about everything. What if this longing of the human soul were to be fulfilled? Then we would know as God knows; we would understand everything about everything.

Or consider that we humans have an insatiable desire for love. We would like to embrace—and even become one with—everything wonderful, marvelous, and lovable in the universe. We would want to be able to love everyone and everything. What if this longing of the human soul were to be fulfilled? Loving everyone and everything with unbounded love, we would love even as God loves. We would not be God because, as creatures, we are not the Creator, but in certain ways we would become like God. The ideal possibilities of our humanity would have been fulfilled. To that extent, we would enjoy perfections that are proper only to God—to understand everything, to love without measure—yet we would still be human beings. We would be godlike, deified. We would be one with God, united with God.

Our minds marvel at the beauty of the universe, and we long to understand everything. Well, Christian belief tells us that God will grant us that fullness of understanding and knowledge. Our hearts long for love, and we want to be close to, to become one with, others and all things. Well, Christian belief tells us that God will give us that total love. We will love unto unity with all, even as God loves. Our union with God would be the answer to the prayer that John (17:21–23) has Jesus pray: "I ask . . . that they may all be one. As you, Father, are in me and I am in you, may they also be in us . . . The glory that you have given me I have given to them, so that they may be one, as we are one, I in them and you in me, that they may become completely one."

The marriage that was going on at Cana is the marriage of the human family and divinity. It is a marriage that would make us one with God. This marriage suggests that already in our daily living we are, indeed, in touch with the power of the universe. Whatever it is that explains where all this world came from, whatever it is that we are step-by-step moving toward, that which in our unknowing we call "God," whatever that mystery is, we are already a part of It. In our everyday ordinary openness to the beauty and wonder of life, we are moving ever closer to It. The marvel in our hearts, our glimpse of the eternal, is not just human. This marvel that we know is not just, as we could very reasonably argue, an expression of our created and completely human capacities. Christianity would say that this marvel is, in fact, the very being of the Uncreated God erupting into our beings. God, the Holy Spirit, has been given to us. In Christ through the Holy Spirit, God and we are made one. This is the new wine on the third day about which John wrote.

THE UNIQUENESS OF
THE CHRISTIAN VISION

That understanding of the union of the human and the divine is distinctive to Christianity. That understanding occurs in no other religion. According to Christian belief, Jesus himself is its paradigmatic instance, for he is both God and human. In him, and particularly at his resurrection, this union finds its first human fulfillment. Christian belief further specifies that, through the gift of the Holy Spirit, poured out in our hearts, we, too, have God within us. Then, following the lead of the Holy Spirit within us, we can implement in our own lives the example of Jesus in his. Like him, we are also destined for glorification in God. We are to share in divinity.

Notice how all the central Christian doctrines are involved in this notion of human deification: the Trinity in God; the divinity of Jesus; his incarnation, redemption, and resurrection; the mission of the Holy Spirit; the need for holy living on our part; the support for such living in a community (church) dedicated to holiness; and the promise of reunion with all the "saints" in God's

own life in heaven. These Christian doctrines are as they are precisely to account for our deification. The point is to insist that we
humans are not divine, we creatures are not the Creator, yet,
through the working of God in Christ and the Holy Spirit, we can
in some way become one with God.

Such mystical union is a challenge to Judaism, which insists on
the awesomeness of God in contrast to us human beings. Judaism
insists on the distance between the holiness of God and the weakness of humankind. Of course, Jacob, Moses, Elijah, and others
were known in some sense to be intimates of God, but their encounters with God do not approach the familiarity of Jesus saying
to all of his disciples "I do not call you servants any longer . . . but
I have called you friends, because I have made known to you
everything that I have heard from my Father" (John 15:15).

Similarly, like Christianity, Islam also believes in heaven, but it
is not a state of union with God. Rather, for Islam, heaven is a
place of sensuous beauty and joy. On the other hand, in its own
way Hinduism does speak of what we might call a union of humanity and divinity. A central belief of Hinduism is: "Atman is
Brahman," that is, the deepest core of the human spirit *is* the Ultimate of the Universe, or, in Western terms, at its core, humanity
is divine. This Hindu belief differs from the Christian. Christianity retains the Jewish insistence that the creature is not the Creator, but Christianity believes, further, that through Christ the
Uncreated Holy Spirit does come to dwell in the created human
heart. In contrast, from the beginning, Hinduism asserts that the
human mind is divine by nature, as does another famous Hindu
belief, "Thou art That." That is, "You are the Ultimate" or "You
are God." Perhaps it is not worth quibbling over the differences,
for in the end both traditions allow that we have God within us,
and these metaphysical matters are well beyond our ability to resolve with certainty.

Still, the implications of these two different doctrinal emphases are at least worth contrasting. The Eastern approach is
likely to downplay the importance of the body and the physical

world: Supposedly, in some way all the world of perceptual experience is an illusion; everything is really consciousness or spirit or divinity, and our goal is to free ourselves from the cycle of rebirths into this base, physical world. In contrast, the Western approach takes the world of space and time, and our single passage through it, very, very seriously: In Jesus, God actually became flesh, so the physical world and the human condition are worthy even of God. Thus, in their doctrines, Hinduism seems to discredit the physical world whereas Christianity seems to hallow it.

Nonetheless, when we focus on practical living rather than on abstract beliefs, ironically Hinduism is much earthier than Christianity, and Christianity, which ought to delight in this world that is said to be created good by God and redeemed by Christ, is notorious for its otherworldly, body-negative moralism. If the proof is in the pudding, Hinduism seems better geared to flesh-and-blood living than Christianity is although, conceptually or theoretically, Christian belief is more coherent.

Then, what would Christianity be if it actually lived its core beliefs? It doesn't live them; it hardly ever has, especially in its institutional structures. Maybe this failure is why many people, rightly concerned more about real living than about metaphysical doctrines, are finding religious inspiration these days in the religions of the East. This comfort of born-and-bred Christians with Eastern religions also suggests that Christianity, Hinduism, and Buddhism do, indeed, have enough similarities that their differences can be bridged. When it comes down to living together on planet Earth, there is no reason for the religions to be at odds.

In any case, human deification is a central Christian concern. Of course, there is no way to prove its reality—just as there is no way to prove the metaphysical beliefs of any religion. As I already noted in passing, on the basis of the capacity of our wondrous human spirits, we could already explain our experiences of beauty and timelessness without appeal to God and human participation in divinity. And, with my non-theist friend, we could hold that, when our brains and, thus, our human minds cease to function, so does our capacity for wonder and awe come to a permanent end.

Nonetheless, as I also noted, these very experiences of beauty and timelessness seem to point to a fullness that goes beyond what electrochemical processes in our brains alone could ever explain. So Christianity capitalizes on the uncertainty in this matter and on the infinite longings of the human heart and proposes for us a vision of life that carries us into the divine realm. With no way to prove human deification, we nonetheless want to believe it, and, as Christians, we make it our hope.

INSPIRATION IN TIMES OF CHALLENGE

It is important to keep that hope of in mind. It provides meaning and purpose in life. It reminds us that our lives are more than what we can see and touch. That vision of fulfillment in God is important to remember especially when we find ourselves in solitary moments, feeling isolated and alone. And all of us have such moments, whether or not we have life partners, family, intimate significant others, and many faithful friends.

That vision is important to remember especially when we face the specter of death. We all know, or soon will know, people who are dying or have died of cancer, heart disease, AIDS, strokes, aneurisms, accidents, or old age. We wait as the clock ticks and the calendar pages turn. We wait for the inevitable news that someone else we know has died. And we know that our own time is coming. In the face of death, however it comes and whether early or late, we are left wondering: "Where's it all going? What's it all about?" Is it possible that we could pass through each other's lives, that we could bond soul to soul, that we could share the most precious and subtle and sacred things and then simply disappear? Gone forever? Never to be known again?

In the depths of our being, we revolt against such a prospect. There must be more. There must be reunion. There must be ongoing life. Even though our fragile humanity denies us any such guarantee, there simply must be something more than this life. At least this is what our hearts and souls protest; this is the insistence of the subtler parts of our being.

John's story of the wedding at Cana tells us, "Yes, you are right. Trust your hearts. Surrender to the deeper longings. You will not be disappointed." The Christian message is that we are already caught up in the power of the universe. When gathered as Christians at Eucharist, we recognize and celebrate the mystery of God's own life among us. Whenever we gather in love, in church or elsewhere, the experience of love sensitizes us to the mystery of existence. We become aware once again. We pause for a moment. We feel our hearts move. We smile, or we shed a tear. We touch the profound realities at the heart of human life—just as if we were at a wedding. We celebrate a marriage, and the marriage we celebrate is our own. We are united with the Power that is behind all things. We are one with God, and in God we have all we have ever loved. And why not cherish such hope?

TEN

The Gain in Life's Losses: Jesus' Ascension into Heaven

AFTER HIS SUFFERING Jesus presented himself alive to the apostles by many convincing proofs, appearing to them during forty days and speaking about the kingdom of God. While staying with them, he ordered them not to leave Jerusalem, but to wait there for the promise of the Father. "This," he said, "is what you have heard from me; for John baptized with water, but you will be baptized with the Holy Spirit not many days from now."

So when they had come together, they asked him, "Lord, is this the time when you will restore the kingdom to Israel?" He replied, "It is not for you to know the times or periods that the Father has set by his own authority. But you will receive power when the Holy Spirit has come upon you; and you will be my witnesses in

Jerusalem, in all Judea and Samaria, and to the ends of the earth."

When he had said this, as they were watching, he was lifted up, and a cloud took him out of their sight. While he was going and they were gazing up toward heaven, suddenly two men in white robes stood by them. They said, "Men of Galilee, why do you stand looking up toward heaven? This Jesus, who has been taken up from you into heaven, will come in the same way as you saw him go into heaven."

Then they returned to Jerusalem . . . When they had entered the city, they went to the room upstairs where they were staying . . . [They] were constantly devoting themselves to prayer, together with certain women, including Mary the mother of Jesus, as well as his brothers.

—ACTS 1:3–14

THE CELEBRATION OF Jesus' Ascension into Heaven is a mixed bag. On the one hand, it is a celebration. Jesus returns to the Father in glory. On the other hand, it is a loss. He is no longer with us. This set of events makes for an emotional roller coaster. Jesus was with the disciples as a wonderful fellow traveler, a support, confidant, and friend. Then he was executed, and his followers were devastated. Then he began appearing again, alive and in the flesh, but strangely so. He came and went, but, as with a good friend who moves away and visits only rarely, at least the disciples were reassured that he was still around. Then there came the Ascension, and Jesus "returned to his Heavenly Parent." He was gone again and permanently. What an emotional ordeal!

The Ascension itself includes a range of emotions. In the Ascension there is both the joy of victory and the pain of loss. Liturgical celebration tends to emphasize the glory, that is, the joy and exuberance of Jesus' exaltation "at the right hand of God," as the stock religious phrases put it. But what do these things mean?

THE IRRELEVANCE OF
CHRISTIAN FEASTS

To be honest about it, most of us have not really sat down and thought about the Ascension. We are hard pressed to appreciate the personal significance of this annual Christian celebration. Truthfully, most of us would not want to do so. We feel no need to do so; the matter seems pretty irrelevant to everyday life.

As with much of religion, we go to church, and the priests or ministers announce some doctrine or "feast": "Today is the feast of the Ascension. We remember Jesus' returning to his heavenly Father in glory, and we are filled with joy. Please turn to your hymnals on page so-and-so."

Our religious leaders tell us that we should be grateful and rejoice over this "holy" occurrence. Or, even worse, presuming to read our minds, they tell us how we (supposedly) feel: "We are filled with joy." Wanting to be religious, sincerely desiring to sense some movement in our souls, we begin to feel that, on the spot, we are somehow supposed to conjure up these emotions and celebrate. But celebrate what? Oftentimes this supposedly life-shaking "event" is just words to us, as meaningful as Phobos and Deimos orbiting Mars.

The Ascension of Jesus, I believe, is a feast of that kind for most Christians. Other feasts, like Christmas, certainly, and Easter, are more meaningful because we have developed personal, family, and even society-wide rituals around them. Our whole social world makes them into real events, just as it does the Fourth of July, Thanksgiving, or New Year's Day.

We are no longer in the medieval world of Christendom, where all of life revolved around the religious calendar. In the contemporary secular world, much of what Christian churches celebrate can be only churchy affairs, merely "pretend" happenings, artificial events that could have meaning only in the church building itself, "celebrations" that have little connection to everyday life.

The problem of the irrelevance of much of Christian ritual is serious, and it pertains to the Ascension. The best that those of us who still go to church can do, I believe, is to use the prescribed liturgical occasions to learn some spiritual lesson. Though we will hardly be able to get up and party over these dead feasts, perhaps they, like the tombs of the pharaohs, the Great Wall of China, or the catacombs of Rome, could, if pondered, still provide useful insight. Pondering them might allow us to forge a spiritual life of our own and, perhaps, even construct a more relevant Christian liturgical calendar.

At this point in history, we are left to mine our religious tradition to uncover whatever nuggets of gold we might find. Perhaps with these we can gild some new events in our lives and actually have real-life reasons for public celebration.

THE LOSSES AND DISAPPOINTMENTS OF LIFE

The Ascension highlights the notion that Jesus was "taken up in a cloud," which is a biblical code for saying that he entered into God's presence. And, we are told, his Ascension is a glorious thing, a cause for rejoicing. However, I think it's important for us to appreciate other feelings that pertain to this feast: the sadness, loss, and sense of abandonment.

Of course, the scriptures do point to that loss. Picture the disciples, if you will, standing there in a daze, staring blankly into space. They were at a complete loss. The two angels appear and speak to them, almost as if to say "Hey, you knuckleheads, what are you standing around here for, looking up in the air?" Then the angels explain things to the gawking disciples. As always, the angels are also a biblical code. They indicate that the disciples received an "inspiration from God." That is, the disciples came to some positive and helpful understanding of the matter.

Of course, this whole scene is symbolic. It is not to be taken literally. It is a way of portraying the early disciples' experience in terms of the ancient Hebrew worldview. In the disciples' dazed stare into heaven, the sense of loss comes through. They were stunned. They had gone numb. Jesus was gone; they did not know what they would do now. Their world was shattered. They could not imagine how they would go on from there.

The disciples certainly felt the loss, but we do not. We have never known Jesus in the flesh. He has never been a part of our daily life and routines. We are not used to seeing him around, talking with him, and going to sleep at night knowing that he will be there again when we wake in the morning. We do not know Jesus that way. So we cannot feel his loss as the disciples did. But there are others whom we have known and for whom we can feel a loss. It is important for us to get in touch with our feelings of loss.

There are friends who have been very dear to us and have moved away. We have so much coming and going in our transient, typically American way of living! How very unhealthy! In my own life, I've moved from hometown Pittsburgh to Syracuse, to Latrobe, to Rome, Italy, back to Pittsburgh, then to Baltimore, Boston, and San Antonio, and then from there to Austin and, most recently, from Austin to Atlanta, to Pittsburgh, and back to Atlanta again. Such moves are costly. They tear from us all our social bonds, all the routines, all the stability. And our departures leave behind friends and loved ones with holes in their own lives. On the one hand, moving around so much—one of the important freedoms we Americans enjoy—makes life exciting. From one point of view, life is exciting when we can move around so much— this is American freedom! But mobility also exacts the sacrifice of the social ties that bring stability and richness to life.

Then, there are also family members who are far away or who have died. These are people who were close to us from our earliest years. Their image, style, and way of being and the times and emotions we shared are woven deeply into our psyches. They are a part of our very makeup. They are people who are especially dear to us, people to whom we feel attached and whom we loved or hated or, most likely, both. Because of the emotional bonds, whether positive or negative, we miss these family members very much.

Sometimes at the most unexpected of times, these people flash through our minds, and we feel the pangs of their absence. Brushing my teeth, walking down a supermarket isle, turning a corner in my car, or looking at a garden, I will remember my mother, or Aunt Louise, or my dad, all long departed, or one of so many friends who have died of AIDS. On holidays and special occasions, the sense of loss can be all the more poignant.

These feelings are so human, so very natural. We really do need to respect them. When they come upon us, we need to take some downtime and let our hearts weep. For we are suffering loss, and losses require mourning.

It is a major mistake today that we think we can ignore these matters of the heart. We move so fast. We travel so easily. We hop to one place this weekend and on to another, the next. And we blur over these repeated uprootings. With a drink on the plane or a pill for "anxiety" or a flurry of travel shopping, we push from awareness the symptoms of separation within us. We turn ourselves into machines.

Strange how deeply we miss people, and how quickly someone can burrow into our hearts. Sometimes we know someone only in passing, a brief friendship, a fleeting love affair, but we remember these loved ones clearly and cherish their memory and always think of them fondly. And we may continue to miss them for years and years after they are no longer active players in our lives. And in so many cases, the losses are permanent, absolutely irreversible. People die.

THE IMPORTANCE OF FEELING EMOTIONS

If we open our hearts and take a look inside, we recognize lots of loss and emptiness. These very feelings, I think, are part of the feast of the Ascension. I also insist that it is very important for us to get in touch with these feelings. Too often we just push them aside so that we don't have to deal with them. They certainly complicate life, but they also enrich it. Pushing them aside leaves us as much less real human beings.

Until we actually feel our losses, we really do not appreciate how much we loved somebody—and how much we were loved. Think about it: We really only miss people who matter to us. Only for somebody loved do we experience grief. So when we miss someone deeply, that must mean that he or she mattered very much to us. Our tears and our heartache are a tribute to our love. Why would we ever want to suppress them? They at least let us know that we are capable of love, and it is important for us to recognize this fact.

There is the story of an Eastern guru whose son died. The man was devastated, distraught, and in tears. His disciple was confused and asked, "Master, didn't you say that all this world is illusion? Why are you so upset over your son's death?" The guru answered simply and profoundly, "My son was a very big illusion!" The guru, but not the novice, knew that enlightenment does not preserve us from life. Rather, it enables us to really embrace and experience life. And life sometimes hurts.

When we allow ourselves to feel those feelings, we remember that we are, in fact, human. There is need and dependence in us. Accepting these inner realities opens us to the real richness of life. It's too easy for us to go out and blow off all that stuff. Then we become hard and rigid. Repeatedly repressing our emotions over the years, we stop feeling. Instead of becoming more sensitive and vulnerable as we age, we think that maturity means having no emotional response. We make a big deal when our president sheds a tear. We even have a telling phrase that applies across the board: "a grown man crying." We say nothing about women who show emotion, but that's only because women don't count! Our society puts women down just as we put down emotion. Don't we call a boy who cries "sissy," and a soldier who chokes or a football player who fumbles vulgar female terms? But, in fact, women are often more deeply in touch with life than the macho men who write them off.

Over the years we can dull ourselves, and eventually we are no longer capable of really relating to anyone. We have, as the phrase goes, "become jaded." People and feeling and beauty and sex and love are all old hat. "Been there; done that." Life becomes shallow and boring. After loss and hurt so many times, we stop feeling. We just go through the motions of life.

It is important to feel feelings because they let us know that we are still human. They are our experience of our own hearts. They tell us that we do need people, that we miss people, and that life is colored with sadness. As Virgil wrote in the single line I remember from fourth-year Latin, *Sunt lacrimae rerum et mentem mortalia tangunt*. Difficult to render in a simple English sentence, a free translation would go like this: "Life has its tears, and the passing nature of things touches the soul."

When we allow ourselves to feel the losses in life, we begin to work through them. We begin to experience what was there. We come to know it better. Then we can tell what needs to be done to take care of it. Usually just letting ourselves experience it is all that is necessary. According to the popular self-help maxim, "You can't heal what you don't feel." Then, after a bit, after some aching and crying and some blue times, the loss is not loss anymore. We have felt it. We know it. We've made friends with the beast. Getting comfortable with it, we deepen ourselves.

Our capacity to feel is all one. The positive and the negative move together. As deeply as we are able to feel sadness, that deeply we can know joy. When we keep ourselves from knowing our sadness, we also flatten out our capacity for happiness. If we don't allow ourselves to go to the depths of our hurts, we will never know the heights of ecstasy. Our joys and our hurts dig each other out as they work off one another inside our psyches, and together they dig deeper and deeper inside us. As we live through the ups and downs of life, we sink a well of human richness into our deepest core. It is important to take the lumps of life and love, and feel the pain as well as the joy.

THE ONGOING PRESENCE
OF LOST LOVED ONES

There is one last thing that happens, I think, when we allow ourselves to know the loss of people in our lives. In some strange way,
we find that the people we love are still with us. Having allowed
the hurt of their loss to pass through, we begin to sense their presence in a new way. I think that is what Jesus hints at, perhaps,
when he says that he will send his Holy Spirit and be with the disciples in a new way. With this promise there is a turning toward
the positive dimension of Jesus' leaving. There is a pointing toward a new sense of Jesus' presence.

The scriptures make clear that the disciples did, in fact, allow
themselves to grieve their loss of Jesus. For a while they were really lost. They spent some quiet time together. For a while they
were stuck in an "in-between" state. They went back to Jerusalem.
They gave themselves over to meditation, reflection on what had
happened. I do not want to say that they spent time *thinking* over
what had happened. Much more to the point, they must have
spent time *feeling* about it. As the scriptures put it, they "devoted
themselves to prayer" (Acts 1:14). They "pondered" these things
in their "hearts" (Luke 2:19). Even Jesus' instructions told them
to *wait*. So they spent this uncomfortable period waiting. It was a
mourning period. The disciples had to let things be until the time
was right. Only then did they again find their bearings and come
to a new sense of life.

When that period of mourning was over, Jesus' leaving proved
to be a gain. The dark cloud of loss did have a silver lining. The
lesson is that, regardless of what happens, we have to dig in and
find the good. If we attach our hearts ever to the good, in whatever occurs, our search for the good will carry us on to the next
stage of life. Open-ended living flows on the path of the good.
That path is the course to the unfolding of the universe, for the
Power behind the universe is a positive force. It opens ever onto
broader fulfillment: Grass will even push its way up through con-

crete. We are equipped with the spiritual radar to detect that path. When we follow it, our lives are in harmony with God. In secular terms, we are moving with the flow of the universe.

Regarding his leaving, Jesus speaks about sending his Spirit. He explains that through the Spirit he will be present again. But his presence through the Spirit is different from his earlier bodily presence. It is a real presence nonetheless. In the Holy Spirit the disciples knew that Jesus was still with them. Exactly what that continued presence of Jesus might mean is difficult to say. We can only understand the things of God in relationship to the things of this world. Still, in making of this relationship, we really can know something about the things of God, for the things of this world are also the creation of God, and God is working in and through them. So knowing them opens onto knowledge of God.

If you have ever lost someone, felt the loss, and worked through it, you may have realized that your loved one was still with you. I have this sense about my father, who died when I was a young seventeen. Every once in a while I experience him inside myself. He has become a part of me. And now and again "he" gives me pointers; "he" shares his wisdom with me. Others have had similar experiences; they have told me so.

When people we love are present in that way, we experience a real gain. Their presence can never be lost again. They have become part of us. They have made a real change in us. When we love someone dearly and allow that person to touch us deeply, even after he or she is gone and once we grieve the physical loss, all that we loved is still there in us. The departed continue to live in us. That is true of family members who are gone, friends we have lost, lovers who moved on, and all who have passed through our lives in the ordinary comings-and-goings of living.

JESUS' PRESENCE THROUGH THE HOLY SPIRIT

Thomas Aquinas dealt with this phenomenon when he wrote about the presence of the beloved in the lover. When you really love another person, your beloved is present in you. The response of love goes to the specific one who is loved, but that response is your very own; the love that goes out is in your own self. Then the love that belongs to the one who is loved is actually the very love that is in you, and this, your very own love, is not any old love but a very particular love, shaped and colored by the uniqueness of the person to whom this love belongs. All the qualities of the beloved make your love what it is. Therefore, insofar as you really love the beloved, insofar as your love has truly appreciated, affirmed, and cherished your beloved, all that you love of your beloved is in you, too. All that is lovable in your beloved is present in you in your own love, for the lovable is precisely what your love is about.

This coincidence of the lovableness in the beloved and the particularity of the love in the lover is what it means, on a spiritual level that the beloved and the lover are one. There is a physical union and there is also an emotional bonding between beloved and lover. More than this, however, because we are human and not just brute animals, our love also has a spiritual component. It consists of an identity between lover and beloved, the identity of the lovableness in both the beloved and the lover's love for the beloved.

The parallel example is human knowing. Knowledge of something requires an identity of the intelligibility (that which is there to be understood) in the thing known and in the knower. Otherwise, if the intelligible content in the knower's mind were not the same as that in the thing known, the thing would not actually be known. So, too, loving someone requires an identity of the lovableness (that which there is to be loved) in the beloved and in the lover. Otherwise, the love in the lover is not really love for this particular beloved. We take our loves to ourselves. We truly become what we know and love.

Human knowing suggests another comparison. If you know 2+2=4 and I do, too, then the very same understanding, the same meaning, is in your mind and in mine. Understanding the same idea, we are identical in that understanding. Our minds contain the selfsame meaning. Similarly, if I love the good that I know in you, that good is also loved in me. Something of you and something of me are one and the same.

That presence in love is what we gain when we dare to love someone, lose him or her, mourn him or her, and allow him or her to live in us again. What used to be bound to the physical presence of someone out there or to an emotional attachment to someone out there is now fully in our hearts. Something of our loved one becomes a very part of us.

Love on the spiritual level—not simply physical or emotional—means choosing, affirming, prizing, valuing. Cherishing someone. Therefore, by loving, by a specifically spiritual act that makes human love human, we take the lovableness of the beloved into ourselves. We choose the goodness, we affirm the value, we prize the beauty in the other, and in so doing, make it our own. We achieve some real identity with the beloved since what is in the beloved, constituting the beloved for what he or she is, now is also in us—chosen, affirmed, and thus incorporated, also constituting us for what we are now: lovers of that particular lovableness.

Thinking those deep thoughts and feeling those deep feelings, Thomas Aquinas was trying to suggest some explanation for the Christian doctrine of the Holy Spirit within the Trinity. The Spirit is God's own love; thus, by love, the Eternal Father-Mother and the Only-Begotten ("the Son") are present in the Holy Spirit. But, if the Holy Spirit is poured into our hearts so that we can love with the Love of God, then, as the beloved in the lover, Jesus is present in our loving hearts. The one we love with the love of the Holy Spirit is within us.

Thus, Jesus' leaving is our gain. Through his leaving and his return in the Holy Spirit, he remains with us in a way that mere physical presence would not allow. Thomas Aquinas' analysis of the presence of the beloved in the lover is simply a way of trying to explain how it is literally true that Jesus lives in us. To express this idea more simply, when we love Jesus and embody his way of living in our own lives, there is a sense in which it is literally true to say that Jesus is in us. He abides with us. His presence remains with us. All that he is and stands for is a part of us.

SOLIDARITY WITH FELLOW HUMAN BEINGS

I think there is also a second gain attached to Jesus' departure. Particularly in Jesus' case—but I think the same is true for every good person—there is a sense in which people achieve a victory through their death. As 2 Timothy 4:7 phrases it in words that are supposedly those of the Apostle Paul, "I have fought the good fight, I have finished the race. I have kept the faith."

Those who have gone before us have succeeded. They have lived this human life. They have known the hardships, suffered the discouragement, overcome the bewilderment, and through it all, like the Energizer bunny, they kept going and going and going, right on to the end. They have become models for us. They inspire us. Through them we know that we are not alone. Others have also struggled as we do, and others are also struggling with us. As we live through these very human experiences, as we identify with others in love and compassion (*cum* + *passio* means "common suffering"), we join the human race. We become one with all the others who have gone before us

I think such thoughts when, on an early morning, I'm driving to my office or the post office and I see people bustling about, waiting for busses, scurrying out of stores, impatient to shift lanes on the expressway. I think such thoughts when, in the locker room at the gym, I overhear the other men talking about their workday, their families, their injuries. I think such thoughts on a weekend night when I'm out at a club, standing alone, wishing I had someone to talk to, someone who interests me, and I look out to see others, some alone, some in couples and groups, but all there just like me, all part of the human race, lost and found, happy and sad, some good at this, others good at that, each into his or her own thing, and all somehow part of the scene.

Here we all are, all engaged in the same project of life, all part of the human race. We not only live *with* one another, but we also live *in* one another. We are all humans expressing life in six billion different ways. We come and go, but life goes on, and we are connected to it all. As Saint Paul would describe the matter, we are one body; we are all members of Christ (Romans 12:4–8; 1 Corinthians 12:12–31; Ephesians 4:1–16).

JESUS' HUMAN PRESENCE WITH GOD

There is more to be said when we look specifically to Jesus. Christians believe that he not only successfully finished his human life but has also been raised to glory and is now seated again at God's right hand. The most important aspect of the whole matter of Jesus is that he is our human brother. He is one of us. On earth we have known him and loved him. He has a human biography, and like every human being ever to have lived, he left his mark on history. Now he is present at God's right hand. He succeeded! He made the grade! He's got it all! There is nothing more that anyone could achieve. He is with God.

Words, all words! It's fine that Jesus is supposedly with God. So what?

That Christian belief in Jesus' being with God suggests that in Jesus the very humanity that belongs to all of us is already present with God. With Jesus' presence at God's right hand, our own arrival path is cleared. A human passage to God is opened. These statements, cryptic and encoded, project a lofty understanding of what it means to be a human being.

We might not always recognize this understanding in these Christian doctrines, and we might not even believe these things or, more likely, not care one way or the other. These Christian beliefs and especially their symbolic expression may well have become irrelevant to us and our technological world. Many of us have recognized that it does not make much sense to quibble over whose doctrines—Hindu, Jewish, Buddhist, Jainist, Christian, Muslim, Mormon, Baha'i, Aumist, etc., etc., etc.—are correct except insofar as these differing doctrines have practical implications for the human family that shares this one planet. Well, the underlying significance of these Christian beliefs is pertinent to every human being.

Buried in Christian doctrine is a vision of the nobility of humanity and the meaning of "the good life." Christianity's message, simply put, is that *we are worthy of God*. We match up to the Supreme Value of the universe. This consideration is important for every person who ever lived, believer, humanist, or atheist: People matter. Our life together is what life is ultimately about: God's eternal seal of approval is on our human enterprise. The Western tradition cannot make this point any more forcefully than by having one of us, a human being, Jesus, enthroned at God's right hand.

OUR UNION WITH JESUS IN GLORY

John 14:2–3 has Jesus say: "In my Father's house there are many dwelling places. If it were not so, would I have told you that I go to prepare a place for you? And if I go and prepare a place for you, I will come again and will take you to myself, so that where I am, there you may be also." The place that we will have is in Jesus' heart.

Because of Jesus' love for us, his human brothers and sisters, we are somehow in a very human way already united with him in his heavenly fulfillment: The same kind of love that bonds us with one another also bonds us to him and him to us. It is this very love, human love, that the Holy Spirit uses to link us with Jesus and, thus, with God. The things of God are intricately tied up with the things of humanity.

All the religious terminology should not distract us from this fact: *Human love is at the core of all these supposed "mysteries" about Jesus and God*. Human love is what matters first and foremost. With it, all the religious details fall into place. Without it, the religious consequences not only cannot follow in actuality, but they also have no meaning we can make sense of. The point of Christian faith about Jesus' ascension into heaven is that, through his love and our human love, we already somehow share in divinity

That would be another gain for us, resulting from our loss of Jesus' physical presence: the assurance that the victory is already ours. We somehow already enjoy—or can enjoy—communion with God. Somewhere in the depths of our hearts, we are in contact with Divinity. In this life, we can experience a divine fullness.

Granted, those are again cryptic and symbolic words, more religious jargon. What does "experience divine fullness" or "contact Divinity" mean?

People often report having had profound spiritual experiences in which their outlook on life was transformed. They might also refer to them as mystical experiences. People speak in terms of being one with God or being filled with beauty and wonder that exceed anything they have ever experienced or being taken into a realm of incredible joy and peace. No one knows exactly what such talk means, and no one is able fully to explain these experiences. Whether or not God is actually the object of these experiences, I do not know. I would certainly be skeptical of any unqualified statement to this effect. On the other hand, Christianity provides ways to talk about such experiences in terms of God, the Holy Spirit, and union with Christ, and in so doing Christianity legitimizes such talk. Whatever the case, to have precise answers to these theological questions is not what matters. The transforming experiences are what matter, and, in the very least, these Christian teachings are describing, legitimating, and somehow explaining these human experiences.

These religious considerations invite us to open ourselves up to the profound human realities within our hearts and minds. We are encouraged to allow our hearts to overflow and to let our minds be boggled. In being told that we are already in contact with God, we are promised wonder, marvel, beauty and awe of life that can enlighten everyday living.

This experience and its overflow are what matter. That these things are "experiences of God," that they will "lead us to heaven," or that they already make us "one with Jesus in glory"—all these doctrinal considerations are to a large extent beside the point. Let these doctrinal matters take care of themselves. Let them not become our preoccupation. Ignoring the doctrinal matters would not be a major tragedy. The only real tragedy would be to miss the transformation of our lives because we are so hung up on doctrines.

At stake in religious doctrines, in the very least, are human realities that are important for us all. Deciphered and decoded, the relevance of these teachings is universal: There is a vision that transforms for the good all that we behold; in contrast to our mundane lives, there is another, richer, more gracious, awe-filled way of living. The down-to-earth, bottom-line point of religious belief is this: We ought daily to be in pursuit of that vision and that style of life!

THE UNIVERSAL HUMAN SIGNIFICANCE OF CHRISTIAN DOCTRINE

There are two sides to the coin of Jesus' ascension into heaven: the glory side and the sorrow side. Christian belief tells us that, united with Jesus in love, we are already in contact with the Divinity. This contact comes through the Holy Spirit, who now dwells in our hearts and energizes our love. We no longer need to look, nor should we, outside of ourselves to the physical Jesus to find guidance and fulfillment in life. The secret of life is buried in our hearts and, through the Holy Spirit, our hearts are one with Jesus in the glory of God. Jesus' saddening departure from earth has put us in a far better situation. There is real gain in Jesus' having left us. Just as people often report after the sad death of their parents, we are now free to trust our hearts, to be ourselves, to live our own lives. This gain is the glory side of the coin.

But there is also the sorrow side. We will only be able to appreciate the gain if we allow ourselves to feel, and the feelings are sometimes painful. Experience of the full depths of our being is not a matter of the intellect, not a matter of doctrines and beliefs, not a matter of religious rituals enacted blindly or slavishly excused as "mysteries." Experience of the depths is first of all a matter of the heart. We need to allow the great loves in our lives, which opens us up and makes us mellow. We need to feel the losses in our lives, which soften and break and renew our hearts. The measure of our openness to the pain is also the measure of our openness to the glory.

Ironically, perhaps, the key to being aware of the transcendent dimension of life is to be open to the emotional dimension of life. Working through loss opens us to experiencing beauty more deeply. Often, after a good cry, we feel more content, centered, joyful. Sighs break emotional barriers; tears wash away drab façades. Then the hidden color and blocked light of the human spirit shine through again.

Attention to Jesus' ascension reminds us of this universal human paradox. The good times and the bad are cooperating partners. The glory and the loss are both facets of the same picture. These things are true for unbelievers as much as for believers. Assent to mere doctrines is not what counts but, rather, engaging the human reality concealed within the doctrines.

One way that believers pursue heavenly things is by gathering with one another for prayer. Not only individual meditation, quiet moments, and personal prayer but group spiritual exercises are also useful. We need one another's support, one another's example, one another's physical and emotional presence. These work together in powerful ways to open us, one and all, to the spiritual depths of the human heart, that territory that we share in common.

Perhaps especially on neglected Christian feasts, like the Ascension of Jesus into Heaven, it would be important for Christians to gather and experience—not just think and talk about—what the occasion really means. Perhaps, then, the profound practical significance of this celebration could be recovered. Or even better, once recovered, that meaning could be expressed in some new way that would actually speak to our secular society and our emerging global community.

ELEVEN

OPENNESS TO NOVELTY: THE HOLY SPIRIT IN CHRISTIAN BELIEF

WHEN THE DAY OF Pentecost had come, they were all together in one place. And suddenly from heaven there came a sound like the rush of a violent wind, and it filled the entire house where they were sitting. Divided tongues, as of fire, appeared among them, and a tongue rested on each of them. All of them were filled with the Holy Spirit and began to speak in other languages, as the Spirit gave them ability.

Now there were devout Jews from every nation under heaven living in Jerusalem. And at the sound the crowd gathered and was bewildered, because each one heard them speaking in the native language of each. Amazed and astonished, they asked, "Are not all these who are speaking Galileans? And how is it that we hear, each of us, in our own native language? . . . In our own languages we hear them speaking about God's deeds of power . . ."

All were amazed and perplexed, saying to one another, "What does this mean?" But others sneered and said, "They are filled with new wine." —ACTS 2:1–13

WE'VE GOT CHRISTMAS: "Here come Santa Claus. Here comes Santa Claus, right down Santa Claus Lane." And we've got Easter: "Here comes Peter Cottontail, hopping down the bunny trail." Pentecost, the feast of the coming of the Holy Spirit, is also one of the great feasts of Christianity. Theologically, it easily ranks with Christmas and Easter. Yet somehow, compared to Christmas and Easter, Pentecost just never made it.

This state of affairs says something about contemporary Christianity. Actually, Christianity has little appreciation for the Holy Spirit. Most Pentecost sermons, for example, turn Pentecost into the "birthday of the church." Then they go on to preach the standard party line: the need to come to church, to belong to church, to follow church teaching. Pentecost sermons seldom actually speak of the Holy Spirit. Would churches really want to bring in the Holy Spirit? The Spirit is a source of novelty; It challenges the status quo.

TWO DIVINE INTERVENTIONS IN HUMAN HISTORY

In fact, the Holy Spirit is as important to Christianity as Jesus Christ, but we have lost the balance. If the Holy Spirit is as much God as the Eternally Begotten One, Jesus Christ, then they are equal. Their coming among us is also equally monumental.

According to Christian doctrine, there are two missions from God to earth. (*Mission* comes from the Latin word that means "to send.") We are well aware of the Incarnation, the belief that God sent his Only Begotten to live among us. As Jesus Christ, he took on a human form and shared our human life. By living his life faithfully, even in the face of death, he rose to new life and, thus, opened up whole new possibilities for the rest of us humans. We know that.

We forget that Christianity also teaches a second mission from God. Just as the Son was sent, the Holy Spirit was also sent. This is to say, according to Christian belief, on two occasions and not just one, God intervened directly in human history.

In two ways God made adjustments in the order of creation. On one occasion, God sent the Eternally Begotten to become human, but God also sends the Holy Spirit to let us become divine. According to Christian understanding, those two missions, those two "dispatches," transformed human history. They change the ultimate meaning of human life. They provide a new conception of the fullest possible human fulfillment. By insisting on the saving missions of both the Son and the Holy Spirit, Christianity accounts for the possibility of human deification: our sharing divine life, our participation in divinity.

DIFFERENT MODES OF PRESENCE IN JESUS AND THE SPIRIT

We have pretty much forgotten the role of the Holy Spirit in the process of human deification. Perhaps this forgetfulness is understandable. There may be two divine interventions in history of equal impact, but there are also differences. When the Son was sent, according to the eternal plan of God, as Christian belief has it, the Son came visibly. He became a human being with a physical body, so he was seen and touched. The disciples knew him face-to-face. We can read his teachings, actual utterances that he made, preserved for us in the scriptures. It is much easier to get our hands on Jesus, even literally so, than to get hold of the Holy Spirit.

However, in the Eternally Begotten One's coming visibly as a human being, there is also a liability. Jesus' physical concreteness means that he came then and there. He entered human history at a particular time and in a particular place. Where that place is distant and when that time is passed, he is no longer present. So none of us has known Jesus the way the first disciples did. None of us has ever walked up to him to shake his hand, pat him on the back, or embrace him, as they did. Actual contact with Jesus is necessarily limited because of the way he came.

In contrast, the Holy Spirit comes invisibly. The Holy Spirit does not incarnate in a particular historical personage. While this kind of presence is free from the limitations of space and time, there is a liability in it, too. We cannot see the Spirit. The Spirit has no physical presence. We really do not even feel the Spirit. Not being a spatial-temporal incarnation, the Holy Spirit is not available as an explicit object of human experience. Of course, we believe that the Holy Spirit leaves tracks of His/Her passing in our hearts, so we speak of the "promptings" of the Holy Spirit. We say that we feel the Holy Spirit within us.

However, such statements are only a way of talking; they are metaphorical. They mean that certain inclinations are of the sort that God would advocate, so we attribute them to God, to the Holy Spirit within us. We might attribute other kinds of inclinations to the devil, and, I would insist even more, again we are speaking metaphorically. What we actually feel inside is our own feelings, our own hunches, our own intuitions. If they do come from God—and, in fact, there is nothing in which God, as Creator, is not present and acting in some way—they are, nonetheless, our own. Who else's could they be? If they are somebody else's, what are they doing in our minds, and why are we the ones experiencing them?

There is no way ever to have an experience of God that is not simultaneously an experience of our own selves. Given that every inner experience, by its very nature, is an experience of our own thoughts or feelings, we cannot simply say that what we experienced was God, period. To be accurate in our statement, we would always have to add some qualification or nuance.

To be sure, some experiences are powerful and peculiar, and we would like to attribute these to some special source. Sometimes thoughts or feeling that come upon us are different from anything we have ever known or imagined in ourselves. We cannot believe that these things actually came from us. Yet the mind is mysterious, and its reach is immense. Its creative power exceeds our meager musings.

Mozart is said to have conceived entire symphonies in a single flash. Kekule understood the structure of the circular benzene molecule through a dream. The mind, our own mind, is "in contact" with things far beyond the awareness of our narrow, conscious, and deliberate selves. Thoughts may be unusual or feelings unprecedented, but this fact is no guarantee that these thoughts or feelings did not arise from within ourselves or are not our own. Whatever the experience, whatever the possible external source, the experience is still ours.

There is simply no way, without significant qualifications and elaborate presuppositions, to make the statement that we have actually experienced God and be correct. We experience things that we believe are from God, and in faith we attribute them to God, but we do not really feel the Holy Spirit Him/Herself. There is no way of getting our hands on the Holy Spirit as we can with Jesus. The Spirit's way of being among us is very different from that of Jesus', so the scriptures use images and metaphors to speak about the Spirit.

As reported in John 3:8, Jesus used the image of wind to refer to the Spirit. The wind comes and goes on its own, and we do not know where it comes from. (Of course, today a meteorologist could explain a good bit about the matter.) On another occasion, again according to John 20:22, Jesus used breath to symbolize the Spirit. He breathed on the disciples and said, "Receive the Holy Spirit." In fact, the scriptural words translated as "spirit," *ruah* in the Hebrew and *pneuma* in the Greek, both mean "breath." In the Acts of the Apostles 2:1–13, another account of the coming of the Holy Spirit, Luke tells the story in terms of a driving wind and tongues of fire. Describing Jesus' baptism, Mark 1:10 speaks of the Spirit descending upon Jesus "like a dove." Except for the dove—but, remember, Mark does not say that the Spirit was a dove or that He/She even took the form of a dove, but that the

Spirit's descent was like that of a dove—those are illusive images: wind, breath, fire, and flight. Perhaps this is the reason why we do not celebrate Pentecost very festively: We are not sure what to make of the Holy Spirit. We have these symbols, but we do not have the Spirit in any specific form. We cannot visualize the Holy Spirit.

On the other hand, there is also an advantage in this state of affairs. The Holy Spirit does not come in any specific time-space form. The Spirit is not sent to be here and now or the there and then. For that exact reason, the Holy Spirit can be everywhere and for always.

Jesus Christ was the Eternally Begotten of God, and only Jesus Christ. But the Holy Spirit is not present in just a single historical individual. The Spirit is sent to each and every one of us, and the Spirit is present throughout the whole of history. The Holy Spirit has been active among us from the very beginning.

The Christian scriptures speak of the Spirit as Jesus' gift to us, and they portray the Spirit as coming only after Jesus. The point is that there is an intimate link between Jesus, the Eternal Child of God, and the Holy Spirit of God. You do not find the One without the Other. However, the fact that the Spirit comes invisibly suggests that the Spirit's presence transcends history. The Holy Spirit works throughout the whole of history. Anywhere anything good is happening, the Holy Spirit is active. At least this is how Christian faith understands the matter, and this understanding allows Christianity to see all good as related to Jesus: through his Holy Spirit.

THE TRINITARIAN STRUCTURE
OF HUMAN SALVATION

From one point of view, the Spirit's elusiveness may be a drawback. But from another point of view, this same elusiveness allows the Spirit to have universal presence, a presence that Jesus did not have. The Spirit's presence everywhere and always is complementary to Jesus' very specific presence in Palestine at the beginning of the Common Era. The mission of the Eternal Son and the mission of the Holy Spirit play off one another.

It is only because the Spirit is working in us that we recognize Jesus as the Offspring of God. The ability to recognize God's presence in human form on this earth depends on being filled with the Holy Spirit. How else would a person be open to such an unexpected occurrence? As Paul puts it in 1 Corinthians 12:3, no one can say, "Jesus is Lord," except in the Holy Spirit.

One only recognizes what one already somehow knows. To recognize God in Jesus or to recognize God's goodness in any earthly expression, a person would have to have something of God within him- or herself. According to Christian belief, it is precisely the Holy Spirit within us who allows us to resonate with goodness wherever it might be. Precisely because it is *God* the Holy Spirit at work in us, we recognize that all goodness is something related to God and not only a praiseworthy human occurrence. We realize that the path of goodness is the path of God. We realize that whoever follows that path moves godward—whether he or she is a believer or not. God within us, the Holy Spirit, allows us to recognize God's presence in any of its many expressions. Thus, Christians can recognize God in Jesus—and also in Buddha, Moses, Mohammed, and the many prophets of our own day, albeit in a different way in each case.

Consider again the Christian understanding of how God leads us to our fulfillment. Because the Holy Spirit dwells in us, we recognize Jesus as someone worth following, and we incorporate ourselves in him. We become like him. We do what he did. We live as he lived. Believing in Jesus is not a matter of proclaiming that he is Lord but a matter of living his way: "Not everyone who says to me, 'Lord, Lord,' will enter the kingdom of heaven, but only the one who does the will of my Father in heaven" (Matthew 7:21).

The movement to God in our regard starts with the Spirit, passes through Jesus, the Only Begotten made flesh, and arrives at the life of the Eternal Parent. The Christian understanding of our life's passage is trinitarian: in the Holy Spirit, through the Son, to the Father. Our goal is to return to the originating Source of all.

SHARING IN DIVINE LIFE: HUMAN DEIFICATION

In Christianity, salvation or fulfillment means sharing God's life. This is the life that the Only-Begotten and the Holy Spirit share in the Godhead. This is the life that we, God's adopted daughters and sons, are also to share through Christ in the Holy Spirit. This is the life about which Peter writes when he says that we are "participants of the divine nature" (2 Peter 1:4). John writes that we will become like God (1 John 3:3). And throughout his writings Paul's repeated phrase is simply that we are "in Christ." Over and over the Christian scriptures make the same point: We share divine life. Thus, our sharing with our brothers and sisters, our giving to the least of our brethren, our hungering and thirsting for justice, our building up God's reign on this earth—through the Holy Spirit the whole of our Christian life is a growing embodiment of all that Jesus Christ was. Through Christ in the Holy Spirit, more and more our life becomes the very life of God in human form. Our everyday activities, from morning rising to nighttime sleep, are a growing expression of the being of God.

The Christian notion that we share in divine life and that our lives are expressions of God occurs in other forms in the other religions of the world. Hinduism, for example—and with it much current spiritual writing in the West—insists that deep down inside we actually are God, that all creation is an emanation or extension of God, and that everything is actually divine. In stark contrast, the Judeo-Christian tradition insists that the creature cannot be the Creator. Only God is divine: Created by God, we cannot be God; we are not divine. Nonetheless, Christianity allows that God is within us precisely as the Holy Spirit poured out into our hearts (Romans 5:5). This Christian insistence both allows God to dwell in our hearts and preserves the difference between divinity and humanity. Eastern philosophy generally blurs this difference.

For many purposes, these theological differences do not matter. What really matters is that people live good and wholesome lives, and in its own way Eastern spirituality often helps people do so. However, these theological differences, like all theoretical differences, do eventually have practical implications. Followed consistently, the Eastern approach carries a subtle put-down of this world and its reality. Christianity's formulations attempt to maintain a delicate balance between the divinity of God and the humanity of men and women while also acknowledging the interaction of Divinity and humanity. Thus, if only for reasons of logical consistency, the Christian accounting is more acceptable. Of course, how these different religions play out in actual practice is another matter, and it is foolish to debate whether Christianity or Hinduism per se is a "better religion." Rather, what we need today is to attend to the identical human concerns that each addresses in its own way.

My point is that we have missed the importance of the Holy Spirit. The growing popularity of Eastern spirituality suggests that Christians are unaware of Christianity's own profound treatment of the very same spiritual matters. Given the rote and legalistic tenor of much popular Christianity today, this state of affairs is no surprise.

CHRISTIANITY'S OVEREMPHASIS ON JESUS

Let me make my point boldly: Sometimes we put so much emphasis on Jesus that we lose Christianity. It really is possible to overdo Jesus. We say Jesus is the center of Christianity. After his name, we call ourselves Christians. But if we have only Jesus, we are not Christian at all. The very name *Christian* can become misleading. Today, of course, the Fundamentalists have taken over this name and appear to control it. Others who claim to be Christian are put on the defensive and have to explain themselves lest they be identified with this twentieth-century, break-away religious movement.

But even when *Christian* is not a code word for *Fundamentalist*, the name *Christian* is misleading. It insists too much on Christ to the exclusion of the Holy Spirit. Perhaps we should have called ourselves Trinitarians, or Spiritans, or something else that would balance the emphasis on Jesus Christ.

According to Christian belief, if we are in Christ, it is so only because of the Holy Spirit. We say that Christ is God's presence among us, that Christ is our contact point with God, that Christ is the way to God. But according to traditional Christian teaching, this oversimplification is mistaken. Our immediate contact point with God is the Holy Spirit. Through the Spirit we are in touch with Christ, and through Christ we are in God. So where is our initial, immediate contact point with God? It is not Jesus. It is the Holy Spirit.

Only in the Spirit are we in Jesus. Clinging to Jesus apart from the Spirit changes Jesus into an idol or, worse, a stick with which to beat others who do not think as we do. There is real need for balance. I am not suggesting that we replace Christ with the Spirit. We need both of them; one without the other gets us nowhere.

If Jesus had come and lived his life and died his death and risen to glory, if he had become the first instance of a deified human being and, thus, had made human deification a human reality, what good would that have been if there were no Spirit to lead us in that same direction? Jesus' passage through history would have been a remarkable achievement. It would have stood out from human history as a fascinating curiosity. But it could be of little real relevance to us.

On the other hand, if the Spirit were in our hearts and had opened us to God, what good would that have been if Jesus had not risen in the flesh and God were not available in historical concreteness for us? Where could the Spirit lead us? There would be no actual and achieved human-divine fulfillment for us to approach. If the risen Jesus is the first instance and supreme model of human deification, the fact is that we need the Holy Spirit to be able to follow that model.

THEOLOGY AND LIFE,
THEORY AND PRACTICE

These thoughts about the Holy Spirit may sound very theoretical: "It's all a nice story, but it might just as well be about some other world. It might just as well be a piece of science fiction." Yes, it is theoretical. Its theology. It is cogitation on religious beliefs, and religious beliefs project another world out of touch with our everyday world. To set up and even defend such a world is one work of religion. Religious beliefs get their weight from faith. Unless people believe them, the beliefs have no significance at all. Yet faith in them does not guarantee that the beliefs are correct. Faith only means that people accept the beliefs as correct. Like any other set of religious beliefs, no one can prove the Christian beliefs to be mistaken or not. As philosophers of science would say, these beliefs are "nonfalsifiable"— they can be neither proved nor disproved—so it is perfectly legitimate to wonder if they make any difference at all. Certainly, no one should hardheadedly insist on acceptance of them. Anyone is free to dismiss this whole discussion.

There is a menagerie of religious beliefs out there, and people are free to choose their favorite. On the other hand, it would be foolish to think that every belief system is as valid as every other. Belief systems can be evaluated in something of the same way that scientific hypotheses can be tested. Beliefs do have practical consequences; thus, they are subject to evaluation. Some beliefs square with the reality of things; others don't. This difference shows in the living. Life will show you which are which.

Remember the Branch Dividians, the cult of Heaven's Gate, and the 9/11 terrorists. There was obviously something wrong with each of their beliefs. And look around at some of the foolish beliefs that are a part of almost every mainline religion. And bear in mind that it is always easier to see foolishness in somebody else's religion than in your own. Then, through it all, realize that, even when our topic is holy religion, there is proof: The proof is in the pudding.

The Christian understanding of the deeper things in life does have practical implications—as do all belief systems. Whether you take the beliefs literally or not, if you are honest about life, at some point or other you will have to confront the matters to which these beliefs relate. If the truth be told, the bulk of religious belief is really about earthly life and not about things up in the sky or a world beyond our death. Religious beliefs are forged in response to the pressing "big questions" of life: Who am I? Who are we? Where did we come from? Why are we here? Where are we going? What is worth living for? What contribution can I make? Unfortunately, over the centuries, encrusted in doctrinal formulas devoid of obvious this-worldly implications, the answers got lost.

Biblical Fundamentalism and Roman Catholicism provide interesting examples. I take Biblical Fundamentalism to be a religion that relies on a literal reading of the Bible and believes that the Bible contains the answers to all of life's questions. In contrast, over and above acceptance of the Bible, Catholicism is noted for insistence also on Tradition, the consistent teaching of the church throughout the centuries. Yet even within Catholicism there is a stream of fundamentalism. Its insistence is not on the Bible but on church teaching. Catholic fundamentalism is papism and dogmatism.

In all its forms, fundamentalism looks to the past. It puts its faith in a formulated teaching that was given as if once and for all, finished and complete. It supposes that it already has a hold on the truth, so nothing else is needed. It looks back and says, "This is it. All the answers are already spelled out here." Of course, no one who knows Christianity at all can avoid making reference to the Holy Spirit. The Vatican invokes the Holy Spirit to confirm its continued teaching of old answers to new questions. Biblical Fundamentalism invokes the Holy Spirit to claim divine authority for its selective reading of the biblical text.

Those appeals actually vitiate the Holy Spirit. They gut the Spirit of any possible creative power. Those appeals use the Spirit to reestablish the status quo. Supposedly, the Holy Spirit leads

you to say, "Jesus is Lord," or "The pope is the vicar of Christ."
Yet once you are back to Jesus Christ, you are right back into the
Book taken literally, right back into the supposedly infallible doctrines and the totalitarian authority of the pope, right back into
the narrow binds of a religion of guilt—right back into the letter
that kills, whereas, as St. Paul wrote in 2 Corinthians 3:6, "the
Spirit gives life."

Christianity without the Holy Spirit takes you right back to
the then and there and leaves no room for the here and now.
Christianity without the Holy Spirit gets stuck in the historical
and cultural limitations of the incarnation of the Eternal Son. On
the other hand, if you allow the Holy Spirit as well as Christ, you
break away from those limitations. You recognize Jesus as one expression—a unique, powerful, and maybe even the definitive expression, to be sure, but nonetheless just one expression—of God
at a particular time and in a particular place. And you recognize
the Bible as a record of varied experiences of God in different
times and places. Thus, you are able to take what happened in
Christ or what you read in the Bible and apply it to situations in
your own life and to new circumstances in the contemporary
world.

According to Christian belief, it is the Spirit within us that lets
us realize what Jesus would do in our own situation. After all, not
even Jesus experienced the life you and I are living. It is the Spirit
within us that lets us know what Jesus would think and say if he
were alive today. It is the Spirit within us that lets us recognize
Christ in places that other people do not. It is the Spirit within us
that enables us to validate goodness in whatever form it occurs.
Or, in any case, Christian belief speaks of such situations as instances of the work of the Holy Spirit.

Following Jesus but without the Spirit, we would be locked
into a first-century Palestinian world, and we would never recognize Jesus in our postmodern world. In fact, Christ would not appear here and now as he did then and there. He would not dress as
he did back then. He would not talk so freely about masters and

slaves as he did back then. He would not surround himself with only male apostles as he did back then. He would not address God exclusively as "Father" as he did back then. He would not be facing the same ethical questions that he faced back then.

Jesus never had to deal with atomic energy. He never had to deal with genetic engineering. He never had to deal with a morning-after pill. He never had to consider stem-cell research. He never had to think about gay liberation and same-sex marriage. He never encountered emancipated women. He never discussed emotional intimacy in interpersonal relationships. He never commented on the global economy or downsizing a corporation or the ethics of advertising through the mass media. He expressed no opinion about air and water pollution or the leveling of the rain forests. He never used e-mail or surfed the Net.

If we limit ourselves to what Jesus said and did, what's written in the Bible, or what the church has already taught, we lose all movement. We lose the freshness. We lose life. Moreover, we lose Christianity. In losing life, we lose the Holy Spirit, for it is the Spirit that gives life. Losing the Holy Spirit, we lose Christianity.

That is not to say that the Holy Spirit magically gives us the answers to life's questions. That is not to say that we should just go with any hunch or intuition we have and claim that it is the inspiration of the Holy Spirit. The Christian tradition does speak about the need for "discernment of spirits." First John 4:1 warns explicitly: "Do not believe every spirit, but test the spirits to see whether they are from God; for many false prophets have gone out into the world." Looking magically to the Holy Spirit for answers to new questions is as mistaken as hoping magically to find those answers in the pages of the Bible or in the Catholic Catechism.

We have to work out the answers for ourselves. What to do about atomic energy? Or campaign financing? Or global warming? Or genetic engineering? Or the morning-after pill? Or preemptive war? We have to study a matter and discuss it with others who are knowledgeable, honest, and good-willed. As a *down-to-earth* community, as people who believe "Jesus Christ has come *in the flesh*" (1 John 4:2), we have to use our minds and trust our hearts to come to some conclusion about the here and now.

Here, then, is a very important, practical implication of this theoretical theology. Believing in the Holy Spirit implies believing in ourselves. Affirming the Holy Spirit means affirming ourselves. Why so? It means accepting and effectively using *our* wondrous humanity, which God created. It means trusting the God-given intelligence of *our* minds and relying on the Spirit-inspired goodness in *our* hearts. It means working out for *ourselves* in collaboration with one another a way to live lovingly and justly in *our* world just as Jesus did in his.

Commitment to the Holy Spirit always implies openness to something new, and it ensures that any novelty is the Christ-like response for our own age. Just as Jesus' shrewd, insightful, and creative responses to challenges surprised his contemporaries— "Give to Caesar the things that are Caesar's and to God the things that are Gods," "Let the one who is without sin cast the first stone," "It is not what people put into their mouths that make them unclean, but what comes from their hearts and out of their mouths," "The Sabbath was made for humankind, not humankind for the Sabbath"—just so, under the guidance of the Holy Spirit, open-minded, honest, and good-willed solutions to today's challenges will surprise us all.

What about people who do not believe in the Holy Spirit or Christ or even God? If they are people who believe in themselves, trust their intelligence, have sincere hearts and open minds, and work with others of similar goodwill to discern a just and loving way, they will also arrive at solutions that others might well call "Christ-like" (Philippians 4:8–9). For the Holy Spirit has been poured out on all God's daughters and sons and, whether acknowledged or not, acts among us (Jeremiah 31:31–34; Joel 3:1; Acts 2:17). For Christ came for the salvation of all God's children (1 Timothy 2:1–6), and, as a fact of history, whether acknowledged or not, redemption must be operating among us all: "Not everyone who says to me, "Lord, Lord," will enter the kingdom of heaven, but the one who does the will of my Father in heaven" (Matthew 7:21; Luke 6:46); "Come, you that are blessed by my Father, inherit the kingdom prepared for you from the foundation of the world; for I was hungry and you gave me food, I was thirsty and you gave me something to drink . . ."—and these latter did not even know who Jesus was! (Matthew 25:31–46).

Then, isn't the good that secularists do also part of God's work in this world? And isn't their way of living what matters, after all? Of course, fundamentalists insist that a secularist's good work is different from that done by a believer, and supposedly the secularist's goodness does not count. I say show me the difference. And furthermore I say oftentimes I prefer the good works of secularists to the supposed "good" that the Bible-believing Christians perpetrate. As the bumper sticker has it: "Jesus, save us from your followers"; and as Jesus himself said, "You will know them by their fruits" (Matthew 7:15–20).

Without believing in Christ, are the secularists not, nonetheless, following the way of Christ (if the matter must be phrased in Christian terms)? Obviously so! Then, to embrace them as brothers and sisters is the Christian thing to do. Such openness to all people of goodwill is one of the practical effects of Christian belief in the Holy Spirit. And such ability to recognize the work of the Holy Spirit even in secular guise is itself evidence that the Holy Spirit is really acting in oneself.

CONTEMPORARY MOVEMENTS OF THE HOLY SPIRIT

Commitment to the Holy Spirit is the key to the wholesome unfolding of a vital Christianity throughout the centuries. Overlooking the Holy Spirit makes for an embalmed and stifling religion left over from a former age. When good Pope John XXIII called for the Second Vatican Council in the 1960s, he made a revealing gesture. Opening a window, he said it was time to let some fresh air into the church. Perhaps the fresh air that he was talking about was the breath, the wind, the breeze of the Holy Spirit.

The changes, the divisions, the conflicts of opinion in Christian circles today are actually what the abstract theology is about. On a highly abstract level, matters debated daily are at stake in the contrast between emphasis on the Eternal Son and on the Holy Spirit. We are living in an age where trinitarian tensions are at work. The equality among the Three in God has been violated. The grinding and shifting in today's world is reestablishing the balance. These matters touch the core of Christianity. They color the process of globalization. They lie at the very heart of daily life and human history.

Make room for the Holy Spirit, and astounding things happen. A glaring example is the religious movement for gay liberation. All indications suggest that this movement flows within the mainstream of authentic Christianity. In fact, the theological underpinnings of this movement are solidly documented. Neither the Bible nor Christian history nor reasoned argument nor scientific findings supports the churches' condemnation of homosexual love. Nor does to the personal experience of today's lesbian and gay Christians. Their gut feelings and life experience square with the best of contemporary research. And the blossoming of their lives in positive contribution qualifies as the "fruits" by which Jesus would gauge the work of God in the world. All the evidence suggests that the emergence of homosexual love is a positive historical development. Does not such a convergence of evidence provide our best indication of the truth? Then, does not such a convergence of evidence amount to a confirmation that the Holy Spirit is at work?

To say *it does not* is to cast aside and discredit all down-to-earth, this-worldly insight and experience. To say *it does not* is to brush aside the very possibility of the Spirit's working in history—because to say it does not is to be blind to God's presence in human form. Close-minded insistence on inherited teaching and myopic disregard for contemporary discovery stab at the heart of Christianity: Christians are those who believe that "Jesus Christ has come *in the flesh*" (1 John 4:2). Genuine Christians find the things of God in the things of earth.

Historical insight into the Bible, the findings of contemporary science, the reasoning of honest thinkers, the life experiences of good-willed people—all these earthly and merely human indicators are signposts of the way of God. Such a convergence of evidence, such a host of witnesses, surely signals the presence of the Holy Spirit in gay liberation.

The same can also be said for other causes that stir our world: dignity of the races, reverence for cultures, equality of women, rights of children, justice for workers, preservation of the environment, emergence of a global village, equitable distribution of the earth's resources, respect for differing religions. In all these matters, the core beliefs and values of the long-standing Christian tradition support the call for rethinking, revamping, regrouping. The Spirit of God is calling us to take another step forward in making our earthbound lives worthy of God. Is this enterprise not the very essence of Christianity wherein God became human so that humans could become divine? Is this enterprise not the very meaning of human community—destined to become divine community—on a shrinking planet?

THE PROSPECTS FOR PENTECOST

Where does this insight into the sweep of God's work leave us today? Well, right where we are, here, living our lives. There is no escaping the vicissitudes of life by appealing to "spirituality" or "religious belief" or "inspired and inerrant scriptures" or "infallible teaching"—at least not in the authentic Christian vision. Such escape is the illusion with which religious leaders seduce followers, spiritual writers sell books, and we all like to deceive ourselves. Life goes on right here where we are with our feet on the ground. No amount of theology changes our earthbound situation. We are still left living and loving and striving as best we know how. We are still left struggling with the religious, economic, and political powers that would darken creative vision. We are still left in the titanic turmoil of our changing times. Pentecost is the center of it all.

Despite its glaring relevance, I do not think that this feast will ever make it big. Maybe that outcome is just as well. If Pentecost became a national holiday, it could be diluted and neutralized just like Christmas and Easter. It would become something big and booming, celebrated and commercialized, but Pentecost is not that kind of thing.

The Holy Spirit's working is something subtle, gentle, quiet. It shows in those little shifts that occur within and among us: the hunches, the insights, the intuitions. It shows in the feelings and motivations that bring new hope, new life, new loves. To be in touch with it, you have to be reverent. You have to be still. When we are still, all kinds of things start bubbling up inside of us.

No big celebration for Pentecost, then, but just consistent faithfulness. Perhaps the best we can do is to continue gathering in goodwill as small communities of kindred spirit, whether religious or purely secular. As people have done through the centuries, we can inspire and support one another and, in this way, keep ourselves open to all that is right, noble, true, and good, or, as Saint Paul phrased it, all that is honorable, pure, pleasing, commendable, and praiseworthy. Then, "the God of peace will be with us" (Philippians 4:8–9). Then, we will also see answered the traditional Pentecost prayer: "Come, Holy Spirit, fill the hearts of your faithful, and enkindle in them the fire of your love. O, God, send forth your Spirit, and new creations will emerge, and You shall renew the face of the earth."

TWELVE

CELEBRATION OF
THE HUMAN BODY:
CORPUS CHRISTI,
THE BODY OF CHRIST

THE CUP OF BLESSING that we bless, is it not a sharing in the blood of Christ? The bread that we break, is it not a sharing in the body of Christ? Because there is one bread, we who are many are one body, for we all partake of the one bread. —1 CORINTHIANS 10:16–17

NO ONE EVER HATES his own body, but he nourishes and tenderly cares for it, just as Christ does for the church, because we are members of his body. "For this reason a man will leave his father and mother and be joined to his wife, and the two will become one flesh."

This is a great mystery, and I am applying it to Christ and the church. —EPHESIANS 5:29–33

"I AM THE LIVING BREAD that came down from heaven. Whoever eats of this bread will live forever; and the bread that I will give for the life of the world is my flesh." The people then disputed among themselves, saying, "How can this man give us his flesh to eat?" So Jesus said to them, "Very truly, I say to you, unless you eat the flesh of the Son of Man and drink his blood, you have no life in you. Those who eat my flesh and drink my blood have eternal life, and I will raise them up on the last day; for my flesh is true food and my blood is true drink." —JOHN 6:51–55

THE FEAST OF CORPUS CHRISTI is a celebration of the Body of Christ. Traditionally, this day focuses on the Holy Eucharist, Holy Communion, the sacrament of the altar, the bread and wine that become for Christians the body and blood of Christ.

In the contemporary world this feast bids us be more down to earth. Rather than speculate about "transubstantiation" or debate the mode of Christ's presence—real or symbolic—in the Eucharist, we might do better to think about Jesus' actual physical body and its role in human salvation. We might do better to face the concreteness of the central Christian belief: the embodiment of God, the physical presence of God in the human Jesus. And acknowledging the material existence of Jesus, we might become more comfortable with our own physical—and sexual—bodies.

CHRISTIANITY'S DETOUR
FROM THE BODY

Somewhere along the way, Christianity lost a sense for people in the physical world. At the price of a sometimes bizarre spiritualization of life, the Christian tradition got lost in an idealized world—even as religion often tends to do and as do many people who find life in this world difficult and prefer to drift into fantasies. This confusion of emphases is obvious in the doctrine of the Eucharist. Consider its history.

In the twelfth century, there was a shift in Christian terminology—a spiritualization as it were. Before then, the words *mystical body* referred to the sacrament on the altar. In the Eucharist, Christ was present mystically, mysteriously, spiritually. In contrast, the *real body* of Christ was the Church, the people in the pews. In the Church was the real presence of Christ. But the terminology switched over. Then Christianity began to say that the real presence was the one on the altar, and the People of God, the Church, was only the mystical body of Christ. Catholics in the first half of the twentieth century grew up hearing that reversed teaching. The most profound Catholic theology of that era spoke of the Christian faithful, the People of God, as the *mystical* body of Christ. What a strange distancing from material existence!

Through the late twentieth century, many of us grew up with even more detrimental ideas. In the 1950s and 1960s, for example, books about sexual maturation and books on moral theology taught that you must never touch the private parts of your body unless absolutely necessary. Seminarians were told to shower in their underwear. It was said to be wrong even to look at your genitals unless you had some good reason. Mere curiosity about your body or the desire to understand it—these were not good enough reasons. It was even said to be wrong to watch two animals copulating if this observation was made out of curiosity—as if interest in nature and its fascination were sinful. The overall impression was that, for the sake of holiness, we were supposed to be wary of our bodies.

I remember that, at one point in my seminary training, I began to realize how foolish that teaching was. My body was myself, yet I found I was afraid of it, afraid of me. I feared to touch myself or even look at myself. I was embarrassed because I was good looking. Somehow, as I was growing up, I learned this body-negative attitude without realizing that I had. I do not remember anybody ever teaching me such negative attitudes outright. What I do remember is an air of suspicion, caution, and secretiveness—something dark and negative—whenever a topic of sex or personal hygiene and health arose, and I quickly learned not to bring up such topics.

I also remember that, as part of our annual retreats at the local Catholic grade and high schools, the priest made vague and ominous remarks about sexual things. The overall impression—indeed, the outright teaching at some points—was that, apart from heterosexual marriage, any sexual interest, thought, feeling, or act was supposed to be seriously wrong, a mortal sin punishable by hell, every time.

What I hear from other people suggests that, in other churches and in other parts of the country, religious upbringing was not much different. Sex-negativism pervades Western religion. Repeated studies have shown that the more religious people are, the more negative attitudes they hold about sex. These attitudes pervade American society.

Today, another wave of sex-negativism has surged. Conservative religion—supposed Christianity—with an ally in the White House, dominates the scene. As a result, the Just-Say-No campaign of the Reagan years is back with a vengeance. The federal government now only funds abstinence-only sex education—despite the fact that studies show such education is ineffective in preventing teen pregnancies and the spread of STDs, including HIV. Asked about this dishonest state of affairs, a White House spokesperson responded, "Values trump data," which is to say, prejudices take precedence over facts, unfounded personal beliefs

count more than program effectiveness. Domestically, over 1.3 billion dollars of federal tax monies has been spent on this religiously
based, abstinence-only, and demonstrably ineffective campaign.

Billboards from this campaign advertise its mind-boggling
message. Yes, now billboards, bigger than life, dissuade people
from having sex! One reads: "Teach your children that virgin is
not a dirty word." The actual lesson, conscious or not, is that sex
is a nasty thing across the board, and that no sex is better than sex
in any form. Another billboard—which I used to see through the
window as I worked a stair-stepper at my downtown gym—shows
a swarm of sperm heading for an egg and reads: "If you don't like
the odds, don't have sex." Under directives from the federal government, the Centers for Disease Control removed reference to
condoms from their websites! The CDC—whose concern is supposed to be national health!

The going message is that sex is bad and that to avoid sex is
virtuous. On whose reckoning? Does anyone realize how pathological this message is? Ironically, the Bible Belt of the South has
adopted the legendary Puritanism of New England. One sex edu-
cator captured the essence of this antisex message in these words:
"Sex is dirty, so save it for someone you love." How could people
so obviously uncomfortable with the very forces of life be playing
so outspoken a role in the life of our society?

Why not sponsor a campaign to foster responsible sex rather
than abstinence? Why not suggest that sex is a beautiful and
wholesome experience that needs to be approached with reverence and respect? Studies do show that such approaches to sex education work better than abstinence-only approaches. The
billboards could have easily said that sex is not a dirty word, and, if
you don't like the odds, use effective birth control. After a century
in which understanding of sexuality has exceeded that of the
whole of previous human history, religious forces with political
agendas continue to wage a medieval war on sex as if it, and not
people's irresponsibility, were the problem.

THE PROJECT OF
RECLAIMING OUR BODIES

Thank God that somewhere in my upbringing I also got a good dose of common sense. I realized that my body-negative attitude was unhealthy and that, therefore, it must be wrong. One such revelation came when I was a budding adolescent. I had just gone to Confession on a Saturday evening and wanted to receive Holy Communion the next morning, but I was afraid that a sexual thought or feeling would arise and, being sinful in its very essence, would pollute my conscience and prevent my receiving Communion. As I agonized over these worries and paced the street to distract myself, somehow it struck me that such thinking is nonsensical. The sexual feelings were there, and they were none of my doing. They just came on by themselves. Was I supposed to be responsible for them? Was I supposed to be sinful for just being myself? Was I to go to hell because parts of my body responded in ways that were beyond my understanding or control? Was I to spend my days and evenings pacing the streets to distract myself?

What a moment of grace this realization was! On the spot I decided that, if God were going to condemn me for things that are totally natural to an adolescent boy, then I did not want such a God. I would not believe in such a God. I would have nothing to do with a God as foolish and stupid as that! This was not the loving and just God that I had heard tell about. Thus, I experienced an important moment of liberation. This decision was a first step on a long journey of bodily self-acceptance.

For years I was afraid to share that liberating experience with anybody. I thought people would think me blasphemous for rejecting the supposed God of religion and for choosing my own God, as it were. And, sad to say, most probably would have! Good sense is not often welcome when sex and religion cross paths.

I called that insight "a moment of grace." With a more discerning mind, I look back on that experience and recognize it, rather, as an ordinary moment of common sense that freed me from religious indoctrination. But grace or common sense—how different are they, really? What difference does the terminology make? Despite the conception, the effect is the same, and the effect is what matters. Wholesome, sane living is what life is about—and what God must be about. Where the one is, there the other must also be. At least this is the lesson I learned that day in my adolescence, and as a result I achieved a new freedom and a welcome modicum of sexual self-acceptance. I felt closer to myself and closer to God.

Later, when I was a seminarian, I was similarly conflicted. Common sense and sane thinking again won the day. Aware that I was really uptight over my body and that this state of affairs was simply wrong, I set for myself a deliberate program that I called "Reclaiming My Body." I began to sleep without pajamas. Horror of horrors! I allowed myself to walk around naked in my room. Ye gads! Little by little I got comfortable with myself. A major victory was my excursion to a California nude beach. After a few minutes of awkward self-consciousness, I forgot that I was in the buff. Jogging naked on the sun-baked sand was a glorious experience. Being dressed or undressed didn't matter any more. I had reclaimed my body. I overcame that damning distance from my physical being that was smuggled into my upbringing.

In the mid-1960s, the sexual balance had begun to shift. The changes were culture-wide. Even Roman Catholicism got some good press. The Second Vatican Council now taught that there are two aspects to sexual intercourse. The one is openness to new life, procreation. The other is making love: the union of spirits, the mutual affirmation, the emotional renewal that is a part of sexual sharing. Whereas before, Catholicism taught that procreation was the primary purpose of sex, now for the first time official teaching said that procreation and interpersonal sharing are of equal importance. Making love is as important as making babies.

This new teaching was a real victory for the human body. This new teaching was an important affirmation of sexuality. Of course, such teaching had been part of Protestantism since the Reformation in the sixteenth century. Both Luther and Calvin lucidly taught that affection and mutual support were sufficient reasons for sexual sharing. The use of contraceptives became common in the mid twentieth century and never was a Protestant preoccupation. Peculiarly, nonetheless, Protestants have been as uptight about sex as Catholics—and even more so, according to recent surveys.

The invention of "the pill" was a milestone in human sexual history. Reliable contraception effectively separated the biological, procreative dimension of sex from its emotional and interpersonal dimension. This achievement set hetero- and homosexual relationships on a par. Women's liberation and gay liberation were aspects of that same historical moment. The distinctively human dimension of sex, interpersonal bonding, was emerging as the genuine meaning of *human* sexuality.

Many psychologists and theologians have argued that making love is the primary purpose of sex and that procreation is only secondary. This understanding makes good sense. If we were talking about barnyard animals, then, yes, producing offspring would be the main event. But when we are talking about people, interpersonal sharing and affectionate bonding take center stage. After all, only people routinely have sex during nonfertile periods. Only in the human species do females routinely experience orgasm: The sole purpose of the clitoris is pleasure, and this same observation applies to no other part of the human anatomy. Only people routinely have sex face-to-face. Only people make love. All these considerations are virtually unique to our species. Love is the key human event. Anybody who knows anything about sex, whether from standard, contemporary textbooks or from personal experience, knows that procreation is a minor aspect of human sex.

In some ways, as believing Christians and part of the larger society, we have begun to balance our attitudes toward our bodies, but we still have a long, long way to go. In fact, contemporary trends suggest that we may be losing ground again. Young people today may be more uptight about their bodies than I was about mine decades ago.

Recent studies show that, in a society that glorifies sex and the human physique, young people are more and more ashamed of their bodies. College kids come to the gym dressed for their workout, and afterward they go back to their dorms to shower in private. The same routine applies to many people who belong to fitness clubs. Public showers are used less and less, and individual showers are now set off with partitions. Sweaty high school athletes rush home to shower after practice and then go back to class.

What is behind this recent trend? Two things stand out. Above all, young people are embarrassed to be seen nude. They are afraid that their bodies do not match the to-die-for models they see on TV, in magazines, and in the movies. Spray-painted pictures of models who are one-in-a-thousand make them ashamed of their looks. Second, more than former generations, today's youth are aware of homosexuality, and they are afraid. Uptight about sex, and encouraged to be so by their elders, they fear one another as much as they fear their own bodies. The antisex agenda of conservative religion is driving a wedge between people of the same sex just as it did for centuries between people of the opposite sex.

Do these statements sound unrealistic? Aren't young people more sexually irresponsible than ever? Perhaps. The figures continue to shift, but repeated studies also show that, compared with the comfortable, people who are uncomfortable with their sexuality tend to be more irresponsible in their sexual behavior. A person who does not want to admit that he or she is sexual, for example, is less likely than others to use effective contraception or take precautions regarding STDs. To be prepared for responsible sex, one needs to admit to oneself that one might actually have sex. People guilt-ridden over sex cannot admit this fact, so they cannot be prepared. This failure is the most serious flaw in the abstinence-only approach to sex education. It leaves kids ignorant of what to do if, one day, they should "happen to have" sex.

Ironically, fear of the body is the embarrassing religious legacy of a society bombarded with images of naked bodies. How strange that such should be the case in a civilization that once called itself Christendom! People make being uptight about sex into a distinctively "Christian" virtue! But fear of the human body implies fear of the body of Christ. Insofar as we are afraid of ourselves as embodied or afraid of one another, insofar as we are afraid of physical contact, we are afraid to be close to Jesus. According to Christian belief, God, at least, thought it worth the effort to take on human flesh in Jesus Christ. Jesus now lives, and we meet him, in one another. We are the body of Christ.

JESUS AS REAL FOOD AND REAL DRINK

Genuine Christianity calls us to celebrate our physical body as we celebrate the body of Christ. Our faith calls us to remember that, when we come together in love, sharing bread and wine, we are communing in Jesus because we are communing with one another. The Body that is on the altar is the Body that is in the pews. It is not only the Body of Christ on the altar, the mystical Body that we celebrate. It is also the real Body of Christ that Christians celebrate, the Christ embodied in us.

Celebrating the Body of Christ, we can also rejoice over the diversity among the members of the Body. In the final analysis we celebrate that we all—men and women, straight and gay, Black and White, Asian, Hispanic, and Native American—belong to one another. We remember that unless we embrace one another and make one another a part of our lives—for we, all of us, are the body of Christ—unless we "eat the flesh" and "drink the blood" of the Lord Jesus and let them enter deeply into us, we have no life in us. For here is real food, and here is real drink, here where brothers and sisters gather together unafraid to reach out to one another, to touch, to embrace, to love. Here our thirst for togetherness is quenched, here our need for sharing is met, and here the very life of God—love—grows among us.

The words that John puts on Jesus' lips make that lesson clear. Jesus says, "I am the bread that has come down from heaven. Unless you eat my flesh and drink my blood, you will have no life in you." Be very careful to understand what Jesus means by "flesh" and "blood." When he speaks of eating his flesh, he does not mean the meat on his bones. We have to understand his speech within the ancient Hebrew mentality. To the Hebrew mind, *the flesh* means "the person." The Greek understanding, which dominates Western thinking, takes *body* to mean "the physical part of a person" as opposed to the intellect, but the Hebrew understanding takes *body* to mean "the whole person." Moreover, again in contrast to the Greek understanding, the Hebrew understanding does not think of the physical body as a barrier that separates us from one another but, rather, as the very means by which we make contact with one another. So Jesus' "flesh" is Jesus himself available to us. For the Hebrew mind the body is the self; it is the whole individual insofar as he or she is here present to us. Similarly, in the Hebrew understanding, Jesus' *blood* means "his life, his self," for the ancient Hebrews understood the blood to be a creature's life.

Therefore, in saying "Unless you eat my flesh and drink my blood, you have no life," Jesus is saying this: Unless you come to me and follow me, unless you make your own all that I am and all that I stand for, unless you take all this into yourself and make it a part of you, unless you live as I lived, unless I live in you, you will not have life. Doesn't that statement make perfect, obvious, down-to-earth sense? Unless you love, unless you share, unless you risk feeling for others—unless you become like Jesus—you will shrivel up and die.

To love is to "eat of his flesh." To commune with others is to "feed on him." The mystery of Holy Communion is not some wizardry by which eating the consecrated wafer magically makes you a different kind of person. The transformation symbolized by the Eucharist results from communing in Jesus, that is, from gathering in love with one another and from sharing (food and drink) in the spirit of Jesus.

In Holy Communion, the Eucharist on the altar and the Eucharist in the pews are one and the same. To commune in the one is to commune in the other. To take the bread and wine is to be one with Jesus; to gather with others is to be one with Jesus. In Eucharist these two come together. To eat the bread and drink the wine (the body and blood of Christ on the altar) in fellowship with one another (the body and blood of Christ in the pews)—to eat and drink in loving sharing with others—is to commune in Jesus. Thus, when Jesus says you will have no life unless you eat my flesh, he means "unless you come and take one another to yourselves, unless you receive one another." Apart from love for one another, there is no life. Love for one another is the true food and the true drink that Jesus proposes.

As we celebrate the Body of Christ, we celebrate not only the sacrament on the altar but also the Body of Christ in the pews. It is by sharing in the *bread and wine* from the altar that we in the pews commune with one another in Jesus. Likewise, it is by *gathering* as loving disciples of Jesus, sharing with one another, that we do, indeed, make Jesus alive again and, thus, commune in him. In so gathering, we lovingly share our own substance with one another and, thus, become the very bread of the altar.

Understood in this way, Eucharist is vitally relevant to our present-day world. Holy Communion is no sentimental recollection of Jesus' last supper with his disciples. Nor is it a pious and private togetherness between the individual "soul" and Jesus. Nor is it a magic ritual that will "save" us from the challenge of living and loving. Rather, Holy Communion is the actualization of Christ's life among people of goodwill who are making a life together today. Holy Communion is the transformation unto increasing love among the people who believe in Jesus' way of living.

If only the churches were more attuned to what they are supposed to be celebrating! If only the churches were concerned about people instead of being so intent on doctrines about God! Then the mysteries of Christianity would mirror the mysteries of human living. Belief in Jesus would be considered a commitment

to our fellow man and woman. Then Christianity, even in its celebration of the Eucharist, would be a partner to all the religions of
the world.

THE BODY AS THE SITE OF CHRISTIAN SALVATION

The body, the flesh, is a central focus of Christianity. You might
never realize this fact by listening to most supposed Christian
preaching. Nonetheless, incarnation or "enfleshment" is at the
heart of the Christian tradition. The essence of Christianity is belief in God's presence among us in our own human form. When
Jesus came to dwell among us, according to Christian belief, he
was God's own life in human flesh. Thus, the physical body is a
key issue in the Christian message.

The centrality of the body is clear in the gospels. Emphasis is
so often on Jesus' body. With his hand Jesus touches the man with
the withered arm, and the man is healed. Jesus spits on the ground
to make mud and anoints the eyes of the blind man, and the blind
man sees. With the tears from her eyes, the sinner woman washes
the feet of Jesus; with the hair of her head, she dries them; and,
through this physical gesture of love, her "sins are forgiven." At
the last supper, Jesus removes his tunic, ties a towel around his
waist, and kneels down to wash the feet of his disciples. Later, the
beloved disciple rests his head on Jesus' chest; two bodies are
united in friendship as they recline together in table fellowship.
And after his resurrection, Jesus bids doubting Thomas to put his
finger in the holes in his hands and his hand into the gash in his
side.

Over and over the scriptures emphasize the body. How important the body is for the communication of God's life to us in Jesus!
His very body is the expression of his own self, and the self that is
expressed, according to Christian belief, is none other than the
Eternally Begotten of God. Since he lives in us through the Holy
Spirit, when we reach out a hand to comfort and console someone
in pain, when we anoint one another to heal and make things bet-

ter, when with our tears we soften a hardened heart or share in someone's sorrow, when the beauty of our hair becomes the source of delight for another person, when we embrace one another and allow someone to rest his or her head upon our shoulder—in all these bodily encounters—we are the Body of Christ ministering to the Body of Christ. If our actions are motivated by real love, the Holy Spirit must be at work in them, and if God's Spirit is at work, Christ is present and acting. God's life is communicated through contact with Christ in our own human bodies. Such an understanding of life easily makes sense of Christian belief, for the one speaks to the other.

The Christian tradition goes deep as it focuses on the body. The fifth chapter of the Letter to the Ephesians actually challenges all our taboos. It does not hesitate to see salvation via the body even in sexual intercourse. And for the truly Christian mind, why not? There is no body apart from sex. Every body is male or female. Every person is masculine or feminine. Whenever we address or touch one another, we reach out as a man or a woman, as a sexual being.

In Ephesians 5, Saint Paul writes that when spouses come together in sexual embrace, the two become one flesh and this unity is a great mystery. And indeed it is! For who can explain how we lose and find ourselves in making love to one another. But Paul says that this marvel is not just a human mystery; it is an image of the union of Christ and his Church. That is, the very love that people experience in making love to one another is an expression of God's own love for us. In that expression of love—carnal, bodily, sexual—the love of God, Christ's own life through the Holy Spirit, the very exuberance that stirs the universe, overflows in us.

SEX NEGATIVISM IN THE CHRISTIAN TRADITION

How sad that appreciation for the body has been lost in the Christian tradition! The culprit was influences that clearly were neither Jewish nor Christian—the Platonism and Neo-Platonism of the

Greeks, the Stoicism of the Romans, the asceticism of the Egypt-
ian desert fathers, and Gnosticism, Manichaeism, and Barbarian
machismo.

Manichaeism and Neo-Platonism, in particular, colored the
thought of that giant of Christian history, Saint Augustine, and
through him influenced the whole of our tradition. We continue to
struggle against the body-negativism that Augustine bequeathed
us. Echoing the sex-negative theme of his age, he suggested that
the pleasure experienced in sex is what transmits original sin in the
human race. He went as far as saying that all sexual pleasure is sinful—Augustine, who, in his youth had both a homosexual and a
heterosexual lover (which was nothing unusual at the time); who
never did forgive himself for having sexual desires; and who, even
when converting to Christianity, was preoccupied with sex and
prayed that God would make him chaste—"but not yet." He
taught that the intention of having children could lessen the wrong
of sexual pleasure to a mere venial sin. Thus, procreation came to
be seen as the only excuse for the experience of sex.

Augustine was the most important Western influence on the
Middle Ages. Following him, the great Saint Thomas Aquinas
took another step into darkness and rationalized procreation as
the essential purpose of sex and penile-vaginal intercourse as its
only natural expression. Aquinas actually taught that rape is a
lesser wrong than masturbation or homosexuality, because, open
to the possibility of conception, rape is at least natural!

How absolutely amazing that minds as great and hearts as deep
as those of Augustine and Aquinas could actually have embraced
the body-negativism that they passed on to us! How frightening
that powerful religious voices continue to urge us to fear and suppress our physical being! How unfortunate that we human beings,
as I've learned from my own experience, are so capable of denying
our own selves! How sad that social pressure and misguided religious upbringing continue to do their diabolical and death-
dealing deed!

CHRISTIAN CELEBRATION
OF THE BODY

Yet, in the midst of this fear of the body and despite the sexual repression among us, annually there intrudes the feast of Corpus Christi, the celebration of the Body of Christ. This feast can be sanitized, its impact intellectualized, its meaning reduced to esoteric dispute over medieval dogma about the Eucharist, but current concerns find broader implications in this ancient Christian feast.

One value of long-standing traditions is that they continue to confront us with relics of the past. In the ebb and flow of history, the relics suddenly become relevant again. Their quaintness eventually strikes us and prompts us to rethink what we have made of our own age. Our forgotten inheritance enriches us again. Thus, Christianity regularly challenges us to honor the body as the very arena of human salvation. Again Christ breaks into our twisted world to bring new light. As before, so now again, salvation comes in the flesh. Christ bids us embrace him as we embrace one another, and, whether we know it or not—and knowing is not what matters—we do embrace Christ when we lovingly embrace one another. The Spirit of Christ in our world urges us to sidestep fear and dare to love. Christ calls us to celebrate the human body. It is his own.

THIRTEEN

FACING THE END:
THE COMING OF
THE DAY OF THE LORD

SEE THE DAY IS COMING, burning like an oven, when all the arrogant and all evildoers will be stubble; the day that comes shall burn them up, says the Lord of hosts, so that it will leave them neither root nor branch. But for you who revere my name the sun of righteousness shall rise, with healing in its wings. You shall go out leaping like calves from the stall. And you shall tread down the wicked, for they will be ashes under the soles of your feet, on the day when I act, says the Lord of hosts.

—MALACHI 4:1–3

WHEN SOME WERE SPEAKING about the temple, how it was adorned with beautiful stones and gifts dedicated to God, he said, "As for these things that you see, the days will come when not one stone will be left upon another; all will be thrown down. . . ."

"When you hear of wars and insurrections, do not be terrified; for these things must take place first, but the end will not follow immediately." Then he said to them, "Nation will rise against nation, and kingdom against kingdom; there will be great earthquakes, and in various places famines and plagues; and there will be dreadful portents and great signs from heaven.

"But before all this occurs, they will arrest you and persecute you; they will hand you over to synagogues and prisons, and you will be brought before kings and governors because of my name. This will give you an opportunity to testify. So make up your minds not to prepare your defense in advance; for I will give you words and a wisdom that none of your opponents will be able to withstand or contradict. You will be betrayed even by parents and brothers, by relatives and friends; and they will put some of you to death. You will be hated by all because of my name. But not a hair of your head will perish. By your endurance you will gain your souls." —LUKE 21:5–19

LUKE'S GOSPEL MAY NOT BE *Star Wars* or *Independence Day*, but the images are the same. They have traditionally been interpreted as symbolizing the end of the world. Falling buildings. No stone upon another. Earthquakes. Wars. Insurrections. Great signs of suffering, plagues. Omens in the sky. Exploding suns and planets. The end of all human life. These traditional images suggest the collapse of the human psyche or the collapse of the human world. This collapse might be literal when, in billions of years, the energy of the expanding universe peters out and implosion results.

The findings of science remain inconclusive on this matter. Alternatively, the collapse might be a symbol for the psychological experience of loss, death, and personal and social undoing.

For us human beings, the "symbolic" case is the most important. We live in a symbolic world, a world of meanings and values; when we lose perspective and life loses meaning, our world collapses. Our world, the human world, really ends. In any case, we must acknowledge that nothing lasts forever. We and our world, however conceived, will eventually come to an end.

SPECIAL PLACES:
THE CENTER OF THE WORLD

The setting of Luke's passage is the temple of Jerusalem. He says that Jesus sat there and the disciples were marveling at its wonder, a structure stunning in its day. Actually, Luke wrote his gospel some time in the early eighties. The Romans destroyed the temple in Jerusalem in the year 70. Luke writes as if Jesus was predicting the destruction of the temple, but, in fact, the temple had already been demolished.

When Luke relates that no stone would be sitting upon another, he indicates what the Romans actually did to the temple. They leveled it to the ground. People were no longer permitted even to enter the area. The Romans wiped out even the suggestion that there had been a temple in Jerusalem. They utterly destroyed the focal point of the Jewish religion. Their intent was, once and for all, to stamp out that pest of Judaism, as they saw it.

The gospel goes on to talk about stars falling from the sky and omens appearing in the heavens. These images of a universe in collapse suggest what the temple's destruction meant to the Jews. Their world really did fall apart.

The words of Psalm 137 give just an inkling of how much Jerusalem meant to the Jewish people: "If I forget you, O Jerusalem, let my right hand wither! Let my tongue cling to the roof of my mouth, if I do not remember you, if I do not set Jerusalem above my highest hope." And Psalm 42 nostalgically recalls a celebration in Jerusalem: "I went with the throng, and led them in procession to the house of God, with glad shouts and songs of thanksgiving, a multitude keeping festival."

We all cherish memories of special moments in special places, and we hold those memories in our hearts: Oh, only to get back home again, to walk that old neighborhood! Oh, to visit the cemetery where family lies! Oh, to spend a few days at the shore with my soul mate! To get away to the lake! To visit the church where I grew up and to pray quietly a few minutes there! Oh, to go back to that favorite park where the family used to have picnics! Places have meaning. They remind us who we are. They link us to our past, and they give significance to our lives. They help hold everything together. As long as we know they are there, somehow we can feel secure.

Oh, if only it were that easy! That security is an illusion. Did you ever go back to visit those places? They are not the same. Even if they remain physically intact, the people who inhabit them change and the times change. Most of all, we ourselves change. The meaning of these places cannot remain the same. The years have brought new experiences and new insights. We no longer think as we did when we were kids or young adults or middle aged. We don't fit there anymore.

We can return to those special places, but the experience is strange. We are like tourists at a historical monument. We know the history, we even know the people involved, but we still look on like sightseers, strangely distant from the scene, uncomfortable because our hearts do not feel the impact that our heads say is there. We feel the loss of our past, perhaps the emptiness of unfulfilled dreams or betrayals, or the quaintness of another time, another life, another hopefulness. The marvel, the wonder, the excitement of the place is gone. It belonged to another era, and fit another worldview. The remembered experience is just history. We are no longer in it.

The attempt to find security by clinging to the past is a doomed endeavor. Such security is bought only at the cost of deadening our feelings and stopping our growth. Nonetheless, nostalgically we look back to former times, and we visit special places. We try to sustain the belief that these things are still a part of our lives. We want to make all the parts fit together in a meaningful whole. We try to make sense of our lives.

Jerusalem functioned as a center of meaning and hope for the ancient Jews. It was the core of their identity. The same must be said for the early Christians who still identified with the Jewish religion. When Jerusalem fell, the whole Jewish world came crashing down. Especially for the Jews, life just made no sense.

PERSONAL WORLDS SHAKEN AND FALLING APART

The lesson of the gospel for us is about those times when our own worlds fall apart, and this image of the end of the world applies on many levels. In some ways our personal world falls apart on the most commonplace occasions: when we stub our toe or have an exam to sit, get a flat tire, say good-bye to a friend, or have a temporary financial crunch. Even worse, we might lose a job or move to an unfamiliar place. These inconveniences disrupt the normal flow, and life seems out of kilter. Our world is shaken. At other times, our world totally falls apart. A love affair ends or a social group breaks up, a marriage dissolves, a loved one dies—these can also affect us in this way.

We live in a physical habitat, but it is not really our world. This habitat is just the setting and props of our world. Our real world is something different. It is the script, the story, the play that unfolds on that stage. Ours is a purposeful world. Significance ties things together, and meanings give sense to our life. So, when people and things important to us, when chunks of meaning fall away, our world comes crashing down. Our world comes to an end.

I heard a report on public radio about a teenage boy named Juan who had come to the United States from Mexico four years earlier. He lived in a Texas border town in a trailer with ten siblings and his parents. He had graduated from high school, but no work was to be had. There was no food on the family table, and the refrigerator was empty. To get a perspective on things, he used to sit by the Rio Grande. But even there he was often hard pressed to find peace of mind. Once, for example, he saw the dead body of a Mexican man floating down the river. Juan speculated that the man drowned trying to cross over to the United States where he might earn money for his family in Mexico. Now, who would tell his family that he was dead? Would they ever know what happened to their father, husband, and son?

What hope did Juan have? What world could he live in? Why had he been born? Of what use was all his potential? He had left his world in Mexico and had failed to fulfill his dream of a secure, comfortable life in America. So he left his family and moved to Denver, where he could find a job. He needed, as he said, to "start a new life," to build a "new world."

That was just one story. Add to it those of people whose marriages fail. Educated and skilled people cannot find work in their field: A lifetime career may mean nothing. Children run away from home, and adolescents commit suicide. Soldiers return from battle wondering what the war was about, their body parts missing or mangled, their psyches damaged forever. The work of artists' is undervalued. Schoolteachers earn less than mechanics. On all fronts, worlds are collapsing. Whole universes keep falling apart.

There is also that time when the world that we know will literally come to an end. We, each one of us, will face our own death. Life as we know it will cease. The morning-sunrise beauty and the winter sunset, the touch of a loved one, the joy of pet projects—all this will be over. As life goes by, we become more familiar with death. Family and friends have had cancer, Alzheimer's, or AIDS. We have sat with those who were injured or just old and worn out. We have watched as the weeks, months, or sometimes years went—or still go—by. We have walked loved ones to death's dark door, gritting our teeth, holding back tears as they slowly pass through, their world dwindling away. They got to a point where they were grateful just to be able to sit up in the morning. Life did not hold much more and then not even that.

In them we see our own dying. We hope our death will be different. If we are to die, let the end come quickly. We prefer not to face hanging on, or at least that's what we say now. It's bad enough that we have to die; we do not want to linger for months or years until death appeals more than life. In others we have glimpsed our own dying. We have touched death and pulled back. Death is the end of our personal world. We all face the end of a world.

THE COMING OF THE "DAY OF THE LORD"

Religion is supposed to provide the glue to hold life together. In the face of life's tragedies, religion offers answers and solace. But more and more people have outgrown their religion. The beliefs that sustained earlier lives have become childhood fantasies. Disillusionment has set in. Why so much suffering? Where is justice? Is God real? Does God really care? Is there life and reward after death? How does one go on when so little is sure anymore?

So many worlds fall apart! We live in difficult times. So many lives are shattered! And what have religion or the scriptures to say in response? To tell the truth, not a whole lot! One sometimes wonders if religion is not a charade. Is one just to believe in a loving God, despite all evidence to the contrary?

The prophet Malachi promised a "Day of the Lord" when divine justice will burn evildoers away. We should not take these words too simplistically. We should not think that, all by itself, somehow our prayer to God will magically right the injustices of our day. We should not naïvely believe that God will miraculously descend from the clouds to smite the evildoers.

Oh, to be sure, those who build houses on injustice's sand will surely see their homes collapse. Of course, many criminals, especially white-collar types, will get away with their crooked deals and enjoy very rich times, indeed—except for having to live with themselves to the end. Their evil ways might take quite some time to catch up with them, and, as in the cases of Enron, WorldCom, and HP or in those of the "princes of the Catholic Church" who allowed the sexual abuse of children to go on, the law might eventually not even inflict a punishment. On the backs of the poor and innocent, they will have their ease.

Should we believe that they will get their just due before the judgment seat of God? Does such a seat exist? Does punishment of the damned do any good to redress the suffering of the poor? Do we really believe that praying "Thy kingdom come" will bring justice to our world? All vengeance aside—it truly is the Lord's— can we just leave it to God to set up a world worthy of God and worthy of us?

In this world, at least, it is naïve to think that justice will somehow be done of its own accord. Of course, to be sure, the forces of justice built into the universe do spontaneously move toward a wholesome balance. Dishonesty and ill will can have no lasting future; they stand on unreality. The entropy of the universe naturally leans toward goodness and justice. But humans are clever, and the devious ones can hold back the tides of justice. Besides, to a large and sometimes frightening extent, the future of the universe lies in human hands. So "God's justice" will not prevail unless we ourselves create a godly world. Unless we ourselves work for justice, peace will not simply sprout up. If the "Lord of hosts" is going to act, He will act through our just hands.

It is sad for me to write these lines that seem to pooh-pooh trust in God and the power of prayer. I see in my mind's eye the images of old women, dressed in dark coats, black babushkas on their heads, their faces wrinkled, and life-worn old men, their gnarled fingers counting off prayer beads. They kneel wearily slumped back on silent church pews and beg God for help. I saw these unsung saints in my childhood church. I see them still when I return to that neighborhood. My mother and my aunts and the neighbor ladies were among their number. I have seen them in every city I have ever visited and on TV screens that dispassionately tell of yet another horror in our inhumane world. Those I've seen are only a few of the millions and millions of anguished souls on every continent, crying desperately to heaven for help. They pray that their meager income and means, despite a life of hard work, will provide them with food on their table. They pray that their sons and daughters who have abandoned religion for more modern ways will find faith again in loftier pursuits and not go the "way of the world." They pray to be safe trudging home from the market as their neighborhood and whole country grow more violent and heartless. They pray. They do not lose heart. They continue to pray—what else have they?—while the violence, corruption, lies, greed, and heartlessness go on.

Do they pray in vain? Do they waste their elder years mumbling to an empty heaven? No, they do not, unless we, the more able to effect social change, turn a deaf ear to their prayers and a blind eye to their sad image. Apart from our action, I shudder to say, they do pray in vain.

Who wants to face this fact? It leaves us virtually helpless in the face of ongoing heartbreak. I tear up to think that my mother's relentless faith and almost unceasing prayer might have gone out to a tranquilizing fiction, and I dedicate my life to making a positive difference in this world so that her faith will not have been in vain. I will have her prayer heard, if only through me. Thus, it turns out, at least in this sense, that trust in God is effective. But maintaining the myth—"More things are wrought by prayer / Than this world dreams of"—that prayer by itself already does what is needed to change our world for the better only obscures our own responsibility for the state of our world.

Nonetheless, the prophet Malachi does offer sound advice as we address the state of our world. Malachi is helpful in reminding us not to lose faith. The temptation is strong. But we must not go over to the dark side, not follow the way of the wicked, not turn to dishonesty and injustice as a way of shoring up our lives. It is true, after all, that deep personal fulfillment depends on honest living. As the Germans say, *Ein gutes Gewissen ist ein sanftes Ruhekissen*: A good conscience makes for comfortable sleep. TV shows like

Touched by an Angel and the annual reruns of Christmas specials lull us into believing that the "Day of the Lord" will come in some magical way. More realistically, the unjust world remains so, unless we make it otherwise. We should expect heartache and hardship along the way, but commitment to justice is a source of strength that is ultimately invulnerable.

THE POWER OF LIFE, THE WEAKNESS OF WORDS

The gospel of Luke offers more sound advice: We are not to plan what we will say in the face of injustice. Rumination over the evils of the day really serves no purpose. How much time and energy do we waste going round and round in our minds over the stupidity and injustice in our world?

The logical arguments we refine in our minds will not change the evildoers. I have given up, for example, thinking that reasonable argument would ever convince Biblical Fundamentalist religion that it is wrong about the Bible and homosexuality. People believe what they want. A mountain of scholarship is dust in the wind to a fiction of blind conviction. The nature of untruth is precisely that it has no concern for evidence and good sense. If it had, it would not be the ignorance or dishonesty or the mix of both that it is.

Do not waste time stewing about the way things are. Oh, to be sure, do your homework and know your stuff. Continue to put out a solid message. But do not waste mental and emotional energy getting upset over ongoing outrages. Recognize that they are unimportant. They make no sense. Categorize them as irrational. Stop seeking explanations for things that are inherently senseless. Put aside futile mind-racking analyses. There are more productive ways to spend your energy.

Stand firm for what is right and good. Invest yourself in worthwhile projects. When the time to defend yourself comes, speak whatever you have in mind. But remember, your words will not matter; your oppressors will likely not even hear your words. Not words, but your very being will make whatever impact you will have, especially if you have moved beyond petty emotionalism and defensive argumentation and become a genuinely good person through and through. You yourself will be the statement that cannot be withstood or contradicted.

Then, according to the lesson that Luke teaches, you will be mistreated, in any case. Should we really expect to fare better than Jesus? Or Mahatma Gandhi? Or Martin Luther King, Jr.? Or Anwar Sadat? Relatives and friends might betray you. In the skirmish you may be "taken out." Let's not deceive ourselves; it happens every day. As if the twentieth century were not documentation enough on how cruel people are to one another and how the limitation of personal freedoms and curtailment of civil protections steadily creep on as a terroristic millennium unfolds. And, increasingly, woe to those who speak from insight, with honesty, and for justice.

STRENGTH TO FACE THE END

Another line in Luke suggests how we can persevere under such circumstances: "By your endurance you will gain your souls." Endurance suggests that there is some suffering to be borne. There are hard times to live through. To endure, to stick in there, is to get through. (It is striking how much Luke's words, written so long ago, apply to the events of our own day.) The ordeal will not end quickly, so do not look for a fast-and-easy solution: a new lover, a new job, a new city, a new car, a new home, more drugs, a new presidential administration, or a spiritual breakthrough that will "make the world go away." Only those who are able to hang in there for the long haul, only they will succeed.

To hang in there you will need support, whatever true friends you might find, fellow travelers on the spiritual quest. You will need daily discipline: good eating, sufficient sleep, and regular exercise, if these are possible. But most of all you will need the harmony of mind and heart that comes from thought, reflection, meditation, and time spent sitting by the riverside to get a perspective on things. The person of solid integrity is the strong one who will endure.

What those who endure will gain is their "souls," that is to say, their selves. They will become themselves. Nothing more is promised. Nothing could be worth more. They will become solid people. They will know what life is about and will be able to live it courageously. They will have depth. Living or dying, they cannot be undone.

I have seen such people in religious circles, in schools and universities, in hospitals and health-care facilities, in the gay community, in politics, in business, in sales, in the home. They are everywhere. Their heroic way of living can thrive under any circumstances. They are individuals who have suffered much. They have grown strong and sure. They know themselves. They know what matters in life. No one can buffalo them. They are simply beyond playing games. Their lives are rich and deep and, most often, simple and unencumbered. They have gained their souls. In comparison, the ending of worlds is insignificant.

FOURTEEN

THE TRIUMPH OF
THE GOOD:
CHRIST REIGNS
FROM THE CROSS

TWO OTHERS ALSO, who were criminals, were led away to be put to death with him. When they came to the place that is called The Skull, they crucified Jesus there with the criminals, one on his right and one on his left. Then Jesus said, "Father, forgive them; for they do not know what they are doing." And they cast lots to divide his clothing, and the People stood by, watching; but the leaders scoffed at him, saying, "He saved others; let him save himself if he is the Messiah of God, his chosen one!" The soldiers also mocked him, coming up and offering him sour wine, and saying, "If you are the King of the Jews, save yourself!" There was also an inscription over him, "This is the King of the Jews."

One of the criminals who were hanged there kept deriding him and saying, "Are you not the Messiah? Save yourself and us!" But the other rebuked him, saying, "Do you not fear God, since you are under the same sentence of condemnation? And we indeed have been condemned justly, for we are getting what we deserve for our deeds, but this man has done nothing wrong." Then he said, "Jesus, remember me when you come into your kingdom." He replied, "Truly I tell you, today you will be with me in Paradise." —LUKE 23:32–43

CHRISTIANS CERTAINLY recognize Jesus Christ as king, sovereign, Lord. He sums up and symbolizes all that is ultimate in our lives. In this sense, we look up to him, we reverence him, we follow and obey him. And not just we. Regardless of their religion, most people who know of Jesus respect him and think him worthy of imitation. Indeed, they say they would find Christianity a much more appealing religion if Christians were only more like Jesus Christ.

A CRUCIFIED KING?

Yet the gospel reading assigned to the feast of Christ the King presents Jesus hanging on a cross between two thieves. What kind of king is that? Certainly, if we saw Jesus in glory, risen from the dead and glorified in heaven, certainly then we could recognize him as a king. But hanging on a cross? Crucified among thieves? In insult and misery? Nonetheless, there is a clue to the meaning of Christianity in that reading. The clue lies in the fact that one of the thieves repents. If you read closely, you will notice that it was "the good thief" who introduced the theme of Christ's kingdom, Christ's reign.

Of course, the notice tacked to the cross read: "This is the king of the Jews." But that notice was put there in mockery, just as the chief priests and soldiers mocked Jesus saying "If you really are the Son of God, come down from that cross." They wanted a miracle. They wanted some show of power.

As it turned out, Jesus was not about setting up some particular political system or other. His concern was to reign in human hearts. Thus, he would hold sway over any and every political system as the changing times called for changing forms of government. His reign was not to be of "this world," which is to say, not about the particular comings and goings of everyday life but about spiritual concerns, and these pertain to all the ever-changing particularities of life.

Jesus' reign was about spiritual issues, and the good thief recognized that fact. He asked to be a part of Jesus' reign, and Jesus said yes.

THE REIGN OF GOODNESS

But how is it that a thief could be associated with Jesus' reign? Simply because he repented. Though he was a thief, there was still goodness in his heart. Compare this thief with the other, who appears to have been hardened through and through. All he knew and could think about—even as he was dying!—were the concerns of thievery. He wanted to save his skin. But the one thief was still good. With reason he is remembered as *the good thief*. There was still enough goodness in his heart that he was able to recognize the goodness in Jesus. He knew that Jesus was innocent and that Jesus did not deserve execution.

Sometimes people who are up to "no good" admire goodness from afar, and when the crunch comes, they will sometimes defend the good. From the days of school desegregation, there is the account of a fourteen-year-old southern male, a self-described "redneck" and "hellion," who objected to the federal judges messing with his "southern way of life." So the boy, a star athlete, along with his buddies, took out their hostility on "the niggers" who were integrating his school. But he began to admire one of them, and in this particular boy he saw "a kid, not a nigger," because this black boy was polite, kept a smile on his face, and walked tall despite the abuse he was given.

One day the white boy saw his friends huddled in a corner over this black boy, and he sensed that what was about to happen was going to be bad, very bad. Without realizing what he was doing, the athlete pushed through the crowd and stopped the happening. His friends all thought he was crazy. He was also surprised, especially when he heard coming from his mouth these words addressed to the black boys: "I'm sorry." From then on, the white boy was the black boy's protector and later his friend. The white boy eventually argued that this whole segregation thing should be abolished. Almost despite himself, the Southern gentlemanliness and the sense of fairness in his own heart moved him over to the other side. Goodness had won out.

Perhaps something similar happened at Jesus' crucifixion. It is interesting that, according to Luke, the good thief addressed Jesus by name. Had he seen Jesus before? Had he listened to him preach? Had he overheard talk about this fellow prisoner? Whatever the case, the goodness in his heart resonated with that in Jesus. Unlike the other thief, he allowed that movement in his heart. He reached out to Jesus. So his last request was one of repentance: "Jesus, remember me, when you come into your kingdom."

Now, there is the answer to the question "How is it that on the cross Jesus could be reigning as a king?" Simply because Jesus was good, and the thief recognized his goodness and bowed to it. Associating himself with Jesus' goodness, the thief was associated with Jesus' reign.

That is all there is to it. It is as simple as that. The reign of God—the kingdom of heaven, about which theologians and preachers can go on and on—is no more complicated than that. It is the reign of goodness. It is the assured victory of openness, honesty, justice, mercy, love. These are the absolutes of life. These are the basis of God's reign. Only these have a future. Closed-mindedness, dishonesty, injustice, hatred and ill will eventually self-destruct. They collapse upon themselves like the house built on sand, about which Jesus once spoke. But heeding Jesus' word and following him—investing in goodness—is like building one's house on solid rock. No storm will topple this house. The powers of hell will not prevail against it.

Eventually and unavoidably, the way of goodness, God's way, will prevail, not just because it is God's, not for some abstract religious reason, not through some punishing divine intervention, but because of the very nature of the good. The good is what lasts. It is what has a future. It is whatever leads to ongoing expansion and growth. This characteristic is precisely what makes the good good. For this very reason it is called "good." Whatever is of this kind is good; whatever is not of this kind is evil, wrong, unethical, immoral, sinful. The meaning of good and evil, their very essences, are built into the universe and into human nature. The reign of God is the reign of goodness. Inevitably, God's reign will come.

WHY JESUS DIED ON A CROSS: THE "ATONEMENT"

Look at Jesus, and you will see the same story. What is he doing on that cross? Why is he hanging there? Christian history has given many answers, but most of them make little sense. Isn't it foolish to say that Jesus died because God wanted him to be murdered? Yet we hear this nonsense. Oh, not in those very words, but we hear it. We hear that Jesus was obedient to God, and the suggestion is that God wanted him to die, so Jesus led himself to the cross. This suggestion evinces sadomasochism, and it makes no sense. What kind of a perverse god would we be talking about here?

Or else we are told that Jesus was paying the price of our sins. The unspoken suggestion is that God really enjoyed the crucifixion. God wanted the misery, the suffering, the scourging. God wanted blood. The more Jesus' crucifixion hurt, the more satisfied God was. God was getting revenge. And again, I ask, what kind of god is that?

If you read the scriptures carefully, there is nothing there about paying a price for sin. Colossians 2:13–14 says, "God made you alive together with Christ, when he forgave us all our trespasses, erasing the record that stood against us with its legal demands. He set this aside, nailing it to the cross." This text does not say that Jesus paid off any debt. It says that the debt was cancelled. There was nothing for Jesus to pay off.

In no way are Jesus' blood and death a payment, a payoff, a compensation, or a remuneration. Despite what any English dictionary says about *sacrifice*, *atonement*, and *expiation*, and despite what biased English translations of the Bible seem to suggest, the Greek words in the Christian scriptures, echoing the ancient Jewish mind, are simply not meant in this way. The shedding of Jesus' blood does not refer to payment or suffering or execution. In the ancient Hebrew mind, which is totally foreign to us, the blood is merely the sign with which Jesus is marked. The sign marks the place where salvation comes to the world, namely, in Jesus. The marking with blood says that God made Jesus into the place where God and humanity are at one.

In the Hebrew mind, as documented in Deuteronomy 12:23, "the blood is the life," and life is from God. So to be splattered with blood is to be connected to God. For this reason the ancient Jewish rituals required that the people be sprinkled with the blood of the sacrifice. The animal was sacrificed, not to make an offering to God, but to get the blood. Covered with blood, Jesus is marked as the point of contact with God's love. As Hebrews 9:13–14 says, "If the blood of goats and bulls . . . sanctifies those who have been defiled so that their flesh is purified, how much more will the blood of Christ . . . purify our conscience from dead works?"

To be sure, these images of blood, sacrifice, and indebtedness are weird. They are not part of our culture. They do not easily make sense to us. They need to be understood in terms of the temple practice of the ancient Jewish rituals. In those peculiar terms the early Christians tried to make sense of the catastrophe of Jesus' crucifixion. Shocked by Jesus' death, they fell back on the only resources they had, their ancient Jewish religion, to interpret Jesus' death. They understood his tragic death as the ultimate instance of the Jewish temple ritual: The people find union with God through contact with blood.

INEVITABLE MISUNDERSTANDING OF CERTAIN BIBLE TEXTS

We should not take those ancient images, totally alien to our mentality, and try to have them make sense in our own terms. When we attempt this feat, we end up with religious absurdity. We have to shut down our critical minds and force ourselves to believe very strange things. Our children have nightmares about being washed in a lamb's blood. Even we wonder what this biblical obsession with blood is all about, and we make up fanciful religious myths to rationalize the thing.

To a contemporary audience, some scripture texts are downright misleading. To get the message that the inspired authors intended, one has to understand the ancient Hebrew history and mind. One has to hear the texts in modern English and make a cultural transposition in one's mind. Only then can one allow those words to pass into one's heart. Few people have the background in biblical studies to accomplish this feat. Besides, who wants to engage in such mental gymnastics while trying to be open to God? I have certainly grown weary of needing to translate so much of what I hear in church. If I want to find the inspiration that I go to church to find, in my mind I often need to rework the hymns, rethink the prayers, and elaborate or reject the preaching. I have to reinterpret the whole ceremony to get a relevant message from it. Taken at its word in contemporary English, much of what Christianity proclaims is in conflict with current knowledge, out of sync with contemporary experience, and even offensive to God.

Some of the scriptures should just not be read in church, such as the passages on Jesus' supposed self-sacrifice in supposed obedience to God or those about wives' being subject to their husbands or the ones that supposedly categorically forbid divorce or those about slaves being obedient to their masters or the antibody texts about the flesh warring against the spirit or the texts about male-male sex being an "abomination" and supposedly excluding people from the kingdom of God or the passage in which God commands Abraham to kill his son Isaac. Heard in contemporary English and without detailed exegesis, these scripture passages present perversity.

In my church, we read the story of Abraham and Isaac every year at the solemn Easter vigil when, more than at other times, the church tends to be full. I've often wondered what the five-, seven-, ten-, eleven-year-olds think when they hear that passage. Old enough to follow the story but not old enough to interpret it, I bet they are terrified. God commanded Abraham to actually murder his son. And Abraham, a good man and, supposedly, a good father, was going to do it. Is this what good fathers do? Why, yes, they obey God. In fact, most explanations blindly present this misunderstood text as a lesson on absolute obedience to God. Well, the children must be wondering "What would happen to me if my father or God got some notion to sacrifice me?" Kids do think about such things!

Of course, there is a sane historical explanation for that text: It marks an important step in ancient Israelite moral development; it marks the turning point when child sacrifice was finally and absolutely forbidden. The point is that God does not want the sacrifice of Isaac or of any child, but who gets this point—what child, especially—on hearing this passage? Even worse, people actually believe God might command you to murder, and, worst of all, they think you should obey.

I spoke once with an intelligent high-school senior who was "Bible believing." Just like Abraham, he insisted, he would kill if he thought God wanted him to. And how is such barbarism different from what happened on September 11, 2001? If such outrage is what "God" stands for, I want a different God.

The churches should not be proclaiming perversity as "the word of God." Such proclamation perpetuates neurotic guilt in believers. Such proclamation works against honest and sane responsibility. Church leaders should acknowledge that these texts are inappropriate for public reading today. They should strike these texts from the liturgical lectionaries and in their place add other more contemporary texts that, on first hearing, convey the authentic biblical message of compassion, forgiveness, and thanksgiving. The objective should be to convey God's message to a contemporary congregation, not to hold fast to ancient texts and subtle theologies. Or is it that our religious leaders don't trust their own judgment as to what is, indeed, the authentic biblical message? Don't they know which other texts would be appropriate? If not, aren't we in a pretty mess!

How much time must Sunday sermons waste on technical explanations of ancient Hebrew thinking! Some people fill their religious lives by "studying the scriptures," that is, by trying to understand those texts. This study has become a cottage industry, and the Bible-believing "Christians" provide the sad example: They spend their time reading, discussing, arguing over the Bible as if this is what religion means and as if there weren't more important issues in our world. Even worse, they don't realize the half of what true historical-critical interpretation takes. So they spin their naïve intellectual wheels over foreign concepts, ancient word usage, symbolic numbers, and arcane cultural allusions. Talk about the "opium of the masses"!

THE VICTORY OF GOODNESS IN JESUS

In fact, the scriptures do not say that Jesus paid God the price of our sins. Yet in a sinful world, those who do good sometimes do end up paying a dear price. They pay the price of their goodness, and they pay it to the wicked, not to God. That is how it was with Jesus. Jesus was too good, too honest, too just. He loved people too much. He was dangerous to have around. His goodness highlighted the corruption, evil, injustice, and manipulation of the powers that be. So they had to get rid of him. That is why Jesus was crucified. It was not because God required it. It was because human corruption required it. Jesus' death was not the will of God. It was the will of sinful humanity.

Yet even unto death, Jesus loved. Even as he died, Jesus remained faithful to himself and, thus, being God the Son, necessarily faithful to God, his Eternal Parent. Remember Jesus' story, and then look at him hanging on the cross. He is not hanging there in defeat; he is hanging there as a hero. Yes, they killed him. Our sinfulness killed him. Yes, we took his human life from him, but nothing could take his soul from him. He was willing to love, to be true to himself, to speak his word honestly and boldly, even to the point of death. This achievement no one could take from him. His very death only confirmed his goodness. In death his stance reached perfection.

Jesus' death gave his words the supreme human validation. His death made his stand for righteousness definitive: He would not, he could not, now change it; he could not put any higher human value on it. Jesus' crucifixion certified his virtuousness. Thus, Jesus is reigning on the cross. There he is in victory. There he is exalted. There he towers in honesty, concern, and justice.

THE REALITY OF THE REIGN OF GOD OUTSIDE OF CHRISTIANITY

Jesus reigns from the cross, and his reign is real. Wherever there is goodness, truth, justice, and concern for what is right and worthwhile, there is the reign of Christ. It is in this arena that Christ does reign.

It is mistaken to think that the reign of God is somewhere in heaven to come. It is mistaken to think that it is some mysterious thing about which we know very little. It is mistaken to think that it is not yet real. Wherever there is goodness, God's reign is already real: It is present; it is active; and it is growing among us.

Likewise, it is mistaken to think that God's reign is present only in the church or only among those who profess to be Christ-

226 · DANIEL A. HELMINIAK

ian. Indeed, the hallmarks of God's reign—openness, honesty, love, and goodwill—are sometimes the most patently absent among those who insist the loudest that they are Christian or who claim infallibility and inerrancy in speaking for God.

Of course, if we wanted to, we could interpret the reign of God in terms that are specifically Christian. We could say that God's reign is the culmination of the life, death, and resurrection of Jesus. We could say that in becoming human and passing faithfully through death, Jesus transformed the meaning of human life. He opened to us a fulfillment in the very life of God: deification. We could say that Jesus and his Eternal Parent poured the Holy Spirit into human hearts to lead us all along the path that Jesus opened up toward life in God. We could say that human life will reach its fulfillment in the divine life. God will be all in all, and in God we will all reign eternally.

We could say all that and, in accord with Christian belief, we would certainly be correct. That would be the strictly Christian way of making the point, but we would be wrong to say that you must believe all that and profess it in those very words before you could be part of this same reign of God. We would be wrong because the workings of God's reign do not depend on what we know or believe or proclaim in religious faith.

If, as Christianity professes, Jesus really has been raised from the dead to the glory of God and if the Holy Spirit really has been poured out into human hearts, human history is not what it would otherwise have been. God's work through Jesus and the Holy Spirit really has changed the meaning of human existence. Then, whether we know and acknowledge this change or not, we are caught up in it. If it is a real work of God, if "the redemption" has really happened, it is now a standard part of the human situation. Then, just by being born into the human race, we are involved in God's saving work in Jesus.

The key to God's reign is not in our saying "Jesus is Lord." As Jesus himself taught, the key is our "doing the will of the Father." Our honest and loving living associates us with Jesus Christ and implicates us in God's reign whether or not we are able to recognize the Holy Spirit, name Jesus, profess an Eternal Parent, and define "reign of God." Honest living is what matters, not the mere words that one can say or the faith that one can profess.

This is a new way of looking at the reign of God. In Catholicism this new understanding emerged in the Second Vatican Council in the mid-1960s. The council made a distinction between the church and the reign of God. Previously, the two were identified; the church was thought to be the realm of God's reign. But the reign of God is that realm where honesty, truth, goodness, justice, and mercy, that is, the qualities of God, hold sway. In contrast, the church is the narrower realm where Christian believers explicitly acknowledge God's working in the world through Jesus Christ and the Holy Spirit. According to this understanding, the church is subordinate to the reign of God. The church is the servant of God's reign. It is the task of the church, the body of Christian believers, to foster and further God's reign in the world.

Wherever there is goodness, wherever there is true love, concern, and justice, there already is the reign of God because goodness is what the reign of God is about. Goodness is what really matters. Goodness is what we as Christians and everyone else are called to. Thus Christ's reign within us is not some mysterious thing that we have to interpret in special Christian terms. It is no Christian "mystery"; rather, it is a human reality with which we are all involved. It marks the difference between love and hate. It marks the difference between good and evil. It raises the question of whether we are going to make this a world of beauty, love, and mutual support or whether we will turn it into a hell of injustice, hostility, and mutual destruction.

The question is that simple. The question is one to which we are able to respond. What will we make of this world? What will we make of one another? What will we make of ourselves? These are the issues at stake when we speak of the reign of God. These are the central issues involved when we look at Jesus hanging on the cross.

HONEST, GOOD LIVING RATHER THAN UNTHINKING RELIGIOUS BELIEF

Of course, it is up to us to respond to those questions. But, again, the response is also quite simple: We are to live justly, honestly, lovingly, and humbly. We need to search our consciences to be sure that what we are doing is right and good. We need to scrutinize our hearts to be sure that we are behaving as we ought to. This require-ment applies across the board: in our relationships with one an-other, in our families, in our jobs, in our neighborhoods, in our civil communities, in our nations, and in our global society.

That much is easy to say, but the devil is in the details. What about the specifics? What about questions that good people them-selves debate? Like abortion, homosexuality, nonmarital sex, di-vorce, certain medical procedures, various business practices, gun control, the "war on drugs," medical use of marijuana, environ-mental pollution, economic globalization, the "war on terror-ism"? What about these?

THE CASE FOR SEXUAL ABSTINENCE OUTSIDE OF HETEROSEXUAL MARRIAGE

Traditionally, the churches have taught: "No sex outside of mar-riage!" Indeed, the "Religious Right" pushes sexual abstinence so much these days—and with the support of the White House—that one wonders if its leaders are just very uncomfortable about their bodies and uptight about sex. One sure reason for the absti-nence campaign is opposition to homosexuality. Think about it. Extramarital sex and homosexual sex involve the same issues: sex for the purpose of relationship and intimacy, not for procreation, marriage, family, or the expansion of the population. In fact, I find no coherent religious argument against loving, same-sex relation-ships. Still, much opposition remains, and it is said to reflect the will of God. Supposedly, lesbians, gay men, and other unmarried people are simply to refrain from sharing sexual experiences. To be fair, we need to realize that in the past century the prevalent meaning of sex has changed from procreation to recreation, from childbearing to bonding. That there would be intense debate about this epochal shift of meaning is to be expected. One would only hope that the debate would progress intelligently and reasonably. However, what is worth noting is not this teaching but the reasoning behind it.

The Vatican suggests that the unmarried are to be obedient to church teaching, and conservative Protestantism and biblical fundamentalism say that they are to be obedient to the literal word of the Bible just as Jesus was obedient to his Heavenly Parent. Jesus had to bear his cross, and we all have our crosses to bear. Outside of heterosexual marriage, people are to suppress their feelings and to suffer quietly within their hearts. Supposedly, this is the will of God. Jesus himself suffered, and, supposedly, Jesus' suffering was also the will of God. Supposedly, sucking it in and bearing the pain is being like Jesus. And the same reasoning gets applied to spouses in bad marriages, children in abusive families, workers in underpaid jobs, poor people with substandard housing, women who seek promotion or religious ordination.

Misguided beliefs about Jesus support misguided advice in our own lives. Supposedly, if suffering pleases God, when we are suffering, like Jesus, we should just "offer it up." Offer it up to what? Offer it up for what? Are we to believe that suffering in itself is valuable to God? Are we to suppose that God is pleased with arbitrary and self-imposed penances? Are we to accept that God delights in the hardships that result from dishonesty, prejudice, and greed? Are we to suppose that pain in itself is somehow redeeming? Is God a sadist? Does God want us to be masochists?

Certainly, Jesus did suffer, and because of the way his life unfolded, he had no other option. Therefore, for him to suffer was the will of God in this sense: Jesus would have been untrue to himself had he run for fear of the suffering, and God would certainly not have wanted him to be dishonest and cowardly. But Jesus' suffering and death are not what mattered. His virtue in the face of death is. It is virtue that is saving. It is Jesus' virtue even unto death that saves us. Suffering for its own sake is useless. So suffering should be avoided unless it is the cost of virtue. One must have a good reason to willingly take up a cross.

The churches say that unmarried people should abstain from sexual intimacy. They should willingly embrace sexual abstinence as their cross in Christ. But the only reason the churches have to offer is that, supposedly, "it is the will of God." If this requirement truly were the will of God, this reason would certainly be sufficient. But the very debate today is whether such abstinence is, indeed, the will of God. Why would God want people to be frustrated, disgruntled, and unhappy?

The only argument the churches have to fall back on is their own self-appropriated authority. In the name of God, they themselves assert that abstinence is the will of God. But in today's world, the very claim to be speaking for God needs to be justified. With nothing to which to appeal except its own self-assertion, the authority of the churches has no credibility.

A LESSON FROM SOCRATES

There is another way to approach this matter of the legitimacy of religious authority. In his discussion with Euthyphro, Socrates posed a question that cuts down the middle of history and religious argument: Is something wrong because God says so, or does God say so because it is wrong? Is it God's naked will alone that makes extramarital sex wrong? Has God just arbitrarily declared it wrong? Or is there something wrong about it in itself? Is it because of its inevitable harm that such sex should be avoided and would be offensive to God?

Certainly, God must say things are wrong because they are wrong in themselves. A mother who forbids her child from playing in the street because the child could get hurt is not just being mean. Similarly, there must be something harmful about nonmarital sex if God really does forbid it. Indeed, in former times there were good reasons to forbid all nonmarital sex, but today, responsibly engaged, what is so wrong with it?

No one has been able to show anything wrong with homosexual love, either, and the arguments against all nonmarital sex are equally shaky. Unless things are wrong simply because God arbitrarily says so, sexual morality today needs radical revision.

OTHER EXAMPLES—ABORTION

Simple-minded appeals to "the will of God" do not convince us any more. We are not moved. We have lived with these issues. We have delved into them deeply. We have seen through the pious rationalizations of spiritual manipulation. We know too much to be swayed by sheer assertion.

Consider another of the hottest issues of the day: abortion. What is the right or wrong of the matter? Surely, the critical consideration is the respect for human life, but the discussion is not very clear about what *human life* means. When we say, "to take a human life," we mean to kill someone. The antiabortion groups speak of abortion as the murder of children, but is the fetus really a human being? Is the fetus really already an infant? Is terminating a pregnancy really murdering a person?

In my mind, the prime issue is whether or not there is a human being, a person, in the womb. Now, there is no doubt that what is growing in the womb is human. If it comes to term, it will not be a cow or a horse but a human being. What is there is human life, but is that growth already a person? Is that tissue that is developing in the womb already a human being, or is it merely a mass of human tissue, like a gall bladder that is surgically removed or a mass of hair that is cut off?

Without doubt, if the fetus were actually a human person, then abortion would be wrong. Abortion would be murder. But if the fetus is not yet a person, then, for sufficient reason the pregnancy could be ethically terminated. Indeed, in certain instances the more responsible thing to do might actually be to terminate a pregnancy. In my mind the telling question is: When does the fetus become an actual person?

To be sure, we cannot give a precise answer to that question. But science can tell us a great deal about fetal development, and it is possible to say when the fetus is sufficiently developed that, as best we can determine, it would be capable of real sensation, emotion, and mental processes. I would take these to be indications of an individual personal life.

Current research shows clearly that before the twentieth week, at the earliest, brain development is so primitive that neural connections do not yet exist to sustain what we know as mental processes. So, until about this time, there certainly is a human form developing in the womb, but it is sheer fantasy to believe that this human form is already a human person.

Former generations were quite comfortable with this understanding. Major figures of Christian history, like Thomas Aquinas, allowed that abortion was acceptable during the early weeks of pregnancy. Expressed in terms of an older theology, the notion was this: In the early weeks, the fetus is too underdeveloped to support the presence of a soul, so there could not yet be a human person there. Only appropriate matter can take on a corresponding form. Mud does not lend itself to being shaped into a bridge. An insufficiently developed nervous system cannot sustain a human mind or soul or spirit. Such reasoning, now highly refined by developmental neurological research, is certainly a legitimate approach to the question of abortion.

Of course, terminating a pregnancy is a serious matter. Who ever said it was not? The women who agonize over their decision certainly know the matter is serious. One would not have an abortion frivolously, without good reason. As President Clinton used to say, "Abortion should be legal, safe—and rare." But when there is good reason and when the pregnancy is in its early stages, though the thought is itself repugnant, abortion may certainly be a legitimate and morally acceptable action. Indeed, it might be the most ethical choice.

You see, we know about these things. We have information that sheds light on such questions. In contrast, religion looks foolish when it simplistically appeals to God or belief without any consideration of the facts of the matter. Then religion becomes hallowed superstition. Religion's insistence that the fertilized egg must be reverenced from the first moment of conception is certainly valid; pregnancy is a serious matter. But religion's claim or insinuation that there is a human person in the womb from the first moment of conception is ludicrous.

Suppose that fertilized egg divides and become twins. Was that fertilized egg a human person who now magically became two people? And what about the placenta, umbilical cord, and the amniotic sack? These all develop from that same initial fertilized egg? Are these, then, also to be treated as human persons? And what about miscarriages? About two-thirds of all conceptions are spontaneously aborted. Are we to believe that God kills off the majority of the human race before they are even born? If so, I want a different God.

Compared to the biological facts of the matter, most religious opposition to abortion is at best uninformed and at worst silly. One only need learn a bit of modern medicine to realize that the antiabortionists are extremists. They appeal to religion, God, and blind faith, and they stir up emotions, but they know nothing. They make no sense biologically, philosophically, or theologically.

We cannot shut down our minds and forget our learning because religion says, "God forbids that," especially when everything we know about the matter supports an opposite conclusion. In the case of abortion and so many other contemporary issues, we know too much to play the role of such naïve and simpleminded believers. It is insulting and foolish—to both God and ourselves—to think that God would require us to do so. God is no megalomaniacal mother who goes around withholding permission from her children just to assert her power and to test the limits of the children's obedience. But, I dare say, this is precisely the kind of God in which some supposed "Christians" believe.

Could we follow such a God in good conscience? Does bearing the self-imposed burden of such ungrounded choices make us virtuous? Must we go against our own better judgment to be faithful to God? Does true religion require us to distrust our own minds and hearts, even at their most honest and sincere? Surely not.

THE CLAIM OF DIVINE REVELATION

At stake in this discussion is a principle that runs through the whole of religion. The principle is revelation, the claim to have messages directly from God. Revelation plays a telling role in Judaism, Christianity, Islam, Mormonism, and, some would say, even Vedic Hinduism. The belief in direct communication from God is common to many religions, but these very religions differ in their beliefs. What they claim God has revealed differs from religion to religion. This state of affairs raises a difficult question about supposed revelation from God: How does one know that it is really revelation from God?

People of generations long past did not need to face this question. They were blissfully unaware of other religions, or, if they were aware, those other religions were distant enough to be ignored and, as necessary, ridiculed. Today, we have no such easy escape. When someone claims that a teaching is revealed by God—the Bible, for example—we cannot help but wonder how anyone knows something is really from God.

As honest and good-willed people, we would certainly believe what God actually revealed, and we would dutifully do what God asks of us, but our very honesty and goodwill now make us ask: How do I know that it is really God who is asking this of me? The only answer can be that we must trust our own best judgment. We must search our minds, probe our hearts, examine our experience, research the matter, and consult with others. On this basis, with the help of others—never simply alone, since we all have our blind spots, limited perspectives, and, yes, biases—we must discern whether a supposed revelation could actually be one of God.

These very disturbing thoughts are symptomatic of our uncertain times. Few other generations, I dare say, have had to deal with such serious matters. Oh, here and there isolated individuals and some great minds have grappled with these questions through the ages, but never before have people in general, across the board, had to make these questions their own. These questions actually transform the whole discussion about religion. Our probing here has shifted all talk of God and religion to a deeper level. No longer can we settle issues by simple appeal to the authority of the church or the scriptures or some other supposed revelation from God. We no longer have the luxury of avoiding personal responsibility for our beliefs and actions by claiming, "This is the word of God." In every case we are now forced to ask the prior question: But is this really from God?

To answer this question we are left to rely on the goodness of our own hearts and on the honesty of our own minds. In our challenging age, the buck stops with us. Ever again we are thrown back onto our own God-given resources, and only our honesty and goodwill can provide some guarantee that we are on the right track. As human beings, we have no other place to stand. We have come to the ground floor. There is no other base beneath this one. Every belief we have and every claim we make are ours alone, the opinion of human beings. In this situation, evidence, honesty and goodwill become the unavoidable bottom line. In our pluralistic world, there is nothing else to which we can appeal.

THE OPTIONS AND THE MIDDLE WAY

The options are clear, and so is the required choice. One option is to blindly surrender ourselves to whatever is said to be revealed by God. This is the path of biblicism, fundamentalism, dogmatism, and totalitarian regimes. It eliminates all questioning, thought, and personal responsibility. It makes mere robots of people. It is a solution unworthy of humanity and of God alike.

The second option takes the other extreme. It relies solely on personal judgment. Unfortunately, however, personal judgment may be no more than whim. In reaction to the problems at the other extreme, our confused and narcissistic world often endorses such whim. We are advised: "Do your own thing," "Everything is relative," "You have to live your own life," "If it feels good, do it." But mere personal preference is hardly something on which good-willed people rely. This second option, like the first, is a cop-out. It avoids the need to act responsibly. So this second option must also be rejected.

The third option is a middle way. It is the path toward which I have been pointing. On the one hand, it does rely on personal judgment, but it insists that one's judgment be informed, that it be made in honesty, love, and goodwill and in consultation with others of similar knowledge and goodwill. On the other hand, this third option is also open to the concerns of religion, but it insists that these need to be weighed and evaluated.

In this third option there is a meeting of present knowledge and past tradition. There is a meeting of one's own mind and the minds of others. This third option unfolds within a community of open-minded, honest, loving, and good-willed people. In this context inherited religion confronts present needs, and honest and loving hearts discern what God's will might be in each case. Such collective commitment to the good is what "church" is supposed to mean.

In this third option we still trust in God, but we presume that God is reasonable. So as our knowledge increases, we have to re-think what we claim God intends. We still live in faith, but our faith is reasonable. As well as having faith in God, we also have faith in the capacity of our God-given minds. We do not suppose that God requires us to be unthinking dolts in order to be faithful servants.

The enterprise I am describing is risky. We are walking along the edge of a precipice. We are taking our lives into our own hands. We are actually tampering with matters of eternal importance. Our tampering will leave us to shine forth in heavenly glory or be lost in the darkness of hell, and, as one wishes, one can take this statement figuratively or literally. The fact is that we are setting the course for the future of the human race. We are making our own future.

We cannot avoid this enterprise. History and history's God have brought us to this point. Our very status as human beings requires a response from us. To retreat into unthinking religion, on the one hand, or into self-centered whim, on the other, would be unworthy of us and of God. We are forced to remain on the narrow, middle path, and the prospect is frightening.

THE ROYAL EXAMPLE OF JESUS

But we are in good company. Jesus acted in the same way. Jesus also challenged his religious tradition, but he did not undo it; rather, he took it a step forward. He transcended it. In the face of the Law of Moses and the revelation of God, time and time again, Jesus boldly said, "But I say unto you . . . "

Where did Jesus get that boldness, that authority with which he spoke? How did he dare challenge the very revelation that his Jewish religion believed to have come from God through Moses?

What Jesus had to go on is what he experienced in his own heart. Allowing that he was the Eternally Begotten of God, as Christian orthodoxy teaches, in the depths of his soul he certainly had some inkling of his Heavenly Parent. He was in touch with God within himself. Deep within himself he had a sense of who he was and a sense of that to which he had to be true. He had that to go on, nothing more, and he followed it. After all, he was a human being; he was one of us. What more could he have had? In this wholly human way, he lived. In this way, he taught. And in this way, he died.

Jesus is the example we are following. We are in good company. Trusting that the Holy Spirit is within us, as Christian orthodoxy teaches, we trust what we experience in our own hearts, as Jesus did. We rely on truth and goodness and dedication to justice, as accurately as we can determine them in all honesty, openness, and goodwill. We do not hedge on any question. We do not fudge our conclusions. We do not misrepresent the data. We do not resort to emotionalism. We do not huckster ideas. We do not impose values. Walking along a precipice, we do not engage in slimy and slippery tactics. We do not want to fall over the brink or cause others to fall.

We look to Jesus, and he is on that cross. What a strange Jesus to look to as master, king, ruler, sovereign: Jesus dying on a cross, hanging between two thieves! But insofar as we understand what was really happening there, we can identify with him. Born of God, he was goodness through and through. As in the case of the good thief, the goodness in our own hearts resonates with the goodness that is Jesus. Therefore, we identify with him, we prize him, we reverence him, we love and serve him. Even hanging on the cross—indeed, precisely as he dies committed to compassion, honesty, and love—he epitomizes our heart's deepest longings. Thus, we bow to him. Thus, he is our Lord, our Sovereign, our King.

As Jesus' followers, we are people attuned to goodness wherever it occurs, under whatever external guise. Far from isolating us from other people or pitting us against those who do not proclaim Jesus as Lord, our allegiance to Jesus as king makes us most valuable citizens of a global society.

FIFTEEN

HOPE AMIDST THE GLOOM OF LIFE: JESUS RAISES THE DEAD

WHEN JESUS HAD CROSSED AGAIN in the boat to the other side, a great crowd gathered around him; and he was by the sea. Then one of the leaders of the synagogue named Jairus came and, when he saw him, fell at his feet and begged him repeatedly, "My little daughter is at the point of death. Come and lay your hands on her, so that she may be made well, and live." So he went with him.

While he was still speaking, some people came from the leader's house to say, "Your daughter is dead. Why trouble the teacher any further?" But overhearing what they said, Jesus said to the leader of the synagogue, "Do not fear, only believe." He allowed no one to follow him except Peter, James, and John, the brother of James. When they came to the house of the leader of the synagogue, he saw a commotion, people weeping and wailing loudly. When he had entered, he said to them, "Why do you make a commotion and weep? The child is not dead but sleeping." And they laughed at him. Then he put them all outside, and took the child's father and mother and those who were with him, and went in where the child was. He took her by the hand and said to her, "Talitha cum," which means, "Little girl, get up!" And immediately the girl got up and began to walk about (she was twelve years of age). At this they were overcome with amazement. He strictly ordered them that no one should know this, and told them to give her something to eat.

—MARK 5:21–24, 35–43

WE HUMANS ARE A STRANGE LOT. We're always complaining about how bad things are, yet we always look for the worst. For goodness' sake, we almost hunt out hardship. Don't we constantly say or at least fear, "This is too good to last?" Or we say, "I never expect too much because that way I won't be disappointed." And of course, we aren't disappointed. We had nothing to lose. We never risk a lot, so we also never gain a lot. We learn to be content with mediocrity. But at least we're never disappointed—and isn't that the most important thing in the world?! Then there's Murphy's Law: "If anything can go wrong, it will." We live by these maxims.

I have a friend who just got back from vacation. He found this T-shirt he really loves. It's black, which is appropriate. On the side near his left shoulder, there's what looks like a small white blotch, a flaw in the field, a glitch in the system, an ominous intruder on the scene, perhaps an unfortunate bird dropping. If your curiosity gets the better of you and you look from up close, you can see that the blur is actually writing. In tiny white letters, it reads, "Life's a bitch, and then you die." Gotcha!

LIVING AMIDST DOOM AND GLOOM

From time to time and understandably, all of us feel discouraged. But worse than the occasional bad time of it, there is an all-out pessimism that can hang over us. It can become quite pervasive and deep—and especially now, in this age of terrorism, when political rhetoric from those who are waging and benefiting from the "war" seems geared to keep us all scared. So a constant fear haunts our unconscious, and in many ways discouragement colors us as a people. We become a depressed and pessimistic lot.

Much of this attitude builds, I think, on our earliest experiences. Because we grow up among a people of doom, we become people of doom. There's no doubt that children pick up things from their parents. Much of this learning occurs before the kids can even. Struck by the perfect stealth weapon, they never know what hit them. Before they can understand anything on an intellectual level, they pick attitudes up on an emotional level.

By tuning in on people's emotions, infants are programmed to follow the patterns of the adults who care for them. When they hold the infants or nurse them at the breast or leave them within earshot of a conversation, the little ones pick up on the emotional tone of the adults. If the infants sense tension and discomfort or anger or hostility or despair, they learn that the world is an uncomfortable and threatening place. Without ever thinking about it, before any possibility of reasoned judgment, infants learn basic attitudes toward life.

Educators say that the most important lessons about life are caught rather than taught. What children "catch" from adults is programmed into their guts. Far below the level of awareness or memory or understanding, the attitudes of the people around us got built into our own psyches.

Newborn infants in a nursery will cry when they hear another baby crying. Studies have shown that it is not the noise of the crying that disturbs the quiet baby. The fact that *another baby is crying* is what disturbs him or her. We humans have a natural empathy that binds us together as a species. This empathy is already at work from our earliest days. One infant's distress disturbs and threatens another infant. Children who were spared the wrath of a cruel parent but saw their brothers or sisters abused will, themselves, later in life show the effects of child abuse. Babies, children, and all of us pick up feelings from the people around us and make those feelings our own.

EMOTIONALLY WARPED FROM CHILDHOOD

Life is not always easy for adults. Things don't always work out the way people had hoped. Oftentimes people don't get what they want. (Is anybody ever really satisfied?) So people dutifully and begrudgingly "make the best of it." They go on bearing the burden of duty, and life becomes a grind.

Having children does not make things easier; on the contrary, it compounds the matter. So it is understandable that many parents are often dissatisfied with their lives. Then, by osmosis, their children also become dissatisfied. After all, the world of the dissatisfied parents is the world into which the children are born. This brooding disgruntlement is everywhere around them. As far as the children can ever know, this is what life is, period. This is the children's world, the only world they know. It is what they experience, and it is what they come to expect. So the innocent and fun-loving children grow up with a dark negativity buried inside them.

A bit older, preschool children become aware of their own thoughts and feelings. They are old enough to begin to separate their own feelings from those of the adults around them. Then others from outside the child's immediate adult circle may tell him or her how wonderful things are, but because this view is contrary to what the child has internalized, he or she may not be able to except it as true. If the child is old enough to realize this fact then the world starts looking like one grand hoax.

Take Christmas, for example. Amidst the hassle of holiday preparations, the worry over expenses, and the tension of frayed nerves, the parents are trying to make a nice Christmas for the children.

Of course, we want to make it nice for the kids. Concern for the little ones must always take precedence over our own needs. But how out-of-perspective things can get! How much we foolishly invest in our children! How much hope we place in their success! And in the process, what unfair burdens we lay on their shoulders! "The children are our future," we say. "All hope rests in them." What we're saying, of course, is that we have already given up on ourselves.

I have a very dear friend whom I sometimes find disturbing. He has little concern for environmental issues. In a way, he is an optimist, and I really love this part of him, but at times his optimism seems naïve. Take plastic, for example. How many plastic or Styrofoam cups of ever increasing thickness have you gotten from fast-food restaurants and contributed to our national stockpile of trash? This nonbiodegradable material will sit in landfills for millennia. When I express concern about this despicable practice, my friend dismisses the matter: "They'll figure out some way to deal with the stuff. They're intelligent. They always figure things out somehow. Why worry about it?" And I fear many people think this way.

So we are to eat, drink, and be merry and kindly deposit our trash in the "Thank-you" bin and let the next generation deal with the problems we are creating. Supposedly, our children will be more intelligent, more creative, and more responsible than we are. Supposedly, our own behaviors and attitudes have nothing to do with the case. Magically, the next generation will generate the strength and virtue that we—and our parents and theirs before them and so on—were unable to muster. We pass the buck to the next generation. We expect the children to save the world. Romanticizing the child Jesus, standard versions of the Christmas story capitalize on this excuse for irresponsibility.

I think we'd get further if we started taking responsibility for our own lives. We'd have a much brighter future if we took the trouble to find ourselves before we started having and investing in children. We'd have a much better world if we created it ourselves as a worthy gift to the next generation. How can we expect the upcoming generation to make that crucial difference when, at the level of the heart, they often have such miserable models to follow?

So, at Christmas, glossing over inner chaos, parents are *ooh*ing and *aah*ing about how beautiful the tree is, how great the presents are, how nice it is to be with the family, how special this day is. Picking up on the inner anxiety, frustration, and sadness that color the event or disappointed with "the presents that Santa brought" or else, having been exposed to a few high-tech movies, hardly impressed by the Christmas decorations, the child may not really be feeling good at all. But the official word is that this scene is really wonderful. Everything is beautiful. This is Christmas, the biggest shebang of the year. This is as good as it gets. And without ever really thinking about it, the child comes to the unspoken conclusion "If this is as good as it gets, I am in for one hell of a life."

On other occasions when parents really want to engage in an adult activity, they drag the kids along and try to keep them happy and quiet. There's the three-year-old at the cinema, who is supposed to enjoy a movie for grown-ups because the adults are enjoying it. This is supposed to be "fun." Or there's the six-year-old in church. The parents are really pious and want to pray (They want a few minutes peace!), but the kid has no interest in the music, the ceremony, or the preaching. (To tell the truth, I've often found religious ceremonies so perfunctory that I wondered why adults, who have a choice, did not just walk out. Who can blame the kids for being restless? Maybe they're just more honest than adults.) And this scene is supposed to be "sacred," an experience of "God's house"—boring! Then there's the outing to the symphony with the seven-year-old, one of the best ways to get children to hate classical music and anything of high culture.

At a parade, fireworks, or a ball game, kids have a good sense of when an event is already getting dull for them. Or maybe they're just tired. In certain circumstances and at certain times of the day, children, especially the very young, tire more quickly than adults. Responsible families with kids will leave an event about a third of the way through or so, because the kids are already tired. But some parents don't seem to know enough, or are not sensitive enough, to respond to the good sense of the kids. Because the parents are having fun, they insist that the kids must, too, so these parents do not leave even if the kids get cranky. After all, these "concerned" parents laid out good money for the tickets and went through considerable effort to get to the event. So they stay to the bitter end. And in their guts the kids learn something about life without ever really questioning it: nobody really cares about me; my feelings do not really matter; the universe is a cruel and heartless place.

For the most part, young children are into basics. Kids need immediate attention. They don't yet know what *delayed gratification* means. They are hungry, and they want something to eat. They get tired, and they want to go to sleep. They have to use the toilet. They want and need to be held. And in the midst of all this, the poor parents (who really do need a break) try to spark the child's interest in loftier things: "*Oooh*, look at that, isn't that beautiful? *Oooh*, look at this. Listen to the music. Watch the clown. Isn't this great?"

Simultaneously, the kids are learning the words that people use to express the positive—*beautiful, great,* and *wonderful*—but what they're feeling inside is neglect and lack of care. Without being able to articulate it, they may even be concluding: "This thing is really dull, and nobody realizes it. I am really not enjoying myself. Is this all there is? Why does everybody say this is wonderful? What's wrong with me that I don't feel good about it?"

Eventually children do get socialized. They learn to smile their own little plastic smiles. They, too, learn to say: "Oh, how wonderful that is!" and "Isn't this lovely?" and "Thank you very much." They know that this response is expected, and they perform on cue. In the meantime, in their secret heart of hearts, they will know that it's all a crock. Programmed at the level of feeling, prior to any ability to think, the self-contradictory lesson takes very well.

THE EXPERIENCE OF INTERNALIZED PREJUDICES

We can see how that early programming works in the case of people who are lesbian and gay. There are antigay and sex-negative messages all around us. From our earliest years we have heard, for example, that gay people cannot keep commitments. So whenever we hit a rough spot in a relationship, the ghost of a self-fulfilling prophecy haunts our minds. We begin to think that it's true: Gay people can never have lasting relationships. We forget that a full half of heterosexual marriages end in divorce and that most of those in the other half stay together out of sheer obligation (which is not always a bad thing).

Or the word is that gay people are always going to be lonely, and this nonsense is widespread. I can hardly believe that a psychotherapist of mine once made this very comment, although he was quite understanding, supportive, and surprisingly liberal in other ways. The ignorance and prejudice surrounding homosexuality run very deep, and this negative thinking takes root in all of us. After all, we grow up and we live in a fiercely homophobic society. Then one day you are feeling very lonely. You are having a very sad time of it. Those words come back, and you feel doubly depressed, thinking despite yourself that you are doomed because you are gay.

Where is the great surprise in the fact that you feel lonely? Everybody gets lonely from time to time. Even happily married couples with loving families and supportive friends experience periods of isolation and loneliness. What do they blame it on? Being heterosexual? Of course not.

Or there is the widespread prejudice that gay and lesbian people are awful, disgusting, and despicable. Growing up, we internalize this prejudice, and deep down inside we actually hate ourselves. We become very apologetic for ourselves. We think that we are bad, that somehow we are terrible people. And this stuff hangs on. It takes years for people to fully come out. It's one thing to acknowledge the fact that you are homosexual and to tell people so. It's another thing to be comfortable with this reality and to be positive about yourself in the face of it. It takes years to root out all the negative attitudes that our society inculcates.

I remember seeing *Making Love* years after I thought I had dealt with my homosexuality, but when two men kissed on the giant screen, right in front of all these strangers filling the auditorium, in redneck South Texas, I felt a shudder go through my body as I slunk down in my seat. Perhaps I was just picking up the emotion in that audience, but the feeling felt like mine, and I wondered how much homophobia had been imperceptibly bred into me and, despite my substantial liberation, how much homophobia was still there.

As recently as a few years ago, I felt a wave of secret embarrassment run through me as I watched a declared lesbian couple speak about their relationship on national TV. And I am out. I'm comfortable in the gay community. I've participated in gay pride events. I've marched with gay contingents. I've given public lectures on homosexuality. I've had years of psychotherapy. I've got the religious angle on this question worked out. I can say outright that the churches are wrong about homosexuality and know that I am right. And to my surprise and chagrin, I continue to find strands of homophobia in my own heart. I have spoken with too many others to believe that my experience is unusual.

Nor is homophobia the only case in point. Other groups of people also daily encounter society's prejudice and hatred that have been bred into them—African Americans, Hispanics, Asians, women, short people, fat people, singles, divorced couples, childless couples, poor people, physically or mentally challenged people. The list goes on. From their earliest years, all carry in their hearts a time bomb of self-hatred planted there by a prejudiced and cruel society and ready to go off anytime they hit a speed bump in the road of life. When the bomb goes off and they experience the negativity, they then have hard evidence that they will, indeed, never be happy. Now actual adult experience confirms the secret gut feeling: "Life's a bitch, and then you die."

On so many fronts, negative attitudes are bred into us. No wonder we humans are such a strange lot, always on the lookout for the worst. No wonder malaise and depression are so common in our society.

PESSIMISM IN THE GOSPELS

Such negativity emerges even in the gospel story. The leader of the synagogue comes up to Jesus asking for help. Jesus willingly goes off with him, but they are met with terrible news: The man's daughter is already dead. Why bother Jesus anymore?

"Just forget it. It's come to its end. Life's a bitch, and then you die. She's dead. Get over it."

Well, Jesus won't hear of it. He insists on going to the house. What does he find? Noise. A din. The wailing of people mourning and lamenting the situation. "Oh, how terrible life is. The poor child is dead."

Jesus looks at the situation in a different way. He suggests that maybe she's not dead but asleep. They laugh outright at him. Well, maybe they should have laughed. We must admit that Jesus' suggestion is pretty far-fetched. It sounds like wishful thinking. But perhaps Jesus' words are there precisely to alert us, in contrast to Jesus' unlimited optimism, to the pessimism that we so often endorse as a given in life.

The point? Our negativism is not a head thing. It is not something we learn intellectually. It is so deep that its roots burrow into our hearts. Therefore, it is not something we can work out just by thinking about it. When push comes to shove, pie-in-the-sky emphasis on positive thinking usually betrays us. Our pessimism goes much deeper than our thinking. It is programmed into our feelings. It becomes part of our spontaneous response. In the end, our feelings, not our thoughts, carry the day almost inevitably.

Oh, we can try and pretend that we are eminently rational. Yet, recall some things you yourself have done perhaps for love or out of anger, actions you would find reprehensible if attributed to somebody else. For the most part, our emotions rule our intellects, and we use our intellects to rationalize what we do. We use our heads just to work out excuses—"explanations," "reasons," we call them—for what our feelings lead us to do.

Our pessimism is a basic attitude that resides in the emotions. Its roots go deeper than any positive thinking we can practice. Like a swamp, ready to absorb us, pessimism surrounds our lives.

THE OPTIMISTIC FRAME OF MIND

We could look at life otherwise if we wanted to. Jesus, for example, said, "She's not dead. She's just asleep." That's a positive and open-ended way of approaching the situation.

I remember this little poem: "Two looked out from prison bars. The one saw mud; the other, stars." What you see depends on where you look and what you're looking for. There's a lot of good going on in life. In addition to the rot, there's beauty and love all around us. What you see depends on your focus. Then what you see is what you are likely to get.

Surely you've heard about the bottle that is half full or half empty, depending on how you look at it. The bottle is an even better example than the view through prison bars. The stars and the mud are two different things that you can focus on. But the bottle is one and the same thing. Then, is it *really* half full, or is it *really* half empty? In this case, the reality depends on how you want to see it, and life is often this way. If you think about the bottle as half full, you can be glad that it's there. If you think about it as half empty, well, you can already start getting sad.

If you want to, you can go right ahead and be sad over a half-empty life. You can go on and make your whole life miserable. There will always be something missing, something more that could have been there. If you keep focusing on what could have been, you will find life entirely empty.

We do that, and especially in this technologically sophisticated world. We are too aware of the options. The very breadth of known possibilities inclines us to be dissatisfied with what we actually have. We watch *Entertainment Tonight* and want to live like movie stars. We go to a movie and find real life dull in comparison. After all, by self-proclamation the movies are "larger than life."

I've talked with people who have traveled to distant and primitive communities. The travelers say that the people there are dirt poor but always laughing and singing. The fact is, they don't know what they're missing. Perhaps they are better off for it.

THE POWER OF POSITIVE THINKING

Of course, we would not want to go back to primitive and isolated conditions, but, in the face of the crazy-making world in which we live, we have to work hard to keep things in perspective. One way to begin is to attend to some of that teaching about positive thinking. It will not make everything right, but it is a good start. We may have lost the volley ball game, for example, but it is not the end of the world. We had fun playing, and that counts unless we were so serious about the game that we didn't even have fun. Then we've really got a problem.

I once asked a student after he finished an exam, "How was it?" On his face I could see his mind working through various responses. Finally he found the right phrase: "It was challenging." (It turned out that he aced the exam.) The word *challenge* has a more hopeful feel than *difficulty* or *problem*. *Challenge* leaves room for success with effort. Those other words suggest only running into a brick wall.

There are ways to developing positive thinking. The method is simple and only requires practice. You need to be tuned in to your internal thinking. At the very first inkling of a negative thought— "Oh, I'll never pass that test," "I'll never get that job," "I'm not good looking enough," "I knew I would mess that one up"—get a hold on the thought and stop it. Admit that you are thinking negatively. Find and admit to yourself the reasons why a negative thought might be appropriate. Realize that you are not crazy for being negative at this point, that there's nothing wrong with you. Then trace that thought back to its very root.

When you get to the root of that negative thought, challenge it intellectually. Come up with some realistic reason to show that your starting point is mistaken: "Why do I think I can't pass that test? When I've worked at it, I've passed others like it in the past." "I've had good jobs before, and in many ways I am a valuable employee. Why not get this new job?" "I may not a model, a twelve on a ten-point scale, but I am not ugly. Besides, I have a good sense of humor, and I can talk about many things. My personality makes up for my looks." "So I made a mistake. Big deal. Everybody makes mistakes once in a while. The world won't come to an end. Besides, sometimes I do very well for myself." Thus, cancel the negative thought at its root.

Repeat this exercise whenever a negative thought arises, and little by little you can break the habit of jumping to negative conclusions. Research has shown that in many cases this "mental hygiene" works as well as today's best medications for treating anxiety or depression.

Another way to combat negative thinking is to use affirmations, short statements of positive impact that you repeat to yourself: "Every day in every way, I am getting better and better and better." Affirmations work to pull us up short when we find ourselves starting down the slippery slope of negative thinking.

Alternative and positive ways of looking at things make life more hopeful. Jesus was into those ways. He was a very positive person. He was always able to find the good, to see the silver lining in every cloud. He saw goodness even where other people couldn't. "She's not dead; she's asleep," he said. And as the story turned out, he was not being unrealistic. It's not as if he was just living in a fantasy.

One detail in that story of Jairus's daughter is striking. This must be one of the strangest lines in all the gospels: When the girl got up, "He told them to give her something to eat." What does eating have to do with something so sublime as supposedly raising a girl from the dead? Not much, as far as any of us can see, and I bet nobody in that household would have thought of eating it either. But Jesus thought of it. He knew that the girl must be hungry after her illness and recent recovery and that she might need something to eat.

The practicality of Jesus is stunning. He is not off in some dream world. The unusual occurrences that happen through him do not blind him. He is squarely down to earth: "Give the child something to eat. She's hungry." Jesus was able to do what he did, not because he was some dreamer but, I think, because he was really down to earth. Of course, we need to admit that the gospels often exaggerate Jesus' accomplishments. They make him out to be a wonder-worker, and we might take their portrayal literally when their real purpose is not to report accurate history but to present a picture that will inspire us not to give up hope. The truth about Jesus that the gospels intend to convey is not factual accuracy about his every deed and word. The truth about Jesus is the saving power of his way of life.

Hardly a dreamer, Jesus was in touch with the depths of life. Profoundly present to his own self, he was also present to everything and everyone around him. Not caught up in his thoughts, fantasies, hopes, dreams, apprehensions, or emotions, he was always right there where he was, in the moment, actually present, attentive to what was actually going on. He was a down-to-earth man. Eastern philosophies would call him enlightened.

Jesus was so fully aware that he was in touch with the very depths of his being. There, Christian tradition tells us, he knew God in a way that no one else ever did. Ever aware of the Power of the Universe and its design for goodness that worked through and around him, he had good reason to trust, or, better said, he had core feelings of security. Then, even in the face of his own death, he trusted. Trusting his gut, he believed that God would somehow vindicate him, that God would not allow him to be simply written off. Goodness would prevail, and, since he identified with the good, somehow he, too, would overcome.

In some situations, we haven't a clue how we'll succeed or even survive. At times like these, raw curiosity sustained me. I wondered how things would ever work out, where my life would be in a year or two, what unforeseen shifts would occur in me or in my world. Luckily, at some level I was sure that somehow something would work out, and it became almost a game to just hold on, to wait and see. I wanted to be surprised. I had to be. I had no idea of a hopeful future.

That believing in "somehow something" must be akin to Jesus' experience on the cross as the evangelists wanted us to understand it. Mark, never afraid to portray Jesus in all his human weakness, does have Jesus expressing the despair that he must have felt: "My God, my God, why have you forsaken me?" (15:34). Mark gives us a Jesus with whom we can readily identify in all our pessimism. But in the face of despair, Luke nonetheless has Jesus trusting as he prays at the moment of death: "Father, into your hands I commend my spirit" (23:46).

Once again, overall the gospels present a positive perspective. Death is no bitter ending, an inevitable dismal demise; rather, death is the return to the Mystery from which we came. Death is the ultimate act of trust in the Gracious Power that gifted and surprised us—if we were able to recognize the blessing—all life's adventure long.

The optimism of Jesus can also be ours. In religious terms we would say that we have learned to trust in God, learned that God is good. The words from the book of Wisdom of Solomon 1:12–15, for example, announce God's goodness in this way: "God did not make death, nor does God rejoice in the death of the living. For God fashioned all things so that they might exist, the generative forces of the world are wholesome, and there is no destructive poison among them, and the domain of Hades is not on earth."

Those words are not a statement of dogma, some dogged insistence on creed. No, they are a religious expression of common human experience. With goodwill and luck—Divine Providence—we ourselves will accumulate such experience over the years. Through the ups and downs of life, hopefully, we will come to realize that "somehow something" does always work out. Life is a positive force. By nature it moves toward unfolding. Slowly but inevitably, it finds ways to rebuild and renew. The Power of the Universe is on the side of the positive. It does not rejoice in the destruction of the living, but all things are fashioned that they might have being.

Therefore, we really do have reason to be hopeful. It's not that we're practicing some hokey positive thinking, trying to convince ourselves that things are okay when they really are not. We know we will get sick. We know we will have heartache. We will lose loved ones. We will suffer huge disappointments. At times we will come near the breaking point. In the end, we will have to face death, and, most likely, also old age and failing health. But these things are not the most important. They need not dominate our lives. The joys and beauties of life can far outweigh the hardships. Oh, life is not perfect, but it is a real adventure. Would any sane person really prefer not to have been born at all? Even W. C. Fields, who had grown up in Philadelphia and absolutely hated the place, wanted carved on his tombstone: "All things considered, I'd rather be in Philadelphia."

Through the school of hard knocks, we can gradually learn that fundamentally life is okay. Then the actual lessons of life reinforce our exercises in positive thinking. As we build up a track record of fulfilled living, our thoughts and events work together and gradually dissolve the pessimism sedimented into our guts.

CHANGING THE DEPTHS OF OUR HEARTS

Still, the negativity among us is deep. Most of us are brought up on it, and some people get an extra dose of pessimism and self-hatred: racial minorities, sexual minorities, artists, and most people who are "different." As a result, it may be hard to learn optimism from the lessons of life and impossible to practice positive thinking without feeling like a fraud. In these cases, it will take something that goes to our core to effect the change. That something, in a word, is spirituality.

Said religiously, we need to be powerfully in touch with God, who is at the depth of all creation, and with the Holy Spirit, who is deep within our hearts. We need to be in touch with the positive Force of the Universe, the radical thrust toward being that works within and around us. Said less religiously but nonetheless truthfully, we need to get in touch with the positive energy that is our own human spirit. It is the most fully realized expression in us of the Power of the Universe, which pushes ever onward toward life, marvel, and delightful expansion.

The spiritual core of every human being is a delicate and beautiful flower that is rooted in the soil of the emotions and depends on these to blossom. When the ground of emotion is polluted and fouled, the spirit must struggle for life. It can hardly bloom. Crass and primitive forces easily overwhelm the spiritual subtleties of openness, wonder, marvel, and awe. So it is that, despite the encouraging lessons of life and our good-willed exercises in positive thinking, often and despite ourselves, we fall into despair when our dark emotions surge. Then, for the life of us, we can hardly manage to maintain a positive outlook. The tension, anxiety, insecurity, disappointment, and distrust that we picked up along life's path all too easily carry the day. The roots of our spiritual capacity are deeper than emotions, so deep, in fact, that they reach beneath the negativism with which we are brought up. These spiritual roots can swell and branch and undermine the ground of negative emotions. Then, the positive can thrive as the negative eventually withers and dies.

Spirituality is about paying attention to the deep and subtle urgings of the spirit. It is about nurturing the roots of the delicate flower of expansion, marvel, and delight within us. Given adequate attention, the radiance, clearness, beauty, and light of the spirit gradually break through and begin to shine. It is really possible to achieve such a positive outcome. Some of us are already on the way toward it. Just grappling with the issues I pose in this book will help us overcome much of the negativity in our social environment. Facing and resolving major questions of faith and ethics is a growth-producing experience. Breaking off an intense relationship, getting divorced, deciding to have a child, coming out as gay or lesbian, dealing with an unplanned pregnancy, making honest and fair business decisions, or facing sickness, death, and loss—any such experience is spiritually enriching when it results from good-willed openness to life. Acceptance of reality as we unavoidably see it is always a self-affirming experience: In effect, we choose to trust ourselves. Thus, we reinforce our natural tendencies toward openness, questioning, honesty, love, and commitment to life—pursuits that are spiritual. We grow spiritually just by living life honestly and lovingly.

Regular prayer and meditation also foster the life of the spirit. That is to say, they allow us time to connect with the subtle forces for positive growth that lie within us and to deliberately reinforce them. The very techniques of meditation help to push aside the cobwebs of negative emotions and enable us to dwell, if just for a moment, with the forces of life. Over the months and years, these moments of peaceful presence accumulate. Bit by bit our spiritual capacity begins to dominate our minds. Gradually, naturally, surprisingly, a positive outlook begins to take hold. Our minds become like that of Jesus. The brightness of the good catches our attention, and the dismal feelings of gloom lose out. I treat this matter in detail in *Meditation without Myth*.

That same transformative process is at work when we gather together for prayer. Public worship is a powerful force: Just like theater, concerts, art shows, pep rallies, sporting events, parades, and political conventions. These secular events often release spiritual experiences for religious and nonreligious people alike. When people pool their enthusiasm, all are empowered beyond their individual capacity. This effect is real whether the gathering be secular or religious. Surefire social mechanisms are at work in public worship. When the music is moving, the preaching inspiring, the ritual finely executed, religious ceremony touches the heart, just like good theater. Memories pour out, emotions soften, tears flow, ideas crystallize, hopes reemerge, and the human heart is renewed. Transformation occurs. The tears wash away the disappointments of the past, and the built-in negativity weakens. At the same time, the life-loving power of the human spirit is released.

Because of my very mixed opinions about organized religion, people are often surprised to learn that I continue to attend weekly Mass. Of course, I make sure to find a church whose liturgies are well done. I go to church because I need to be inspired, and I need to be reminded periodically about the spiritual dimensions of life. Good liturgies fulfill these needs in me, so I gratefully take advantage of the services. I do not expect anything magical to happen in my life because I go to church, and I do not believe that God is "angry" or "punishes" people for not going. I certainly do not attend Mass out of any sense of obligation or guilt. I find going to church helpful, so I do it. I only wish that everyone could find a church that makes a positive contribution to his or her life.

It is important for us who have outgrown our religion to be committed to spiritual practices. We need to set aside time on a regular basis to attend to the things of the spirit. This is something we have to do. Just as we eat every day and just as we exercise regularly, we also need to attend regularly to our spirit in prayer, reflective reading, meditation, and public events. When we do, we gradually transform ourselves. Only in this way can we finally secure a positive outlook while living in a negative world.

DEALING WITH SERIOUS DEPRESSION

Yet, from time to time, even this advice is all too optimistic for many of us. Some of us labor under the heavy burden of clinical depression. Biological weaknesses may have been inherited, years of oppression mount up, ongoing stress exacts a cost, ingrown hostility solidifies, and together these forces take their toll. The power of negative forces so overwhelms us that we are simply unable to transcend them on our own. Luckily, today there is help even for clinical depression; no one needs to live in that darkness. The solution in this case is to seek professional help. The practice of psychotherapy has come a long way since Freud, and many skilled therapists are available to help us exhume and discard the garbage of our past and, by so doing, free our spirits to soar and allow us to delight in the adventure of life.

The mechanisms of psychotherapeutic change are the very same ones that are at work in prayer, meditation, and liturgy. The key is to unlock the psyche so that ossified emotions and memories can flow freely. Then, by virtue of the spiritual drive within us, healthy and positive, resurrecting occurs. Life reasserts itself. This same process occurs on many occasions in life: intimate conversation, vacations, theater, concerts, civic celebrations, school programs, political rallies, sporting events. In psychotherapy, a trained professional triggers these mechanisms, focuses their effect, and helps the client to stick with the process. When we are too bottled up inside ourselves, the natural healing processes of life are not enough to loose us. We need professional help. Such help can cautiously disarm our defenses and open us up to needed healing and growth.

Religious believers will readily recognize the workings of God in the psychotherapeutic process, for, indeed, *God* means precisely the Creator of, and Power behind, everything that is. So faith in God should not keep us naïve regarding spirituality and its natural processes. Enough of these limp religious responses to depression: "Trust in God," "Don't lose faith," and "God's grace is sufficient." When people are deeply discouraged, such exhortation rings absolutely hollow. The very problem is that people are no longer able to trust or believe or hope. This very effect is what depression means!

Appealing baldly to grace as some miraculous nostrum is reaching for pie in the sky. Of course, in some way we can rightly call the psychotherapeutic process "grace." It is ultimately from

God, as is everything in some way. It rescues people from despair, and it opens doors to unexpected new life. Truly, it is an amazing grace. However, we now have some understanding about how God's "grace" in this case works, so we have the responsibility to foster it actively. The day is long gone when theological jargon can pass for effective help. Today, religion without psychological understanding is like navigation without a compass or medicine without biology or long-distance communication without electronics—a hit or miss affair.

Another blessing of the current age is the development of psychotropic drugs. People who are deeply depressed need them and often benefit from them. Yet some religious people are reluctant to take antidepressants; they prefer to "trust in God." What a sham of religion such thinking represents! These recent discoveries are precisely the help that God is now offering. To wait for a miracle when more routine assistance is available is not religion but superstition.

People sometimes hesitate to use psychoactive drugs because they are not natural, but what does *natural* mean? If we were to shun anything that did not come with us out of the womb, we would soon be dead. In this sense, eyeglasses and contact lenses are not natural, but we wear them without batting an eye. But from another perspective, eyeglasses are completely natural, for they work by respecting and applying the laws of nature called *optics*.

Of course, introducing synthetic chemicals into the central nervous system is a much more serious matter than putting on eyeglasses. Granted, too, our mechanistic society is all too ready to solve our problems with pills, and for motives of greed, the pill pushers downplay the seriousness of taking medication. Every drug has side effects, and the long-term side effects of many psychotropic drugs are still unknown. No medication should be taken casually. Nevertheless, when all else fails and a wasted life, or even suicide, is the likely alternative, popping some pills is the sane, wholesome, and responsible thing to do. The risk to life outweighs the risk of side effects.

To my mind, antidepressants are like a crutch: Nobody likes to use one, and everybody looks forward to throwing it away, but until you can do without it, a crutch is a handy thing to have. It gives the healing processes a chance to work. Coupled with good psychotherapy—and it is frightening to realize that the managed-health movement often just dispenses pills and refuses to pay for therapy—modern medications are another of God's graces. By altering the very chemical balance in the brain, they can short-circuit negative thinking and ward off depressive emotions. Then we are provided a breathing space and with professional help we can learn to look at life more optimistically. Then, the ineluctable process of spiritual emergence has a chance to reassert itself.

THE PROMISE OF FULLNESS OF LIFE

Living among a people of doom, we often become people of doom ourselves. We are a strange people, more alert to what's wrong than what's right. Jesus offers a different picture. His focus is on the good. Attuned in his heart to the positive Power of the Universe simply by being himself, he exhibits optimism even in the face of death. Similar optimism can be ours as we become more spiritually integrated.

SIXTEEN

THE CURRENT CULTURE SHIFT: MOTHER GOD, SISTER MARY, AND HOMOSEXUAL PROPHETS

BELOVED, let us love one another, because love is from God; everyone who loves is born of God and knows God. Whoever does not love does not know God, for God is love. — 1 JOHN 4:7–8

THEN HIS MOTHER and his brothers came; and standing outside, they sent to him and called him. A crowd was sitting around him; and they said to him, "Your mother and your brothers and sisters are outside, asking for you." And he replied, "Who are my mother and my brothers?" And looking at those who sat around him, he said, "Here are my mother and my brothers!

> Whoever does the will of God is my brother and sister
> and mother." —MARK 3:31–35

EVERY MAY WE CELEBRATE Mother's Day. We honor
mothers throughout the nation. The occasion is relevant to us all.
Everyone has a mother, known or unknown, liked or disliked,
happy or sad, however it may be. Besides, many who are reading
these words are or will be mothers. It is important to reflect on
motherhood.

When we reflect in a religious context, a broader theme
emerges, or at least this broader theme emerges for me. I think
not only of our mothers on this earth, but I begin to think of God,
too, as the source of life. I think of our being children of God, and
so I begin to think of God as mother.

CHILDREN OF GOD

The scriptures point in that direction. They say that whoever
loves is begotten of God; those who love are born of God. Then
Jesus gives us his supreme commandment: that we love one another. Elsewhere in John's gospel, Jesus speaks about how God
would come and live in us who love and keep his word. The overall idea is that all of us in Christ are born unto God's life. We are
God's children.

Let us briefly recall what our being children of God means. It
does not mean only that we were created by God, because everything in the world was created by God. According to Christian
belief, it also means that, over and above our created, human life,
God has chosen to give us a share in eternal, divine life. It is not
just that we have human life, and even the best of what human life
might offer, but in Christ we are destined to share in Divinity. We
are to become like God. We are to be deified. I explained this
matter in the chapter on the wedding at Cana.

In a very profound sense, then, we can say that we truly are

God's children. God has adopted us. God has introduced us into the divine family. We belong with those three divine ones—Father, Son, and Holy Spirit—who live in eternity. Sitting alongside Jesus, the only-begotten child of God, we adopted children, his human brothers and sisters, take our place at the heavenly table. It is as if Jesus took us, his playmates, home with him, and we have become members of the family. With God's own Spirit in us, with the gift of Divinity in our own hearts, like Jesus we can rightly look to God as Father. This is the specific sense in which Christians speak about being children of God.

GOD AS FATHER—AND MOTHER

When the evangelists wrote about this matter, they used the word that Jesus himself used. Even as Jesus taught us to pray—"Our Father, who art in heaven"—the apostles spoke of God as "Father." We even find the Aramaic word for "father" in some places in the New Testament, though the Christian Testament was originally written in Greek. This remnant of Aramaic suggests that this word really was Jesus' own. It is one of the few words about which we can say: "This is the very word that Jesus himself used." The word is *Abba*. It means "Father," but a more accurate translation is "Daddy."

Strange that Jesus would refer to God in that way. However, he was not absolutely the first to do so. In fact, that usage was offensive to the Jews of Jesus' day. It was common for a child, even a grown person, to address his or her father as *Abba*—Daddy—but no one would address God in that way. The word is much too intimate. It suggests too much closeness. Yet Jesus talked to God as father, daddy, abba.

Jesus could not have done much better in his day. Saying Mommy or Mother would just not have worked. The reasons are sad. The place of women in the culture of Jesus' day was even worse than in our day. In the time of Jesus, the father was the center of the family, who provided the family with an identity. The father was the source of love and compassion as well as the source of discipline. The father owned everything. The wife and children, as well as animals and other property, belonged to the father. Thus, it would only make sense in Jesus' day, when he wanted to speak of God in a very intimate way, to speak of God as daddy, usage that worked perfectly well in his culture. But cultures change. Couldn't we use different words today to express what Jesus said in his way in his day? Of course.

Women do not have the place they used to have. Now we are beginning, at least, to see that women can be equals with men. We certainly revere mothers as much as (and probably more than) we do fathers. Under these circumstances it could be quite appropriate to address God as Mother.

Addressing God as Mother would also be correct theologically. Traditional trinitarian theology holds that the relationship between Jesus as the Son and God as the Father is that of being born. This relationship is the sum and substance of the distinction between Father and Son: The one begets, and the other is begotten. Therefore, they both are God, yet, as individuals, the one coming from the other, the one could not be the other.

There is a peculiar phrase in the decree of the Council of Constance (1414–1418). It speaks of the Son as being born of the "womb of the Father." Now isn't that a real mix of male and female! Doesn't it put the feminine into God! The reason for those unisex words is to emphasize the fact of being born, the generation of one person from another.

However, if the essence of the relationship between the Father and the Son is "bornness," talk of God as Mother would certainly preserve that essence. Thus, theologically, it would be perfectly correct to speak of God the Father also as God the Mother. Talk of God the Mother retains the notion of generation.

ANTIFEMALE BIAS IN
SOCIETY AND RELIGION

In our day there is good reason to change the way we talk of God. Not only is the place of women in society at such a level that we could appropriately speak of God in feminine terms, there also seems to be a need to do so. We have come to realize that a powerful male bias rules our culture. Our culture is patriarchal, run for and by men.

The fact is blatant in church services when there's a man up front, in charge of everything and surrounded by male assistants. Only rarely will we see a woman leading a religious service. In the Catholic Church it is alleged that Christ's will forbids the ordination of women. Other Christian churches advance similar arguments. There is considerable historical evidence and theological opinion to the contrary, but the Vatican and many Protestant denominations or segments within them have taken a hard line. This very fact makes obvious how patriarchal Western society remains. Almost anywhere in our society, men are dominant and women are subordinate.

Antifemale attitudes lie at the core of Western tradition and Christianity. The Greek poet Hesiod, a contemporary of Homer, wrote of women, "Awe filled immortal gods and mortal men when they saw the sheer trick, irresistible to men. . . . High thundering Zeus made an evil: women, the partners of evil works." And elsewhere Hesiod wrote: "He ordered Hermes Argeiphontes, the messenger, to put in her a bitch's mind and deceiving behavior . . . lies and sly stories, and deceitful behavior." Aristotle's opinion, almost the very opposite of what contemporary biology knows, was that a woman is a mutilated male. The influential, second-century Latin Father of the Church, Tertullian, said of women: "You are the devil's gateway! . . . What is seen with the eyes of the Creator is masculine and not feminine, for God does not stoop to look on what is feminine and of the flesh." Similarly, the fourth-century Greek bishop and saint Epiphanius wrote: "The female sex is easily seduced, weak, and without much understanding. The devil seeks to vomit out this disorder [sexual desire] through women." Negative stereotypes about women have embarrassingly impressive pedigrees.

Masculine dominance is also blatant in the core symbols of

Western religion. We speak of God as male: God, He; God the Father; God the Son. Even in reference to the Holy Spirit, we say "He." (I am not suggesting that the Holy Spirit is female. God is neither. I am only pointing out the consistent masculine bias in our language about God.) The overall impact of this usage is to suggest that God is masculine. The suggestion is that the highest, the supreme, the most sublime, the most important of realities, God, is identified with the male. Until flagged and challenged, this masculine bias operates subtly but powerfully. Silently and corrosively, it seeps into the psyche.

A parishioner once told me a "cute" story about her four-year-old daughter. While saying her prayers, with deep concern the little girl looked up to her mother and asked, "Mommy, was Jesus always a boy? Wasn't he *ever* a girl?"

You could write this comment off, as the mother herself did, as an indication of the fluidity of gender identity at that young girl's tender age. Yet the girl was already well aware that she was a girl, not a boy, so she was not like Jesus, who was not a girl. There is something else that caught my attention here. In her spontaneity and innocence, this little girl was saying that she found it difficult to identify with a Highest Power who is always male.

Her mother explained to the little girl that Jesus was a man, not a woman, so he was never a little girl, but that he loves her nonetheless. Undoubtedly, within a few years, the spontaneous resistance to patriarchal bias was stamped out of that insightful girl, and she stopped asking embarrassing questions and, like her mother, learned to play the gender roles that society imposes. But she was right to raise that question, and others are doing the same.

We all know in our minds, of course, that God is neither male nor female, but when we picture God, what do we see? When we have feelings about God, what do we feel? Our rational mind is not really what controls us. Our heart is what controls us, and in our hearts we tend to imagine God as male—just as we were taught to do in our most impressionable years. The unavoidable

implication of that training is that women are really not as important as men because God is male, not female.

That unspoken teaching has a negative effect on people, both
women and men. Subtly it gives men a demeaning notion of
women. The fact that women can be set on a pedestal is only an
exaggerated reaction to the put-down. The need for the token
pedestal only proves that the put-down is real.

Consider how men insult other men by calling them "girl" or
"sissy" or some other more vulgar names associated with the female. Such hostility toward anything feminine has been standard
in military and athletic training. Many boys and men understand
their masculinity only in the negative terms of "nonfemale." To be
a man one must harbor hostility to all that is womanly. Such an attitude produces a culture of rape. Our boys grow up in a society
that nurtures and supports the physical abuse of women. Cross-
cultural studies of rape have shown this situation to be so.

At the same time, a patriarchal culture also puts a burden on
men. Everything rests on their shoulders, and they can hardly afford to let go, relax, and just be themselves. One of the main reasons that transvestites cross-dress is to be free for a while from the
pressures of being a man in our society and to be able to enjoy
pretty clothes as women do. More commonly, men use alcohol as
a way to "break the tension," a practice that we promote, and then
we wonder why we have a drug problem in our society. Blatantly
supporting the dysfunctional patriarchy and subtly undermining
the men's liberation movement, a two-page *Newsweek* ad for De-
war's whiskey read: "You don't have to beat a drum or hug a tree
to be a man." The unspoken message was that all you need do is
drink. An ad on a restaurant table pushed desserts with these
words atop pictures of cakes and pies: "Too full, sissy?"

In the meantime, little girls grow up with a secret sense of infe-
riority. To achieve success, they are made to believe that they must
marry and stand behind a "good" man. Thus they learn to be coy,
attractive, and sexually enticing. Attempting to match the impos-

sible models they see on TV and in magazines, they stop achieving in math and science when they get to high school; they starve themselves into bulimic and anorexic slenderness; and they spend billions of dollars on cosmetics and other beauty products. They make themselves into sex objects, and all this just seems natural. We smile to see girls grow up and start primping themselves for the boys. We think it sweet when they begin to act like "mature women." We never stop to think that the reddening of lips and cheeks and the mascara-enlarged eyes mimic facial features during sexual arousal. We expect our women to walk around as if they are always turned on, ready and waiting for a man. Recent studies of TV programming, music videos, and teen magazines show that, despite some androgyny here and there, these gender stereotypes control the media as much as they ever did.

It is easy for women to accept their place because, from earliest childhood, they are taught to look up to a male god just as they are taught to respect their husbands and obey their male bosses. The whole system holds together quite consistently, and, as a system, it works beautifully. The only problem is its incalculable human waste.

THE MALE GOD

We are now well aware of destructive forces built into our society, and, make no mistake, they are linked to our masculine image of God. The image of the Father God puts the ultimate seal of approval on the patriarchal system that we have inherited and that we so dutifully maintain.

Since we are now aware of these facts, we have a responsibility to do something about this situation. It is wrong for us to go on speaking of God always as male, period. This way of speaking hurts all of us, so we are morally bound to change it. Not only is it theologically correct to broaden our image of God, our culture is opening up to such a change. We have a moral responsibility to effect it. We need to talk of God as Our Mother. The Vatican's pronouncement, that on Jesus' example God must always be imaged as Father, must be seen for what it is: a blatantly self-serving, political move to protect the all-male power structure of the Catholic Church.

Here's another, little-recognized facet of the problem: There are women among us who are not particularly attracted to men. They have little affection for men in the romantic sense of the word. But if lesbian women have only a male God to relate to, what does this state of affairs do to them? Bad enough that Jesus was always a boy and never a girl! There is no getting around this reality: He was male, not female. He had to be one or the other, but there's no need to make a point of it.

The emphasis of Christian tradition has always been on Christ's *humanness*. The point was never that God incarnated as a male. Until the 1977 Vatican document *Inter Insigniores*, which forbade the ordination of women, I had never seen an official church document, in Greek or Latin, that linked Jesus' saving work to his maleness. But to describe Jesus, that document used the Latin term *vir*, which means "a man, a male." In consistent contrast, Christianity always used the generic terms for a "human being"—*homo* in Latin and *anthropos* in Greek—to refer to Christ. Unfortunately, in Catholic documents these words are translated "man," so in English the Vatican's shift in teaching has gone unrecognized. The Vatican made a major change.

No longer insisting that Jesus was human, one of us, the Vatican now emphasizes that Jesus was male and, for this reason, forbids women's ordination. Similarly, the current translation of the Nicene Creed, dating back to 325 and recited every Sunday in many churches, still states: "For us men and our salvation, he became man." But the original Greek and its Latin translation read: "For us humans . . . he became human." The recent Vatican emphasis on Jesus' maleness is a blatant departure from Christian tradition. By all standard criteria, it is heresy! Christianity had always celebrated the all-inclusive humanity of Christ, not his maleness.

If not only the human Jesus but also the Eternal God are portrayed as male, where does that leave women who have no spontaneous attraction to men? It leaves lesbian women in a particularly difficult and unnecessarily unfair situation. If they are to be religious in any standard way, they need somehow to relate to God. Yet a male god must be of little interest to them.

This problem of gender in God is relatively recent. For centuries Christianity has more or less gotten along without these complications. Thus, conservative types wonder what all the fuss is about. They suggest that people just "suck it in" and go along with the (supposed) traditional formulas. Such an attitude is unacceptable for anyone concerned about the welfare of people. Contemporary psychology has made us aware of the profound implications of these matters; it is psychologically destructive to force people into prefabricated conceptual boxes.

This psychological insight is certainly relevant to issues of God and religion. Thus, the churches' diehard insistence on masculine images of God shows that the churches are, in reality, not concerned about people.

I sadly realized this cruel fact in the case of the Catholic Church when I was a naïve, newly ordained priest. I watched the official church systematically destroy a best friend and his colleagues, priests of the Archdiocese of Washington, D.C., involved in a controversy over birth control. More recently, the silencing of the already silenced Sr. Jeannine Gramick and Fr. Robert Nugent—founders of New Ways Ministry, an educational service to gays and lesbians, absolutely orthodox, the most respectful of Catholic teaching among all gay-supportive Catholic outreach programs—demonstrates that the Vatican continues its ruthless ways into the third millennium.

From Methodist and Baptist families, as well as Catholic ones, I have heard stories of how people were rejected from their church, cut off from friendship and social support, declared anathema to "faithful church members" because of a divorce, ho mosexuality, or some other "failure unworthy of Jesus." Too often the churches conveniently forget the real Jesus so that they can emphasize their own teachings, close ranks, exercise power, and make big money. Often the churches do not seem really to be concerned about people.

GOD THE MOTHER

In fact, God is neither male nor female; so we can speak of God as Father, but we can also equally well and equally correctly speak of God as Mother. We can even mix and match our metaphors. I have come to like the combination "Mother-Father-God." I vividly remember the first time I heard that expression. I was living in Boston, and I went to see a multimedia promotional called *Where's Boston?* It was wonderfully done with music and narration and a whole array of screens and multiple images. It highlighted the many sides of Bostonian life. Religion was one of the topics. Along with pictures of churches, steeples, and choirs, there boomed the voice of a progressive minister. He prayed in a liturgical lilt, "Oh, Mother-Father-God!" and I could not keep myself from laughing out loud. The thing sounded so silly to me, so artificial, so contrived, and, I thought, so unnecessary.

How our upbringing, habits, and comfortable routines control what our minds and hearts will allow! I could not take that prayer seriously, not the first time I heard it. I had never considered that one might pray to God as Mother.

I remember another occasion when a community of young religious women asked me to say Mass for them and to do it with only feminine images for God. The experience was uncomfortable for me, but I changed in the process. As I got more familiar with the novelty and grew in understanding, not only did I open to new formulas, I have become adamant about them.

I like the title Father-Mother-God precisely because the notion is weird. It is shocking to speak of a mother-father; there is no such thing in our experience. That unfamiliarity is appropriate because God is not like us. When we have to use a strange and cumbersome way to talk about God, we are reminded over and over that God is not like us. Trying to deal with God, we constantly have to adjust ourselves and adapt; we continually have to open ourselves to broader understanding.

In much the same way, the ancient Hebrews struggled with talk about God. They forbade pronunciation of the Holy Name, so they had to find circumlocutions. The ancient Jews substituted *Adonai* for "the Name". To this day nobody is sure how the tetragrammaton, the four-letter name of God, YHWH, is to be pronounced. Some say Yahweh; some say Jehovah. Out of respect for Jewish tradition, we should say nothing. The point is that no one should pretend to know God's name. No creature can name God. No one can declare what God is. Said secularly, no one understands what it's all about.

In a similar fashion, the ancient Jews were forbidden to have images of God. Images turn into idols. Images let people think they know what God is like just as names let people think they have a hold on God. Many religious people have not learned that ancient Jewish lesson. Somehow we think we know what God is, so we reject new names, and we laugh at strange names for God just as I did. But the oddity of the names is the very point: God is not anything we can name.

Avoiding the gender issues of Mother or Father, sometimes I speak of God simply as Parent. Perhaps this name sounds too clinical, like referring to your sisters and brothers as "my siblings." But even that, we are getting used to. And we can expand the name Parent and soften it to form Loving Parent or Eternal Parent.

I am suggesting that we might consider God as mother: warm, caring, compassionate, loving, taking us to her breasts, holding us closely, wiping away our tears, communicating a secret strength, providing a sense of security, being there in constancy. All these qualities that we associate with mothers apply very, very well to God. God is mother to us, and more.

MARY: MOTHER OF GOD
AND SISTER TO US

Begin to think of God as mother, and other devotional issues arise. This new understanding of God casts Mary, the mother of Jesus, in a different role.

John (19:26–27) recounts how, on the cross, Jesus asked the beloved disciple to take care of his mother, or so it might seem: "When Jesus saw his mother and the disciple whom he loved standing beside her, he said to his mother, 'Woman, here is your son.' Then he said to the disciple, 'Here is your mother.' And from that hour the disciple took her into his own home."

John's portrayal of this scene at the foot of the cross expresses a gospel theme noted first in the earliest of the gospels, Mark 3:35: "Whoever does the will of God is my brother and sister and mother." So, even from the cross, as portrayed by John, Jesus is still in his teaching role. His message is that his biological mother, Mary, and the beloved disciple are united in the spiritual family of the true followers of Jesus. The point is not that Jesus wanted someone to take care of his mother, though such concern is certainly a worthy consideration. The point is that spiritual commitment is what constitutes true family.

The beloved disciple in John's Gospel may not be an actual historical person but is, or also functions as, a symbol of all faithful Christians. Thus, in light of Jesus' words from the cross, "Here is your mother," Christian tradition has taken Mary to be the mother of all Christians, and devotion to Mother Mary has become a part of Christianity, especially in Catholicism and Eastern Orthodoxy.

From a psychological point of view, in the churches where God was and is officially conceived unfailingly as male, devotion to the "Blessed Virgin Mary" always filled a vacuum. It supplied a feminine image. Unfortunately, because of excesses in Marian devotion in Catholicism and because of hostility toward Catholicism, that vacuum was left unfilled in the mainline Protestant churches. Their services often have remained stark, emphasizing preaching—that is, the intellectual—and lacking the warmth and softness of the heart.

There seems to be a natural human need for a feminine dimension in religion. So Mary was exalted, sometimes to an extreme, it must be admitted. The feminine aspect of religion is so important that the great psychologist Carl Jung suggested that Mary herself actually be acknowledged as divine. This change would supply the missing feminine dimension in traditional notions of God. Theologically, Jung's suggestion has major problems, but psychologically and historically, it is right on target. We need a feminine focus in Christianity, and Mary filled that role.

Anyone familiar with Mexican-American culture will recognize the important role that Mary plays as Our Lady of Guadalupe. This devotion emerged precisely to fill a gap. Very soon after the Spaniards had left the Americas, French missionaries, for the most part, organized the churches. At least this is true for the areas that now comprise Texas and the southwestern United States. The Sisters of Divine Providence, the Sisters of the Incarnate Word, the Oblates of Mary Immaculate, the first bishop of Galveston—all these people were French, and they brought with them a tinge of their Jansenism. Jansenism was a very legalistic, strict, ascetic version of Catholicism that emerged in seventeenth-century France. The warm, indigenous peoples could not relate to it. The God of a Jansenist clergy would just not do, so the religious sentiment of the native peoples flowed toward the *Guadalupana*, Our Lady of Guadalupe. This devotion thrived and gave their Christianity a heart. For Hispanic Catholics and others, as well, Mary provides a feminine complement to the hypermale image of God.

What happens when we allow feminine images of God and begin to see God as mother? One significant result is that Mary gets displaced. There is no longer a need to exalt her in her motherhood. This statement is not to minimize the fact that Mary was the mother of Jesus, that she played a pivotal role in salvation history, and that, as such, she is often acknowledged as a spiritual mother to Christian believers. Yet, if God is mother, we do not need to look so insistently to Mary as mother, and we become aware that the motherhood of God and Mary must be taken in very different senses.

As a devotion, the motherhood of Mary declines. Then, as Catholicism's Second Vatican Council portrays her, Mary becomes, rather, a sister to us, a fellow believer, a model for Christians. It is precisely in this sense that the Gospels portray Mary, especially the Gospels of Luke and John. For Luke, Mary is "full of grace," a "highly favored one" (Luke 1:28), not because she was the biological mother of Jesus but because she "believed that there would be a fulfillment of what was spoken to her by the Lord" (Luke 1:45). Mary is seen as a disciple of Jesus; she is one of "those who hear the word of God and keep it" (Luke 11:28).

Luke actually portrays Mary as the first disciple. The moment of discipleship for her came when she heard God speak to her "through an angel," as the scriptures tell it. As portrayed by Luke, her response was similar to the one that Jesus taught in the Lord's Prayer: "Thy will be done on earth as it is in heaven." Mary said to the angel, "Here am I, the servant of the Lord; let it be with me according to your word" (Luke 1:38). So, before all else, she who is the mother of Jesus is one who does the will of God. According to Jesus' criterion, she is family to Jesus, not because of biology, but because of willing response to God.

This recent recovery of Gospel teaching is of major importance for contemporary Christianity. The Catholic emphasis on Mary has been a serious stumbling block for the ecumenical movement of the twentieth century. Now new appreciation of the Gospels' picture of Mary balances the understanding on both the Protestant and Catholic fronts. Recognizing that the New Testament itself holds Mary up as the model Christian, Protestantism can acknowledge that it has neglected the figure of Mary, and Catholicism can acknowledge that its devotion to Mary has often been excessive. Both can now move to a middle position and meet in agreement there. Bible-based consensus on Mary becomes a unifying point among Christian churches.

SPIRITUAL, NOT BIOLOGICAL, FAMILY

On an occasion when the disciples came to Jesus to say that his mother and brothers were outside looking for him, Jesus announced that fidelity to God's will is the criterion of family. In fact, his family had come to take him away because "people were saying 'He has gone out of his mind'" (Mark 3:21). Jesus' somewhat offensive response insisted on a difference between biological and spiritual family. He said, "'Who are my mother and my brothers?' And looking at those who sat around him, he said, 'Here are my mother and my brothers! Whoever does the will of God is my brother and sister and mother'" (Mark: 3:33–35). Luke, Matthew, and John soften this response of Jesus as reported in Mark and increasingly understand Mary as a faithful disciple who does, indeed, belong to that inner circle.

Consistent throughout the Gospels, however, Jesus' point is challenging: the bond of physical relationship is not what matters but, rather, a spiritual bond of common commitment to God, to all that is right and good. Those who do the will of God are Jesus' family, and in this way Mary qualified as family to him. Whereas we say, "Blood is thicker than water," Jesus says that fidelity to God is more telling than blood.

Jesus' way of thinking is encouraging to many people who have difficult home situations. His teaching speaks to abused children, alcoholics or drug addicts, and gays and lesbians—all who might need to leave their families to maintain sanity and health. Sad to say, rather than being a loving support system, families are sometimes a bad influence, so people cannot afford to remain in them. For survival's sake, people sometimes need to cut all ties to family members and find new friends who are like mother and father, sister and brother—a new family.

This very same teaching of Jesus can be an inspiration to people who, for whatever reason, suffer the loss of their loving biological families. If "home is where the heart is," then, for people of good-will, *family* means people who share a common commitment to goodness. Distant from family and feeling the loss, people often need to turn to such spiritual family for support and companion-ship. In these situations, people can find the support they need to follow the teaching of Jesus. On the word of Jesus, if not yet through personal experience or official legal recognition, they can rest assured that loving housemates and friends truly make a family.

GOD'S CALL TO THE UNCONVENTIONAL

The lesson thus far is clear: As disciples of Jesus, we are to stand in the same position as Mary. We, too, are to say yes to God even if our circumstances are strange, and, if such be the case, we need to identify that strangeness correctly. The peculiarity was not that Mary saw an angel. I certainly do not believe that an angel literally appeared to Mary and spoke audible words to her. I do not believe that we come to know God's will by hearing voices, seeing visions, or having extraordinary religious experiences, altered states of consciousness. These would more likely—and deservedly so—lead us to a psychiatrist.

Religious talk of visions and voices should be taken metaphori-cally. Luke's portrayal of the matter in Mary's case is simply the biblical way of saying in images what we would say in words: The work of God surrounded the birth of Jesus. How Mary's realiza-tion of God's call actually occurred, as in our own cases, had none of the magic and glamour that Renaissance paintings attribute to it. Nonetheless, let's play with the narrative as it stands and see what more we can learn.

The strangeness of Mary's case as portrayed in the Gospels was this: Her visit from the angel involved sex. It was a question of conceiving a child in an unconventional way, which was bound to be misunderstood, to say the least. She was having a child out of wedlock. This birth could lead to all kinds of complications. She knew that it would, and despite it all, she said, "Thy will be done."

Thus, Mary becomes relevant to us. She makes a fine model for us. She is the one who tells us to say yes to God's will, even in unusual and sexually related circumstances, like struggling with one's sexuality, going through a divorce, or dealing with a pregnancy.

Mary still remains an important figure in Christianity. Although she is traditionally used as a model of sexual "purity," this "virgin mother" is also important to us who are dealing with sexual questions. She becomes our model, our big sister, our spiritual mother. Her story inspires us to trust in God. Seeing her in this way, we can look to her as one who encourages us to be ourselves. She wants us to do exactly as she did. Accept the will of God. Be honest about our situations. Accept ourselves as we are. Trust God's wisdom in all cases. Find the good in whatever happens. Make the best of every situation. Dare to take a courageous and creative stance.

AT A CULTURAL TURNING POINT

How far-reaching these matters of gender and religion are! How monumental this overturning of centuries-long understandings! These matters touch and shake the very core of Western civilization. They call for rethinking the very meaning of *man* and *woman*, the masculine and feminine, God and humanity.

To think of God as Mother introduces into Protestantism the long-absent feminine principle. To think of God as Mother displaces devotion to Mary from a central position in Catholicism. To think of God as both Mother and Father and as neither challenges all men and women to shift their way of relating to one another. Being male or female begins not to matter as much as being a human being, a person. The physical gives way to the spiritual. Gender and sexual orientation cease to be significant. The biological makes room for the interpersonal.

If our times are turbulent, if strong emotional conflicts arise, if people resist the new ways, if others are impatient for change, if many are dazed and confused, if we fear that the very ground under our feet is giving way, none of these matters should surprise us. Our generation is experiencing one of the greatest culture shifts in history. Perhaps more than at any other time, our psyches are being assaulted. We are being forced to restructure our most basic perceptions of reality.

It is very difficult to put forward to most people considerations of gender such as these. One would have to be very careful raising such issues before most Sunday congregations or parent-teacher associations. Yet people who are already on the outside looking in tend to grasp these matters intuitively. I've seen this very effect when working with the gay community. I've been surprised at how easily gay audiences understand my approach to spirituality and, in contrast, how other audiences are downright baffled, if not offended, by my thoughts. Among gays, such thinking comes easily. Such sensitivity, such penetrating awareness, is part of a spiritual giftedness that often accompanies homosexuality. Not fitting in from an early age, we tend to see through societal trappings more quickly than others do. We know that the emperor has no clothes. We tend to get to the heart of social matters more easily and to focus on deeper realities like honesty, love, and justice. We tend to look on people as people and not as social categories. Thus, in many ways the lesbian and gay community is prophetic—which is one of the premises of this book.

But these issues of gender roles and stereotypes are important for everyone, not just for gays. These issues go to the very core of our religion and to the very core of our culture and society. When one touches the raw nerve of sexual identity and sexual and gender stereotypes, the whole of the body politic begins to twitch.

Understandably, people on the fringe of church and society are more open to these considerations than are people who are invested in the establishment. In a unique way, God calls the outcasts to be God's children, even as Jesus noted in rebuke of the chief priests and elders of his day: "Truly I tell you, the tax collectors and the prostitutes are going into the kingdom of God ahead of you" (Matthew 21:31). Seeing through the trappings of social and religious "requirements" is difficult, but less so for those whose very constitution relegates them to the sidelines: homosexuals, African Americans, women, Jews, Muslims, disenfranchised immigrants, disillusioned youth, artists, all so-called outsiders.

THE LAST SHALL BE FIRST

Irony of ironies! Blessed are the poor! Blessed are the meek! Blessed are those who suffer persecution for justice's sake! We religious and social outsiders have insights that others do not. Thus, we, of all people, become the pathfinders. We are the prophets. We are the spiritual and social guides for our brothers and sisters. We need to pray for, that is, maintain goodwill toward, all of them. And we need to remain true to our special calling and vision. We need to remember what our gifts are.

Although the churches tend to reject us, we must not, in turn, reject ourselves or squander the spiritual wealth that has been our peculiar gift. Precisely because of our outsider status, it is we who have the spiritual insight that church is supposed to foster. Turning perhaps away from the church, we must not turn from the spiritual path. Lonely, at first, on this path, we will surely find fellow travelers. Like Mary, the "big sister" whom we look up to, we can accept ourselves, embrace our situation, and see an occasion for good in our particular lot. Like Mary, we can say "Yes, Thy will be done," as we look on God as a loving Mother. Thinking outside the religious box, we and others like us—let this be noted!—*we* will blaze the spiritual trail for our global community into the third millennium.

SEVENTEEN

THE POLITICS OF RELIGION: THE POPE AND CHRISTIAN UNITY

NOW WHEN JESUS CAME into the district of Caesarea Philippi, he asked his disciples, "Who do people say the Son of Man is?" And they said, "Some say John the Baptist, but others Elijah, and still others Jeremiah or one of the prophets." He said to them, "But who do you say that I am?" Simon Peter answered, "You are the Messiah, the Son of the living God."

And Jesus answered him, "Blessed are you, Simon son of Jonah! For flesh and blood has not revealed this to you, but my Father in heaven. And I tell you, you are Peter, and on this rock I will build my church, and the gates of Hades will not prevail against it. I will give you the keys of the kingdom of heaven, and whatever you bind on earth will be bound in heaven, and whatever you loose on earth will be loosed in heaven."

—MATTHEW 16:13–19

THOSE WORDS FROM the Gospel of Matthew are printed in massive Latin letters around the inside base of the dome of St. Peter's Basilica in Rome: *Tu es Petrus et super hanc petram aedificabo ecclesiam meam*: You are Peter, and upon this rock I will build my church. For centuries, Roman Catholicism has relied on this text to support its understanding of the papacy.

Traveling around the world as he did, Pope John Paul II was frequently in the news, and Pope Benedict XVI continues the tradition he set. Religion is still very important in the lives of many people. So even in this postmodern and supposedly secular world, the papacy remains a matter of interest. Of course, the interest is not always supportive. Many groups oppose the Pope and the Vatican, many within the Catholic Church itself. The basic criticism is that the Vatican is outdated, and on many counts there is no denying the fact.

We who find ourselves on the fringes of the churches of whatever Christian denomination we have chosen easily become critical of the pope. In many ways, he stands for staunch, conservative, authoritarian Christianity. Claiming to be the vicar of Christ and leader of a powerful, worldwide institution, his statements have an unavoidable impact on all Christian churches. Chafing under such leadership on many counts, we have good reason to be critical. We have been misunderstood. We have been rebuked. Our struggles have been glossed over. We have been hurt. Again and again we are told outright that we are wrong when our only alternative is to surrender our common sense, to deny our experience, and to ignore our conscience. We have reason to feel hurt and angry.

Our generation is living through very turbulent and difficult times, and our church leaders—with some welcome few exceptions—are really doing little to make things easier. They respond to the turbulence defensively, protecting not only what they claim to be Christianity but also their own power bases. Their simplistic and pious messages ignore the real human issues of the day. While clergy, ministers, and people on the firing lines in the churches struggle to be real Christians from day to day, the higher-up leaders—at least in the Catholic Church, which I know best—appear to be living in another world. Still, it would be useful to keep these matters in perspective.

"UPON THIS ROCK"

We can begin by looking at that text about Peter and determining exactly what it means. It is made out to be the biblical basis for the papacy. Catholics are taught an oversimplified understanding of the thing: that Jesus picked Peter to be his spokesperson, his vicar, and so, succeeding in Peter's role, the pope takes the place of Christ. Therefore, the pope has absolute authority in the church. And since the pope appoints the bishops and the bishops ordain the priests and the priests control the parish life of the Catholic faithful, it appears that all religious power and authority flow down from the pope and that the pope has a direct line, the only line, to God even as Joan Osborn's pop song "What If God Was One of Us" says: "Nobody calling on the phone, 'cept for the pope maybe in Rome."

Conservative Catholics and the hierarchy would protest that summary. They would come to the defense of Catholicism: "That summary is too simplistic. It's an exaggeration. It's the caricature of the Catholic Church that Protestants have been proposing for centuries. In fact, recent Catholic theology emphasizes a more co-operative form of governing the church."

Well, protest as they will, anyone who knows the inner work-ings of the Catholic Church knows that it is an authoritarian, sometimes heartless, institution that Pope John Paul II worked overtime to keep it that way, and that Pope Benedict XVI seems to be following suit. The Catholic system is a leftover from the Middle Ages and the Renaissance, wherein kings, princes, lords, knights, and peasants made up the hierarchical order of society. In his own realm (rarely hers), each person at each level of the hier-archy had virtually absolute authority. Higher-ups would repri-mand only egregious excess, and loyalty was prized above all else. The Catholic Church functions in this very way today. As is evident in the current sex-abuse scandal. Systematically, as a matter of policy, the bishops protected and covered up the misdeeds of errant priests, and the Vatican gave asylum and a plum pastoral position in Rome to Bernard Cardinal Law when, under investigation, he was forced to resign as Archbishop of Boston. This hierarchical, authoritarian system protects authority and power at every level. The supreme consideration is to preserve the institution. Obedience and loyalty are the prime hierarchical Catholic virtues.

Yet if you look at the text about Peter, some questions need to be asked. What does that text really mean? And is it really Jesus who is speaking, or rather Matthew? Are we reading a theology that grew out of the Matthean community, or did Jesus actually say those things that way?

First of all, notice that this text uses the word *church*: "Upon this rock I will build my *church*." The Greek word is *ekklesia*, and it means "the gathering of those who have been called." So, in its root meaning, the church is the people who hear and respond to God's call.

There are only two places in all the Gospels where the word *church* occurs, and they are both in the Gospel of Matthew. This quote in chapter 16 is one place, and chapter 18 is the other. Chapter 18 lays down a policy for resolving conflicts among individuals. The text teaches that, if you cannot settle a difference between disputants, as a last resort take the matter to the church, and let God's chosen ones, the Christian community, resolve it. Like Chapter 16, Chapter 18 also deals with the proper use of authority in the church.

A second point to be made about that text in Matthew 16 is that it is based on the earlier Gospel of Mark, which reports the same scene at Caesarea Philippi. What is interesting is that in Mark's account the point of the story is different. Mark recounts the discussion at Caesarea Philippi to teach that the Messiah must suffer, but the disciples do not understand. In fact, Peter objects. Then, far from calling Peter the rock on which the church will be built, in Mark's account, Jesus calls Peter a tempting devil: "Get behind me, Satan! For you are setting your mind not on divine things but on human things" (Mark 8:33). There is good reason to believe that Jesus' words were as Mark reported them rather than as Matthew did, for Mark's account casts Peter in a bad light. The early church would not have made up or reported such a thing about Peter unless it had actually happened, and a subsequent generation, like Matthew's, would have wanted to tone down any negative report about Peter.

Put these observations together—that talk of church occurs only in Matthew and that Matthew reinterprets the event at Caesarea Philippi—and it appears that the text about Peter as rock is Matthew's theology, not the actual words of Jesus. Indeed, a close reading of Matthew 16 and 18 reveals that Matthew is presenting his own understanding of what church should be.

That conclusion does not imply that we can totally disregard Matthew's words about Peter or the church. To be consistent, we would likewise have to disregard most of what is in the Gospels. Matthew and the community whose faith he expressed certainly believed they understood the mind of Jesus. After all, they were Jesus' faithful disciples. They believed that Jesus did intend what Matthew wrote, or, to say it more accurately, they believed that what Matthew wrote is what Jesus would have said had he been there with them in their own day. They also believed that "through the Holy Spirit" Jesus actually was with them as the times changed and as the church emerged and formed. So, understood in this nuanced way, the Gospel of Matthew could be said to represent Jesus' mind regarding Peter and the community of Christian disciples. In this particular text and throughout the Gospels, although the evangelists did not report the actual words of Jesus himself, they expressed their understanding of the mind of Jesus. For this reason, the Christian tradition reveres these accounts as true to Jesus and God. Of course, for centuries, Christians had taken the Gospels as a literal report of the words of Jesus. Only historical studies in the past hundred and fifty years have enabled us to get behind the Gospels and sort out the theology of the evangelists from the actual words of Jesus. This sorting out provides us with a new understanding of church. The same kind of sorting out is also the basis for my presentation of sexual ethics in *What the Bible Really Says about Homosexuality* and for my highly human portrayal of Jesus in chapter 9 of *Sex and the Sacred*. The application of historical-critical analysis to the Bible has had an impact that can hardly be ignored. It casts all the major tenets of Christianity in a new light. No wonder the conservatives are retrenching, the religious fundamentalists are strategizing in fear, and all of us are juggling spiritual uncertainties.

THE EMERGING STRUCTURE OF THE EARLY CHURCH

Despite its checkered history, we must not simply disregard Matthew 16. What we must do is understand and apply it correctly. The founding of the church was not as simple as we are led to believe. Jesus did not pick out Peter and "crown" him the first pope, and Jesus did not decree that the successors of Peter should rule over the church as his absolute vicars. These notions developed over time. They arose as different times called forth different responses. To be sure, insofar as these notions "arose under the inspiration of the Holy Spirit"—that is, guided by human honesty, goodwill, and responsibility—these different responses were in accord with the "will of Christ," for whatever is the right and good thing to do in any situation would surely be the will of Christ. But this is not to say that at Caesarea Philippi Jesus Christ himself confirmed Peter and his successors as the popes of Rome. Surely, Jesus had no such detailed plan in mind.

Then here is the point: If the structure of the church emerged and changed as different historical situations arose, then the structure of the church can be adjusted again as the times continue to change. Contrary to official Catholic teaching, on the one side, and contrary to the some anti-Catholic teaching, on the other, there is nothing absolute and eternally fixed about the structure of Christianity. The Catholic and the anti-Catholic claims are political and self-serving.

When we look at what Jesus himself was about, it is clear that he had no idea of a church as we understand that institution today. Certainly, he could not have imagined the world as it is today. Because orthodox Christianity believes that Jesus was the Son of God made flesh, many like to think that he had a blueprint of all history in his mind and knew everything that was ever to happen. But if that were the case, he wasn't really human, was he? But orthodox Christianity insists that he was. As a real human being, he would have had to live his life in hope and trust as we all do, and he would have had to wait and see where his life would lead him. So he certainly could not have had in his human mind an understanding of the whole of history. He certainly did not foresee the fall of the Roman Empire; the rise of medieval Europe; the Protestant Reformation; the emergence of nation-states; the beginning of modern science; the industrial, technological, and electronic ages; and the globalization of our own day. And he certainly did not set up a structure for the church that was to remain fixed throughout these epochs.

To be sure, Jesus did know something of what his life was about. He had a sense of mission; he had wisdom to share. Clearly he wanted to reform his world, to bring on "God's reign," that is, to foster a more just and equitable society. But to think that he had everything planned out to the end of time is really to attribute too much to him. It is to deny that he really was a human being.

Did Jesus ever intend to found a church? Not in any explicit way. Yes, he was a teacher. He did have particular ideas about how life ought to be lived. He did gather a group of disciples around him, and we have a list of twelve men who made up an inner circle. This list of twelve occurs in all the Gospels. This confluence of testimony constitutes credible evidence on the matter. It is also quite clear that Peter stands out among that group, sometimes making a fool of himself but always speaking up. Even in the group that Jesus set up, Peter was the leader; the change of his name from

Simon to Rock confirms his leadership role. But these facts do not mean that Jesus explicitly intended to set up a church with specific structures as an ongoing institution to carry on his work.

Still, the fact that Peter's name was changed from Simon to Rock (*Petra* in Greek, and hence *Peter*) is significant. In the scriptures the change of someone's name always marks a new role in salvation history: Abram became Abraham, Jacob became Israel, Saul became Paul. That Simon's name was changed to Rock suggests that somewhere, at some point, Jesus himself picked him as leader.

But the actual development of the Christian church depended largely on the unfolding of history. Jesus was crucified. His followers were dumbstruck. Then they experienced this man, whom they loved and mourned, acting among them again in a way they had never imagined. They proclaimed that "He has risen." They found themselves filled with vision, purpose, and motivation, and they spoke about the "Holy Spirit" come upon them. They found themselves moved to go out and preach a powerful message.

By the time we get to the church about which Matthew was writing, sometime in the sixties, Peter was, indeed, playing a key role. To explain this fact, Matthew theologized it. He explained it in terms of God's doing, for he knew in faith, he believed, that things happen according to God's will. So he wrote about Simon as Rock. However, in those early years, different segments of the Christian community were structured in different ways. There was no single understanding of how the church should be organized. Clearly, Jesus did not leave any such specifications. For example, Paul's churches were governed by groups of leaders, not by single "bishops," and some of those leaders were women. In contrast, the community behind the Gospel of John conceived church as a rather unstructured group of believers for whom the most important requirement was to be a "beloved disciple" and to follow the lead of the Paraclete. Yet even the Gospel of John gives deference to Peter: For example, having outrun Peter to Jesus' tomb, the beloved disciple waits for Peter and allows Peter to enter the tomb first (John 20).

We lack the historical data to describe the emergence of the Christian church precisely. We do know that the church of Matthew respected Peter as its grounding rock. What Peter's role entailed, of course, depends on what you want to make of that rock. What kind of authority should be attributed to Peter and his successors, the popes of Rome?

THE STYLE OF THE PAPACY

One other observation has to be made to keep this matter of Peter and the popes in perspective. There is no doubt that Jesus chose Peter for a special role and that in the early church Peter had a position of respect and authority. But if you go to the eighteenth chapter of Matthew, to that second place were the word *church* occurs, you find that the authority given to Peter was also given to the other disciples. In Matthew 16 Jesus says to Peter: "What you bind will be bound, and what you loose will be loosed." In Matthew 18 those same words appear again, and this time Jesus is addressing all the disciples. Speaking to the whole Christian community, Jesus says: "What you bind will be bound, and what you loose will be loosed." Evidently, that saving authority, the power of binding and loosing, was not intended for Peter alone. It was intended for the whole church. Accordingly, the authority of the Catholic Church that is currently invested so completely in the papacy could be divvied up in different ways.

The Catholic Church continues to follow the medieval model of the divine right of kings. According to this model, the ruler, whoever he (or, rarely, she) might be, is appointed by God and must be tolerated and obeyed until Divine Providence provides a successor. This pyramidal model invests all authority at the top and attributes the ultimate authority to God.

This model, however, is only a product of history. For specific reasons, it emerged at a particular time and served a particular purpose. For its time and place, it was useful, but there is no absolute requirement that church structure follow this model. Despite the official line of the Vatican, as already suggested, the scriptures simply do not require this particular form of government, which evolved for the good of former times. Something else could be—and needs to be—developed for the good our own times.

Almost all of the Christian, that is, non-Fundamentalist, churches today understand those texts as I have just presented them. The Lutheran Church, the Presbyterian, the Episcopal, the Methodist, the Disciples of Christ, the United Church of Christ—today they would concur that Peter did have a special role among the disciples, that in some way the pope is the successor of Peter, and that the pope should continue to exercise some central role among Christians. The role they envisage is suggested in John 21:15–17, where Jesus says to Peter three times "Feed my sheep," and in Luke 22:32, where Jesus predicts Peter's denial but says to him: "I have prayed for you that your own faith may not fail; and you, when once you have turned back, strengthen your brothers [and sisters]." These texts see Peter, and thus the pope, as a focus of solidarity and unity within the church.

The point of debate is the manner in which the pope might exercise this role. Should the pope be autonomous, have absolute authority, and maintain unity by imposing uniformity? Or should the Pope act as a facilitator who fosters harmony, and cohesion, works toward unity by encouraging mutual respect and understanding? Apart from official Catholicism, the other Christian churches do not see the pope as the bearer of absolute authority. They imagine the pope as someone who works to resolve differences, to mediate disputes, to represent all sides, and to maintain community, something like the secretary-general of the United Nations or the archbishop of Canterbury within the Anglican Communion.

In fact, that collaborative model of the papacy is very much like the one that functioned in the early church for about five centuries. The patriarchs of Alexandria, Antioch, Constantinople, and Jerusalem, and the patriarch of Rome (the pope) all exercised independent authority within their own jurisdictions, but the patriarch of Rome was regarded as "first among equals." The pope was honored with respect that made him the focal point of harmony among the Christian churches. As is obvious, the history of Christianity exhibits various styles of "papacy."

Protestant churches are not the only ones looking for a new style of papacy that would allow for a united Christianity. On these matters, many individual Catholics and many Catholic lay organizations are in open conflict with the official Catholic Church. John Paul II significantly abandoned the changes solemnly decreed at the Second Vatican Council in the 1960s and returned the Vatican to its prior autocratic style. It is unlikely that Benedict XVI will reverse course. There is widespread Catholic opposition to this retrenchment. There are divorced and remarried Catholics who feel excluded from the sacraments. There are Catholic couples who, in good conscience, continue to practice birth control despite official teaching. There is CORPUS, the organization of married priests who want to return to active ministry without giving up their wives and families. There is Dignity, the national organization of lesbian, gay, bisexual, and transgender Catholics, who have been evicted from church property. There is the Women's Ordination Conference, which continues to discuss a topic forbidden by the John Paul II. There is Call to Action, an organization of lay activists seeking a range of changes in the church, some of whom a rogue bishop has threatened with excommunication. There are Voices of the Faithful and SNAP, Survivors Network of those Abused by Priests, which were formed in response to the Catholic sex-abuse scandal and the bishops' cover-up and are demanding more lay involvement in the governance of the Catholic Church. Many in the Catholic Church and the other Christian churches are ready for change.

LIVING CREATIVELY IN
A FLAWED SYSTEM

I am told that a Chinese curse runs like this: "May you live in interesting times." Well, we are certainly living in interesting times. Our times are exciting and promising on the one hand but very distressing on the other. The upheavals of our day will not be settled for quite some time.

I venture to say that our world has never known the kind of turmoil that we are currently experiencing as we move toward a global society. Restructuring our world and Christianity will require a whole new conception of revealed religion and of human solidarity, something like what I suggest in this book and in *Spirituality for a Global Community*. Only a harmonious, global vision will meet the present need, and the emergence of a working solution will be long in coming. In the meantime, continued Catholic insistence on its superiority to other Christian churches and continued Christian insistence on its superiority to other world religions are now blatantly part of the problem. Insisting on their uniqueness, Christianity and the other world religions are not contributing to the solution.

Maintaining perspective makes it easier to live with the day-to-day frustrations of contemporary Christianity. A broad perspective reminds us that life is bigger than our problems with the churches.

I am inspired remembering the comment of a young, Hispanic, gay man who was interviewed for a documentary on being Catholic and gay. Filmed socializing with friends at a gay bar, he was obviously at peace with himself and his life. He readily revealed that he prays regularly and also goes to Mass. Asked how he remains in the Catholic Church, he confidently asserted, "It's my church. I grew up in it. I am comfortable being a Catholic." And here's the relevant line: "The pope's not breathing down my back."

Similarly, with heroic compassion and a touch of humor, another beleaguered Catholic friend of mine expressed this opinion about the pope: "He's a busy man. He has so many things to attend to all over the world. The pope can't help it that he doesn't understand everybody."

Of course, conservative Catholics, bishops, and the Vatican object to such attitudes. They negatively label that emphasis "cafeteria Catholicism": Take what you like and leave what you don't. They attempt to make others kowtow to their own narrow version of the faith. However, as is ever the case in political push and pull, the Catholic conservatives themselves are also selective about the teachings they honor: They downplay Catholic insistence on the inviolability of personal conscience before God, and they tend to homogenize all church pronouncements into that one, exceedingly rare form: infallible teaching. The same kind of political maneuvering goes on in all the churches. Besides, religious conservatives are generally ignorant of the whole sweep of church history, which is filled with honest controversy. The New Testament itself enshrines differences and disputes: for example, those regarding the structure of the church, as noted above.

Indeed, the true Christian way seems to allow for differences and to foster discussion and through these to clarify truth and arrive at workable policies. If Christianity is not a religion concerned for the good of each and all, Christianity is not a religion worth following. Respect for individual conscience is the way of authentic Christianity. Read Romans 14 on the matter. A conservative demand for uniformity—especially regarding sexual ethics, including the role of women and policy on abortion and other reproductive technology—is splintering the churches.

Any honest appraisal of the current debates must admit at least this much: The available evidence on many fronts no longer clearly supports the old teachings. Our data base has expanded. Our understandings have broadened. Our world has changed. Under these circumstances, sincere goodwill must at least leave room for honest discussion and for good-willed diversity. The conservative hoopla about preserving embattled Christianity is a defensive and self-serving maneuver, at best, and a politically motivated charade, at worst.

Those who have found integrity of conscience grant themselves freedom of soul within the churches. This "soul freedom"—a Baptist phrase—does not require disrespecting or rejecting traditional faith and practice. A worldwide Christianity can even find room for a pope if the papacy is conceived as a focal point of spiritual unity. In the true spirit of Christianity, a transcended Christian must outright reject only those things that prove to be downright humanly destructive, as must any Christian and any person of goodwill.

Achieving deep spiritual peace, knowing the mind of Christ, arriving at psychological and Christian maturity—substantively, these words all mean the same thing—a person can remain affiliated with a church but must take membership with a grain of salt. Despite its oversimplified official line, Christianity includes many facets that are simply the products of historical accident. Current research in religious faith shows conclusively that church teaching and policy simply have not "always been that way." They were not eternally decreed by God, and they can certainly be changed. If you want to insist that the Holy Spirit inspired these things and that they were not mere accidents, well, yes, you can legitimately understand the matter in this way: Religious faith sees God acting in all things; the believer sees as Divine Providence what the unbeliever sees only as chance. By the same token, one must also allow that the old ways may have already served their purpose and that the Holy Spirit may well be inspiring new things in our own day.

Change in the outlook and practice of Christianity is inevitable. The writing is already on the wall. Not even the churches—with their appeal to the Bible. Tradition, and God's eternal decrees— can forever resist the tides of time. After all, the churches are not the Lords of History.

There is a Power bigger than us all at work in our universe, and, in its own gentle but firm way, that Power will have its way. It will continue to push for harmony, justice, and peace, and its push will eventually counter every destructive human force. Working with It, our task is to hasten positive change and to minimize collateral damage. We are to live lives of personal integrity and make what contribution we can to the common good. In this way, members of a church or not, we are actually what "church" is to be. We are a city built on a hilltop, whose light cannot be hidden. We are the beacon that lights the path toward global community in the third millennium.

EIGHTEEN

EPILOGUE: THE MIND OF THE TRANSCENDED CHRISTIAN

AS OUR WORLD gets smaller, I think about a global community, and I suspect religion is the key to creating it. Talk of a "shrinking world" used to be metaphorical. It suggested that expanding communications media and faster travel make contact among distant lands and people easy. Today, such talk must also be taken literally. At least in terms of habitable land, the world actually is shrinking. Daily, the melting of the polar ice caps reduces the actual square footage of dry earth. According to experts, we have a window of about ten years in which to reverse the effects of our environmental irresponsibility. If we do not, catastrophic and irreversible climatic changes will occur. Storms, floods, and rising temperatures will forever alter life as we know it on planet Earth.

But humankind will not reverse course unless diverse peoples and world leaders can work together in shared concern for the common good. Hence, thought about the global community becomes urgent, and, hence, concern for religious cooperation becomes imperative.

In this book I have focused on Christianity and its potential for outreach and connection with other spiritual traditions. Concern for the planet was not my initial motivation. As happens with most of us, I started with more self-centered interests. In my own Roman Catholicism, I watched as Pope John Paul II—remarkable for his outreach to the world but disturbing for his relentless conservatism within the church—reversed the openness to the modern world that Pope John XXIII had envisaged, the Second Vatican Council had prescribed, and Pope Paul VI had begun to institutionalize. Under these discouraging circumstances, precious years of my life wore on. Ordained a priest, officially representing the church and opposed for my critical thinking, I was relentlessly forced to grapple with pivotal religious issues. In the process I moved beyond my naïve, pious, natal Catholicism, and I began to transcend my religious upbringing.

My concerns were the denial of the rights and dignity of women, especially in regard to ordination; the prohibition of condoms in the era of AIDS; the rigid culture of unthinking loyalty and absolute obedience in the Catholic hierarchy, evinced most recently in the sex-abuse scandals; close-mindedness to the implications of fast-moving medical research on fetal development, abortion, stem cells, the human genome, and the like; and, above all, unbudging insistence on the essentially procreative nature of human sexuality.

This latter concern was the kicker, the time bomb that eventually went off in me. It was the tottering domino that inevitably started the others to fall, because I discovered I am homosexual and, according to Catholicism's increasingly mean teaching, I was doomed to a lifetime of loneliness, something with which I had already lived too long.

FORGING A PERSONAL POSITION

My burdened study, thought, prayer, consultation, and personal experience all converged to convince me that, on the matter of sexual ethics, the Catholic Church is simply wrong. The vast majority of married Catholic couples, all practicing birth control in good conscience, had also concluded as much. If wrong in one area, the Church could also be wrong in others. So the dam of religious control over my mind and heart broke. I was now set on a path of responsible freethinking. Finally, I was growing up, and, like anyone facing the wide-open horizon of self-determination, at times I was scared. Luckily, providentially, I had the inherited personality traits, the loving and stable upbringing, the long and expensive education, and the extensive life experience needed to grapple with such big questions and emerge solid, confident, and reasonably intact. And I did.

Having worked through the issue of sexual orientation, I constructed a model for approaching other issues. In the questions that regard our life together on this planet, only reasonable appeal to relevant evidence ought to carry the day. The credulous reliance on claimed revelation, inspired books, divinely chosen leaders, long-standing traditions, or customs and personal preferences to answer important questions is centuries outdated. The only approach that could hope to win universal human approval must appeal to good-willed open-mindedness, ever-renewed insightfulness, and reasonable reliance on evidence. In a word, the scientific ideal must reign, even in matters spiritual. Indeed, especially with regard to spiritual and religious questions, if our world is to survive, we must come to a consensus, at least insofar as these questions have practical implications for life on planet Earth. This is the understanding I developed over the years, and this is the understanding that supports what I have written in this book.

I have come to think about religion in three categories: **inconsequential, indispensable,** and **indeterminable.** In my mind, the challenge is to sort these three out and then treat them as is appropriate in each case.

The Indispensable within Religion

Obviously, **the indispensable** aspects need the greatest attention. These are the matters that I have been emphasizing, those that relate to life on this planet: matters of ethics, values, and morality and matters of knowledge, truth, and correct understanding.

Knowledge and morality, always go together: What we claim to know colors how we behave, and how we behave controls what we will know. Truth determines values, and values influence the determination of truth. Named still otherwise, these two are beliefs ethics. They are the central, spiritual components of religion, are the distinctive products of the human mind without which we cannot live. They are our window on life. They frame our living in this world. Religious or nonreligious, we all live by some set of them. Everybody, rightly or wrongly, holds some understanding about life and has some commitments in living. If we are to live together in peace, we must find a set of beliefs and ethics that any and every person of goodwill could accept in good conscience.

How do we derive such a set of universally valid beliefs and ethics? The only option I know is an open-minded, insightful, good-willed, and responsible appeal to relevant evidence—the attitude of the scientific ideal. This is my central principle. Matters about the running of this world should be decided on the basis of realities in this world. Appeal should be made to evidence from our world as it is today. Appeal to heaven and hell; afterlife, karma, and prior lives; "God," gods, goddesses, angels, celestial entities, libraries in the sky—all such metaphysical suppositions should play no role in determining life on this earth. There is no way to resolve questions about such metaphysical matters. They are essentially indeterminable. As such, they cannot provide common ground for successful living.

We must resolve matters of beliefs and ethics that are relevant to the real world if we are to live in peace. They are indispensable. They are unavoidable in human living, and every religion carries some wisdom about them. This spiritual wisdom within the religions is what needs to be brought to the fore. This is the aspect in all religions that needs to be emphasized and consolidated today.

The Inconsequential within Religion

The **inconsequential** in religion are all those matters that are actually just accidents of history. They are aspects of culture or tradition that happen to be as they are just because that is the way they happened to develop. In themselves, they carry no particular weight. They could be changed, and no harm would result.

I am thinking of things such as holy days, dietary rules, dress codes, ritual languages. No religion has the right to expect that everybody should observe its particular customs and traditions. Whether Friday, Saturday, or Sunday is the proper day for worship is hardly worth quibbling over. Anyone who steps back for only a moment from his or her own tradition will recognize that there is nothing about any one of those days that is inherently more valid than the others—like driving on the left or right side of the road or preferring chocolate to vanilla ice cream.

These are matters of sheer convention, agreement, preference, custom, habit, tradition. These matters and all others like them are ultimately inconsequential. They may have personal significance to particular believers; they may have deep sentimental value; they may have important historical roots in a tradition, but in themselves, in the big picture, they really make no difference. They are not worth fighting over. Hard as it might be to hear, this is the fact of the matter. Take these inconsequential or leave them, and life goes on. That's why they are inconsequential.

Of course, in matters religious, it is not always easy to sort out the inconsequential from the indispensable. Religious traditions have always entangled the two, and as long as the traditions existed in isolated enclaves, they served their purpose well enough. But when, as today, diverse religious traditions and secular perspectives all interact, some sorting out is required.

Take homosexuality as an example. Some church groups have absolutely insisted that it is wrong, so much so, in fact, that one would think the whole religion turned on this belief. Indeed, appealing to the Bible or historical pronouncements, some churches do insist that they stand or fall on the question of homosexuality—a ludicrous prospect, in my mind.

The fact is that sexual practices—just as all ethical questions—pertain to life in this world. Therefore, they are among the indispensables. We will not live in peace with one another, respectful of all persons, unless we reach a consensus on these matters.

What would that consensus be? Again, according to my understanding, only an appeal to evidence that is relevant to this world is pertinent to the indispensables. What does the evidence suggest? In fact, there is no evidence whatsoever that homosexuality per se is destructive to humans, and there is plenty of evidence that, when people come out, their lives blossom. In light of the overwhelming bulk of available evidence across an array of sciences and disciplines—medicine, psychology, sociology, anthropology, history, theology, biblical studies—to call homosexuality wrong or evil is irrational. The evidence is clear and so, then, must be the spiritual implication: Whether one is heterosexual or homosexual is irrelevant. What matters is that people be respectful of one another—in whatever sexual relationship. Mutual concern, not sexual orientation, is the focus of wholesome living in this world—because the social system collapses when people are abusive to one another, and the social system is buttressed when people, even homosexuals, love one another.

Thus, it turns out that the religious prohibition of same-sex relationships is only a cultural convention, a custom, a taboo. It is a remnant, as we now know, of a misinformed and mistaken tradition. Furthermore, since this prohibition pertains to the indispensables but since it conflicts with a reasonable consensus, it is disqualified, so the religions must eradicate it.

The difficulty is that we tend to be so wedded to—and blinded by—our own tradition that we cannot imagine that most of our learned sexual prohibitions, and many other religious teachings, are merely cultural artifacts. Prying these matters apart, the inconsequential from the indispensable, and resolving each in its appropriate way, is precisely the delicate and difficult challenge of spiritual commitment in our pluralistic world.

Another difficulty is that religions tend to involve God in everything. But God is the paradigmatic **indeterminable**: Nobody knows what God is or what God wants. All appeal to "God" is really appeal to some human conception, theory, or opinion about God. Some opinions might be better than others, but deciding which is which throws us right back onto the indispensable of this world: reasonable appeal to evidence within coherent, insightful human thinking. In themselves, beliefs about God are completely indeterminable.

Nonetheless, invoking God, religions freely connect the inessentials and the indispensables to the indeterminables: God revealed that Friday—or Saturday, or Sunday—is to be the day of worship; God forbids divorce or abortion or same-sex love; God disapproves of women who wear slacks; and so on. Religions invoke the authority of God to justify their particular teachings about both inessentials and indispensables, and the religions hardly think to sort out the differences.

To be sure, in former times, the linking of God with culture was commonplace. Every society claims that its ways are from God simply because every society must believe that its ways are right, good, wholesome, productive. But when different religions meet and conflicting notions of God and God's will emerge, appeal to God becomes useless. Once again, the only way to resolve the differences is to fall back onto human openness, insight, and reasonable appeal to evidence. Once again, not God—or supernatural revelation or metaphysical entities or otherworldly beliefs and claims—but this-worldly goodwill and good sense must carry the day. In the last analysis, at least for the time being, that is, while we live in this world, only the indispensables really matter. The rest is secondary. Indeed, the rest must be deemed invalid to the extent that it conflicts with the indispensables.

According to my understanding—this point is pivotal—the indispensable is supreme: if some opinion is irrational, in conflict with the existing evidence, it could not possibly be of God. Human goodwill and good reason trump not only societal and religions conventions but also any supposed appeal to direct contact with "God."

This, then, is how I have come to sort through religious matters, and this is how I propose a way that fosters life and supports global community. Part and parcel of this way is the ability to transcend one's own religion: to go beyond inherited teaching, to sort out the pieces, and to give to each its proper weight. Thus, I have written about *The Transcended Christian*.

The idea is not that people should abandon their particular denominational Christianity but that, digging deeply into it, they should find the spiritual insight to see beyond it. They should learn to hold on lightly to the religious inconsequentials and indeterminables. Above all, they should commit themselves, with the rest of humankind, to furthering the indispensables.

To go this way and not get lost requires profound spiritual maturity: courage, honesty, goodwill, study, thought, consultation, prayer, faith, trust, forgiveness, patience. To take this journey is to leave the safe, religious flock, which now wanders about, as Jesus said, like sheep without a shepherd, and to trek off, virtually alone, with only one's inner compass—and the Holy Spirit—for guidance, forging a new path that veers back toward the authentic advance of the tradition in a direction, however, that, in light of the status quo, will be said to be off target. To follow this path is to be "like the master of a household who brings out of his treasure what is new and what is old" (Matthew 13:52). It is to realize that "no one sews a piece of unshrunk cloth on an old cloak" and "no one puts new wine into old wineskins" (Mark 2:21–22)—and to dare and act accordingly. The challenge of our times is great. Again, according to Jesus: "The gate is narrow and the road is hard that leads to life, and there are few who find it" (Matthew 7:14).

Yet our era is forcing us in droves to find this new way. My hope is that what I have written here will serve as a guidepost.

The Indeterminables of Christianity

Among the **indeterminables** of Christianity, throughout these chapters I have included the core doctrines of Christianity: the Trinity in God, the divinity of Jesus, life after death, and the very existence of God. In no way do I deny these doctrines or even to suggest that they are not believable. I began my professional career as a priest and theologian. I know well what these doctrines mean and what bases they have. I know that through the centuries theologians have worked out the questions that surround these Christian beliefs, and none of them is incoherent. I treated these matters in *The Same Jesus* and in *Spiritual Development*, and other theologians present comparable explanations.

People make fun, for example, of Trinitarian doctrine. They caricature it as the assertion that three is one and one is three. Christianity says nothing of the kind. The insistence that there are three distinct Subjects or Persons in only one God places the three in one place and the one in another; there is no suggestion that the one is the other. The differences between the Divine Subjects and the Divine Nature can be specified on the basis of their constitutive relationships such that there is no contradiction in the doctrine. Of course, these subtleties are beyond most of us, and, even granted their mastery, the doctrine is challenging. The same can be said for the traditionally orthodox statement that Jesus Christ is both fully human and fully divine. In this case, the distinction between one Subject and two natures dispels all contradiction but, once again, does not remove the challenge of the doctrine.

The Christian doctrines are clearly plausible: One need not be a fool to believe them. Though not fully understandable—after all, they are about God—they are not irrational. One does not have to surrender human intelligence and reason to affirm them.

Thus, my point was not to deny or reject these doctrines but to bracket them, to respectfully leave them out of the discussion. Whether they are true or false could never be shown. There is no way to definitively settle questions about such otherworldly, metaphysical matters. Insisting unwieldingly on them—or, worse, insisting that others also accept them—does no one any good. These beliefs, and similar beliefs from other religions, cannot be adjudicated.

I outright reject the Biblical Fundamentalists' claim that no one can be "saved" without explicit faith in Jesus Christ. If God is going to damn everyone who is not "Christian," I want another God! I will not reverence unfairness and barbarism. Even more, I deplore their parallel suggestion in some circles that, once one accepts Jesus as "Lord and Savior," one will get to heaven regardless of how one lives. Such claims are religious nonsense. Far from making people better, they invite irresponsibility. In the name of Jesus, they give people license to do whatever they feel like doing and to still believe they're okay because they are "saved." In my mind, insistence on, and argument over, doctrines is mostly a waste of time.

> » Whether God is Trinity or not, the world still goes on, and we are left to live in it.
> » Whether Jesus was truly God or not, we still need to live virtuous lives, and Jesus still provides a powerful example.
> » If redemption through Jesus really changed the meaning of life, whether we know of this change or not, born into human life, we are involved in the change. If not, why claim such a change actually happened and is real?
> » Whether the Holy Spirit really inspires us or not, confronted with the same question and given the same data, any honest and good-willed person will come to more or less the same conclusion. Such is the defining nature of reasonableness. The Holy Spirit need not be part of the mix.
> » Whether one affirms the existence of God or not, life is what it is.
> » Whether there is an afterlife or not, one must still live this life and live with oneself, and the very structures of one's being and any hope for fulfillment in this life require that one live virtuously.

It makes no sense to suppose that the truth for Christians is different from the truth for other people: Truth is truth, and, if not, it's not true. The same goes for goodness. Christians have no inside track on life. Religious faith does not relieve a person of responsibility for his or her own life.

THIS-WORLDLY WISDOM IN OTHER-WORLDLY DOCTRINES

The beliefs of religion that are other-worldly are indeterminable. As such, they can play no role in specifying the good life on planet Earth. Moreover, I insist, other-worldly beliefs could be valid only to the extent that they actually help people lead a truly good life here and now. To the extent that those beliefs do not, they cannot be true, and they could not possibly be of God.

You see, in my understanding, good living here and now is the criterion of all else. I will not believe that living irrationally because of some article of faith could ever be pleasing to God: God would not have created us as intelligent, rational, and self-determining beings only to require that we act contrary to our nature and believe and behave in ways that make no human sense. Rather, good living on this Earth must be the criterion of personal fulfillment in any possible life to come. If I am correct, concern about realities and lives beyond this one are superfluous and distracting.

I said that other-worldly beliefs are valid only to the extent that they foster good living in this world, and I even suggested that much of religious doctrine really serves to portray a worthy picture of modern life. Led by this light, I mine the indeterminables of religion for insight into the indispensables of life.

I gave numerous examples in this book. In most cases, my general strategy was to highlight the psychological or personal-growth aspects of a belief and to play down or bracket the aspects other-worldly. Here are key instances:

» Prayer to God also requires communing with one's own spirit, and the human spirit is our immediate guide to good living. Highlighting this mechanism, I tend to encourage meditation and contemplation over standard prayer with words.

» The mystical wedding between God and humankind projects an ideal of perfect love and unity among all persons, divine and human, in heaven. This ideal keeps before us a worthy goal to pursue in our life together on earth.

» The Ascension has to do with Jesus' return to heaven, but I presented it as a lesson in the need to internalize Jesus' teaching and to live virtuously from the inside out.

» The celebration of Corpus Christi, the Body of Christ, involves God's becoming flesh in Jesus Christ and Christians' communing with Christ through the Eucharist, Holy Communion. In contrast, I emphasized the union of Christians with one another in Christ and the importance of comfort with one's body—and sexuality—for good living in this physical world.

» Belief in God means trusting that a good Power is at work in our world and surrendering ourselves to It. So, in practice, belief in God is belief in life. It is to take things as they come and, always finding and furthering the good, to make the best of every situation. Thus, every person of goodwill, whether a believer or not, is actually involved in the same commitment.

» The correct meaning of scripture depends on the original intentions of the authors, as accurately as it can be determined, in their own time, place, language, and culture. That is, only a historical-critical reading provides authentic biblical teaching for the current age. The "literalist" or Fundamentalist reading methodically ignores the inputs that the human author and the human interpreter bring to a text and, thus, cannot be unbiased, cannot be accurate.

» Jesus is the way because he is the embodiment of all that is right, true, and good. The human goodness of Jesus, not his divinity, is what makes him the saving model for us. Therefore, the way to life is to seek out the right, true, and good in our own time and place rather than to slavishly imitate Jesus, saying, "Lord, Lord." Thus, anyone, believer or not, knowingly or unknowingly, could be following his way.

» Redemption through the cross does not apply only to Jesus' saving work but also to anyone who attempts to reverse the course of injustice and wrongdoing. It is not that suffering in itself has any particular value, but justice in a corrupt world always has a cost, and someone must pay it. The innocent will have to pick up the slack because evildoers never will. Those who are committed to furthering goodness in our world must be ready to shoulder an unfair portion of the burden. Thus redemption occurs.

» If it is true, if it squares with reality, the message of Jesus and of the religions is pertinent to every person if only it is translated from religious jargon into everyday language. If it cannot be so translated, one must assume it is irrelevant.

When emphasis shifts from the indeterminables to the **indispensables** within a religion, one's perspective must broaden. Then, being a member of the human family takes precedence over any other identity, even one's Christianity. (But isn't such universal identity precisely what Christianity is about?) To live this universal human kinship while remaining rooted in one's particular religion is the essence of being a Transcended Christian. Thus, again and again in this book, I highlighted the indispensables hidden beneath the crust of standard Christianity.

» Renewed reverence for the human body and human sexuality is essential to a wholesome and fulfilling life in this world.

» The society in which we life—fast-paced, mobile, materialistic, unfeeling, routinized, superficial—is psychologically and socially unhealthy and spiritually destructive. Forging a saner way of life will contribute more to contentment and peace, to the "things of God," than any attempt to convert people to God and religion.

» Our human minds include a spiritual dimension that is geared to open-ended growth in all that is true and good. Religion and the discovery of God are products of the human spirit. Thus, the inclination of the human spirit—openness, wonder, honesty, and goodwill—is the key to all spiritual growth, human well-being, and social harmony, and alignment with God.

» Every individual is unique. Each must find her or his own way of being in this world, and each has a distinctive contribution to make. All preferences, behaviors, and ways of life are permitted as long as they respect and contribute to the overall well-being of all concerned. People must stop condemning others merely because their paths are different. Unless real harm is being done, no wrong or sin is being committed.

» It is not enough that individuals become good people individually. The very structure of society needs to be transformed because society forms, guides, and restricts individuals and because, without new social structures, no change for good can survive. Like a prophet or a John the Baptist, truly spiritual people will tend to be activists, decrying social injustice and promoting needed societal change.

» Commandments, laws, and directives or fear-filled adherence to religious teachings will not save people or our world. Positive change comes from the human heart and the goodness therein. Therefore, religions should emphasize virtues—open-mindedness, wonder, honesty, goodwill and love, forgiveness, justice, compassion—rather than a list of "Thou shalts" and "Thou shalt nots." Only a truly virtuous person, internally free to respond as she or he sees best, can meet new situations with life-enhancing responses, which might not always follow standard procedure.

The Inconsequential within Religion

I spent only little time in this book on the *inconsequentials* of Christianity. Some of them would differ from denomination to denomination. Others, such as keeping Sunday as "the Lord's day," would be so common as to be taken for granted, and the Seventh-day Adventist' keeping Saturday as the Sabbath stands out as a distinguishing mark of the group. Dispute over such matters of times, dates, and customs, as common in Christian history as it is in everyday life, becomes more significant and will call for greater flexibility as society becomes increasingly diverse.

One example of inconsequentials in this book would be the religious holy days that gave occasion to a number of the essays: Ascension, Pentecost, Corpus Christi. These are specifically Catholic feasts; they are virtually unknown in Protestant churches. These feasts are remnants of Christendom, that medieval era in which the whole of society was Christian and the holy days were the culture's holidays. Today, holy days and holidays hardly coincide. The season of Advent offers a striking example: While, liturgically, a month-long penitential Advent leads up to twelve days of celebration of Christmas (still archaically recognized from the carol by that name), the secular world uses that lead time for celebration and sales, and the stores dismantle Christmas decorations on December 26. The secular and sacred worlds are badly out of sync.

To the good, Catholicism has attempted to make its liturgical season more relevant to the modern world. Some of the Holy Days of Obligation, for example, which usually fall on weekdays, no longer strictly require attendance at Mass, and some have been moved to Sunday or have been dropped altogether. New Year's Day is the most intriguing case. Falling a week after Christmas, the day used to be celebrated as the Circumcision of the Lord—hardly an appropriate theme for hung-over New Year's revelers. More recently, the feast was dedicated to Mary, Mother of God, but celebration of a Mass for World Peace was also allowed, and thoughtful priests take this option. It clearly matches the secular holiday better than those other religious themes. Still, officially,

New Year's Day remains a solemnity of Mary on the Catholic liturgical calendar; to relinquish religious pieties and inbred practices is difficult.

The Spiritualization of Secular Society

Quaint as it might seem, the medieval notion of Christendom carried profound wisdom. It suggests the interpenetration of the secular and the sacred in society. This notion should not be threatening to us who have become used to the separation of "church and state." The medieval arrangement is but one example of the most standard of arrangements among early societies, in which culture and religion were one. The wisdom is to realize that spiritual concern—shared beliefs and ethics—is natural to human living and is a feature of every society. Under the guise of religion, the spiritual used to interpenetrate all societies. Now, because of a pluralism of religions within any one society, religion can no longer fulfill its traditional role, and we have awkwardly shunted religion—and, with it, virtually all accountability for truth and goodness—to the sidelines of life. But that traditional role still needs to be filled, and a nonreligious spirituality, could fill it. No society can stay afloat for very long, let alone stay on course, without a spiritual compass and a moral rudder.

In these twenty-first-century circumstances, the most promising strategy I know if the following:

» First, to tease the spiritual apart from the religious; to disentangle the spiritual core of indispensable common beliefs and ethics from the particularistic religious structures of inconsequential or indeterminable doctrines, traditions, scriptures, rituals, calendars, offices, and ordained staffs;
» Next, to install at the heart of secular society this universally valid, generic or core spirituality;
» Then, to retain organized religions, as varied as cultures and languages, to foster this generic spirituality, each in its own way.

» And finally, to enlist all people of goodwill, whether religious or not, in this global spiritual enterprise.

Thus, society would retain an explicitly conceived, spiritual core: the indispensables of human living in this world. At the same time, an array of religions would foster this universally accepted core through judicious use of the religious indeterminables and inconsequentials. Secular society would include spirituality without privileging any of the many religions. I elaborate this vision in *Spirituality for a Global Community*.

Some such arrangement is, I believe, what we must eventually achieve—a global community explicitly based on the indispensable requisites of human living: justice, honesty, fairness, mutual respect, gratitude, compassion, care. Apart from any religious connection, Christians could support these ideals in a secular environment, and these same spiritual ideals could simultaneously be the focus of the churches' prayers and rituals: the message of mutual love and caring that Jesus preached, which, through the Holy Spirit, involves us all in the unifying life of the Eternal Parent.

The Transcended Christian as Global Citizen

To hold such a vision, one must move beyond one's parochial Christianity and conceive a global community of human sisters and brothers not by abandoning one's Christianity, not by forgetting that those sisters and brothers are sibling daughters and sons of God, but by digging deeply into Christianity and grasping its truly saving core: love, as it applies in different ways to different facets of life: inconsequential, indeterminable, and indispensable. To maintain such a vision, one must become a Transcended Christian.

Thus, speaking from the fringes of contemporary Christianity and learning spiritual lessons among the outcasts of religion, I have proposed a vision of Christianity that is open to all the outcasts and, perforce, to all the people of the world. There can be no cordoning off of these diverse concerns, because they naturally go hand in hand. The agenda of the Transcended Christian is not only the in-house task of updating Christianity and not only the religious challenge of building bridges to other religions but also the human imperative of forging a global community of the third millennium. If such a community is to be viable, it must be grounded in some way in spiritual realities. The Transcended Christian is precisely the one who authentically discerns the spiritual within the religious, grants the spiritual its natural priority, and, moving beyond his or her religion, reaches out in genuine spirituality to the whole world.

The specific result of such an endeavor may not be what Matthew had in mind when he had Jesus say, "Go therefore and make disciples of all nations, baptizing them in the name of the Father and of the Son and of the Holy Spirit, and teaching them to obey everything that I have commanded you" (28:18). Nor may the specific result look anything like a contemporary Christian congregation at worship. But the substance of the result must certainly be what Jesus, Matthew, the churches, mature Christians, and all people of goodwill have felt calling out to them in their hearts from time immemorial: "May they all be one. As you, Father, are in me and I am in you, may they also be one in us" (John 17:21). Such a result is the aim of the *Transcended Christian*.

ACKNOWLEDGMENTS

THIS BOOK WAS long in the making. Its beginning lie in the early 1980s, when I was the officially appointed chaplain to the lesbian and gay Catholics of the Archdiocese of San Antonio. In that capacity, I preached almost weekly to a small band of women and men, still hopeful at that time that the Catholic Church would change its teaching on sexuality and welcome lesbian, gay, bisexual, and transgender (LGBT) individuals. I exercised my ministry mainly through Dignity/San Antonio, the local chapter of the independent, lay-organized, national Catholic support group for LGBT people, their families, friends, and supporters. From time to time, Nickie Valdez, the "spiritual mother" (founder and long-time sustainer) of Dignity/San Antonio, would ask me for copies of my homilies. I had none. I prepared my sermons in my head and spoke them from my heart, and they drifted off into the universe. Someone suggested hat I tape-record them, and I began to do so regularly.

Over the years—not just in San Antonio but also in Austin, Boston, Pittsburgh, and anyplace that I might be preaching to Dignity—I collected a large number of recordings. I long had the idea of publishing the homilies because priests occasionally asked me for help with their ministries: What does one say to a group of lesbian and gay congregants?

In the late 1990s, Dr. Bruce Jarstfer, then of San Antonio, a retired surgeon, had some time on his hands. He offered to transcribe a stack of homilies on tape so that I could rework and publish them. I dedicate this book to this wonderful man, not only for his help with this project but also for the many other contributions of generous service he has made on so many fronts over the years.

By the turn of the millennium, Catholic ministry to LGBT people was hardly a going enterprise. There was no market for gay homilies. The Vatican had virtually shut down all such creative LGBT ministry. Yet the ideas in those homilies remained relevant, powerful, and needed. Prompted by the thoughts of those original creative moments, I turned the homilies into essays on contemporary Christianity and worked and reworked them. In 2003, Alyson Books contracted to publish the manuscript, but the vicissitudes of publishing delayed the project until 2007. I am grateful to Alyson executive editor Joseph Pittman for his expeditious work on this book in the past year.

From time to time, many other people have also contributed to this project. In addition to Bruce Jarstfer, I offer special thanks also to my dear friend Raymond Machesney, for his generous support in general and of this book in particular. I am also singularly grateful to the Reverend Professor Peter J. Gomes, minister in the Memorial Church, Harvard University, for his insightful foreword to this book; I am honored to have the endorsement of so pivotal a religious figure in this time of religious uncertainty. Moved by the same sentiment, eager gratitude for the institutionally committed but forward-looking spiritual leaders, I thnk Prof. Richard P. Hurdy, Drs. Arianni and Oreaon Masters, and the Rev. Dr. Jean Richardson for their kind endorsements and invaluable, self-effacing minstry. Bill Bennett, Sharon Cabeen, and Geoff Corbin offered substantive criticism and encouragement regarding various drafts of the manuscript. Margaret M. Graff and Judy West helped in a similar way, as did also Tommy Gallick, Clarence B. Johnson (R.I.P.), Dick Marshall, and Dennis Weakland. For other kinds of support, help, and suggestions, I am also grateful to Doug Bradford, Jim Bussen, Lee Cox, Eileen Duff, Kirby Garner, Don George, Jesse Gomez, Marcus Fleishhacker, Allam Helminiak, Daniel J. Helminiak, Paul Drew Johnson, Toby Johnson, David Jones, Cecelia McHirella, Joey Mills, David Przeracki, Dan Rauzi, Jack Simpson, and Urvashi Vaid.

May the kindness of these friends and colleagues channel through the words of this book, and may these thus-hallowed ideas, before radiating out once again into the far-flung universe, help to transform you, my dear reader, along with the Christian religion and our emerging global community.